Also by Michael Ruhlman

Boys Themselves

The Making
of a Chef

THE MAKING OF A

Chef

Mastering Heat at the
Culinary Institute
of America

Michael Ruhlman

An Owl Book
Henry Holt and Company
New York

Henry Holt and Company, LLC
Publishers since 1866
115 West 18th Street
New York, New York 10011

Henry Holt® is a registered trademark
of Henry Holt and Company, LLC.

Library of Congress Cataloging-in-Publication Data
Ruhlman, Michael, date.
The making of a chef: mastering heat at the Culinary Institute of
America / Michael Ruhlman.
p.   cm.
ISBN 0-8050-6173-8
1. Ruhlman, Michael, date.   2. Cooks—United States—Biography.
3. Culinary Institute of America.   I. Culinary Institute of America.
II. Title.
TX649.R8A3   1997   97-30078
641.5'092—dc21   CIP
[B]

Henry Holt books are available for special promotions and
premiums. For details contact: Director, Special Markets.

First published in hardcover in 1997 by
Henry Holt and Company

First Owl Books Edition 1999

Designed by Betty Lew

Printed in the United States of America

7   9   10   8   6

For my father,

Rip,

provider of the feast

Everything is relative but there is a standard which must not be deviated from, especially with reference to the basic culinary preparations.

A. Escoffier
The Complete Guide to the Art of Modern Cookery

Contents

Acknowledgments

First, my thanks to Ferdinand Metz and Tim Ryan for allowing me into the Culinary Institute of America. I do not remember a single significant request that was turned down. Dr. Fred Mayo was generous with his time and offered valuable guidance through the labyrinthine Institute. Andrea Harding likewise worked hard on my behalf, as did Janis Wertz. All chef-instructors were generous with their time in answering my questions; many, however, such as Todd Philbrook (sorry about the show plate!) and Tom Griffiths, do not appear in this narrative though I owe much to them. Of the many reference books I used, the most valuable was the Culinary's own, *The New Professional Chef;* as far as basic cooking methods and standard ratios, I know of no better cookbook. Finally I am grateful to all the chefs and students who appear in this book for their time and their willingness to be a part of this story.

I would like to thank my agent, Elizabeth Kaplan, to whom I am permanently indebted.

No one can know how judicious and intelligent Bill Strachan, my editor, has been in his work because his effect is so subtle as to be invisible and yet he improved the manuscript enormously. I am grateful to him.

Thanks forever to R.P.

I would like to thank my mother, Carole, who, besides being an awesome mom, is the personification of human generosity and high spirits.

Words do not exist to adequately thank my wife and daughter, as the reader will soon appreciate. They are to me the most miraculous duo on earth, and I would be lost without them.

The Making of a Chef

Part I

Skill Development

 Secret Sharer

The bundle waiting for me on the couch had been secured with butcher's string and looked as ordinary as laundry. I tucked it beneath my arm and strode out of the office and through Roth Hall, the main building of the Culinary Institute of America, slipped into a bathroom, and closed myself off in the farthest stall. I removed my sweater and jeans and stuffed them into my leather shoulder briefcase. I untied the bundle, shook out one of two pairs of houndstooth-check trousers, and stepped into them, then buttoned the immaculately white, double-breasted chef's jacket over my white T-shirt. I jammed the extra set of pants into the briefcase along with my street clothes, snapped it shut, grabbed my black overcoat and knife kit, and pushed out of the stall.

I stopped at the mirror. I had not been in a uniform since high school football and I sent myself an ironic lift of the eyebrows, then an uncertain shrug. The figure in the mirror—dressed as a culinary student—looked like me and did not. The figure seemed more a secret sharer. I could not dwell long on this uniformed other self—I had only a few minutes to find K-8, the Skills kitchen run by Chef Michael Pardus.

I hustled down a dark brick corridor—to my right a long, glassed-in kitchen, to my left display cases inlaid into the brick facade. I turned left at Alumni Hall, the main dining room, once the chapel of this former Jesuit monastery, strode past a dishwasher's station, and turned left again. The first kitchen on my left was K-8 and I would arrive, thankfully, a minute or so before two, when this class was scheduled to begin.

I stepped through the doorway and eighteen pairs of eyes cranked in my direction.

Chef Pardus halted in mid-sentence. The seventeen students, already lined at attention along four large stainless-steel tables, two on either side of the room, regarded me curiously. Chef Pardus wore the standard chef-instructor uniform, similar to the students' but with fancy round white buttons on his chef's jacket running up each breast, green and gold stripes along the collar, a green name tag pinned above his breast pocket, and a paper toque that was an inch or two taller than the students'. He was trim, measured about five feet ten inches without the hat, which revealed a few light brown curls kept well above his collar, and he wore wire-rimmed glasses.

"Michael," the chef said. We'd been introduced the previous week, and he had given me course information and homework assignments.

"Yes, Chef," I said. "Sorry I'm late."

"You're number eighteen. I've put you at Table One." He pointed to my spot, smack in front of him at the head of the class. He stood in front of a beat-up, circa-1960 metal desk. Behind him on the board in bright ink marker he had written:

Day One

2# mirepoix

2 tomato concassé

1 sachet

$^{1}/_{2}$ minced onion

I took my spot and shoved my belongings on the shelf of the steel table.

"Do you have a hat?" Chef Pardus asked.

"They didn't give me one," I answered

"A neckerchief?"

"No."

"You need to have those in this kitchen. I'll call central issue in a minute and see if we can hook you up." Chef Pardus seemed a little annoyed. I was late *and* my uniform was incomplete.

But I was here, and that's all that mattered now, the physical fact of my presence. This was a physical place.

I'd made it to Culinary Skill Development One, the first kitchen in the intricately scheduled curriculum at the Culinary Institute of America. It was a move I felt that, in some ways, had been foreordained a decade earlier.

Shortly after I graduated from college and began work in New York City, my granduncle, Bill Griffiths, wrote a letter to me outlining some definitions of art, and in doing so, he described a meal he'd had at Gallatoire's in New Orleans decades ago. "The total meal involved many things," he wrote, "but what I have never forgotten is the potatoes. There were no fancy sauces, no tricky seasonings, no admixture with other ingredients—just plain small cubes of potato cooked in such a way that the surfaces were delicately crisp and crunchy and the inside, rich, smooth, and flavorful. One was simultaneously aware both of exquisite texture and marvelous taste. The lesson it taught me was that the chef hadn't used the potato as a basis for displaying flashy, flamboyant skills, but had placed his skills as an artist in the service of the potato."

I found a fundamental truth in these words and I wrote the last sentence on a three-by-five-inch card and stuck it to the wall beside my desk.

Nearly ten years after my uncle Bill wrote those words to me—faded but still affixed to my wall—I intended to learn how to cook and to write about *how* one learned. And I hoped to use my uncle's words regarding art and potatoes as a kind of lantern to light my way. I would not strive to learn the sort of stuff being photographed for food magazines, but instead how to make the kind of potatoes Bill had described.

My goal was both humble and presumptuous: I wanted to learn how to put myself in the service of the potato. This was to me the key phrase, *in the service of*, the axis, the unmoving shaft, of a statement with many ramifications. Is great cooking really art? Are chefs artists? What is wrong with flash and flamboyance? How could the lowly potato become so important in a meal as to be the one thing my uncle remembered decades later?

Also, I love to eat potatoes.

Given these two qualities—the desire to learn to cook and to write about it, with all the notions of artistry, history, gastronomy that inevitably orbit this learning, and a simple and perhaps atavistic love of eating—I had

hatched a plan to attend the Culinary Institute of America, the most prominent cooking school in the country, a food-knowledge mecca. What did they
teach here? According to the Culinary Institute of America, what did a chef
need to know above all? What was the inviolable core of a culinary education? What were the secrets of truly great cooking?

All this I wanted to know, and I'd come here to impersonate a student. I
would learn to cook as though my future depended on it. When I entered
Chef Pardus's Skills kitchen I stepped into a new world. I would learn what
it took to be a professional chef. I would start at the beginning, and the
beginning of Culinary Skill Development was stock.

"Making stock is one of the primary purposes for being in this class,"
Chef Pardus said as we began our tour of the kitchen. Our first stop:
the steam kettles. The three enormous tanks, each a hot tub for one, were
bolted to steam pipes and accommodated by two water faucets. Each day,
the center kettle would be filled with 120 pounds of chicken bones, $22\frac{1}{2}$
gallons of water, and 15 pounds of mirepoix, along with bay leaves, peppercorns, parsley stems, and thyme wrapped in cheesecloth and called a *sachet
d'épices*. This combination would yield 15 gallons of chicken stock by the
end of class, to be cooled, labeled, and stored before lecture.

"You want to cook stock at what?" Chef Pardus asked.

Several voices called out, "At a lazy bubble." Everyone in the class
should have learned this from the video assigned for homework. The library
contained about twenty-three hundred videos, some of them made for television by the Culinary Institute—*Cooking Secrets of the CIA*, a cooking
show featuring individual faculty, had recently begun to air on public stations throughout the country—but most were utilitarian, made solely for
the students, such as "Making Brown Stock," "Shucking Oysters," and "Calf
Slaughter."

"Right, a lazy bubble," Chef Pardus repeated. "A few bubbles breaking
the surface every few seconds. Why? Because we don't want to emulsify
the fat into the stock and stir up other impurities. We're looking for
clarity here."

Chef Pardus squatted at the end kettle's spigot, opened and closed it,
saying, "Make sure this is closed all the way or you're going to have wet
shoes." He turned the knob on the steam pipe and the kettle began to clank
like an old radiator as its jacket filled with steam. Chef Pardus hefted a

large white tub from table to kettle and dumped its contents, forty pounds of beef bones. He pushed the faucet over and turned the water on.

"We're going to blanch the bones first," he said, "to get rid of impurities, mainly blood. The water's going to get a rich, funky, gray color. We'll skim that off and then we'll empty it. In Skills One, I want everybody to make stocks to measure. By Skills Two, you can do this by sight." On an easel to the left of his desk was a large pad of paper with the stock ratios on it— water to bones to mirepoix to tomato. For the first three weeks, Pardus wanted us to measure in order to know how high seven-and-a-half gallons of water rises above forty pounds of beef bones. "After four hours, we're going to add what? Mirepoix, right. An hour before finishing, the sachet d'épices." The stocks would be about 145 degrees when we strained them, he said, and we would cool all stocks—typically thirty gallons a day—to 70 degrees in two hours and to 45 degrees in four hours, as sanitation guidelines require. "But don't worry," Pardus said. "We can go from kettle to cooler in eighteen minutes. The record I think is sixteen minutes."

"Make sure you skim the fat before you cool it," he added. "If you forget, and you're making consommé, your classmates are going to hate you because you dropped the consommé grade by two points."

He introduced us to the ovens. Two banks of ranges ran nearly the length of both sides of the room. "When you come in, make sure your oven *works*. Students don't light pilot lights. We have someone come up from mainte-nance. If you do it wrong it will blow you across the room." He crinkled his nose and grinned. "It's kinda scary. You lose all your facial hair."

He then addressed the burners and cast-iron flattops, particularly the latter: "You don't always know if they're hot. If this were hot," he said, feeling for heat, then pressing his palm to the black metal, "my hand would probably stick to it. These get very hot, and you'll need to use tinfoil rings to regulate the heat when you've got a lot of pans going."

Chef Pardus returned to the beef-stock kettle, which had begun to steam. Behind him, taped to the wall, a giant piece of paper read:

A great stock is judged by

—Flavor
—Clarity
—Color
—Body
—Aroma

"A lot of blood is coming out," he said, peering into the enormous kettle. "As soon as it comes up to temperature it's going to turn gray."

Chef Pardus continued the tour of the kitchen, moving clockwise past the ranges to the sinks, three basins for hot soapy water, hot rinse water, and cool water with sanitizing fluid. The sanitation steward, a position that changed daily, was responsible for keeping them clean, not easy when eighteen people are making béchamel sauce. Before leaving the sinks he said, "Please help everyone out here if you're not completely in the weeds. You'll get a lot more out of this class if you're not here washing pots all night."

The food steward, the other position assigned daily, and the sanitation steward were responsible for making sure people helped out. "They are second in command," Pardus said. "They are the sous chefs in this kitchen. If they ask you to do something—if anyone asks you for help—you don't say, 'I'm too busy, I have a headache, my dog ate it, I lost it in the *sun*.'" He paused, scanned our faces. "You say, 'O.K.'"

We passed the ice machine, which faced the huge maple cutting boards we would be using; passed the dry storage, where food that didn't need to be kept cold was located; and then went to the cage, which was the size of a large closet and filled with stock kettles, food mills, china caps and chinois, ladles, skimmers, colanders, Robot Coupes, and one giant ladle that we would use for shoveling steaming bones and vegetables out of drained stock kettles. He held or pointed to each item. "This is a solid spoon," he said. "This is a slotted spoon. This is a perforated spoon." He alternately held up the slotted and solid spoons. "In some places they call this a female spoon. They call this a male spoon. If you're working with a guy who spent his formative years in Nazi Germany, he may start yelling, 'Give me a female shpoon, give me a female shpoon!' And you better know what it is. *But*—it's ancient *history*. We don't use that term here, but you should know what it is."

He held up bain-marie inserts, hotel pans, and spiders.

Sensing that the large, carbon-encrusted roasting pans he'd put in the oven earlier were hot, Pardus pulled two tubs of veal bones from the reach-in, to the right of his desk at the head of the kitchen. The bones had been delivered Friday and sat for the three-day weekend. He smelled them, turned a few in his hands, scrutinizing them. "These are a little off, but I think they'll be O.K.," he said.

Adam Shepard, a tall thin student with a narrow face, sharp nose, and dark hair, asked, "Is this a flavor issue?"

"Yeah, we're talking flavor here. We're going to be cooking it so we don't need to be worried about any residual toxins, like, I don't know, staph toxins. It would just have an off odor."

He removed one hot pan from the oven and poured Wesson cottonseed oil from a large white jug into the pan. "It's the cheapest oil you can buy. We use it only for this." He dumped half the tub of bones in. They hissed as they hit the oil. "You want an even layer, not stacked. Why is that?"

"So they caramelize evenly?" one student asked.

"Well, yes," the chef said. "But you could get that by turning them frequently." He waited. "The reason is that the bottom and top layer would caramelize but the middle would sweat and release liquid, and the liquid would form at the bottom of the pan. So instead of a good fond, you'd end up with a crust of blood and coagulated protein. Don't try to squeeze eighty pounds of bones into three pans."

The final stop on the tour was the pot room, filled with sauteuses, sautoirs, marmites, sauce pots, rondeaux, and plastic two-gallon stock containers. He held up a sauté pan with sloping sides and asked for its name. "Sauteuse." He held up a pan the same size but whose sides were at right angles to the bottom. "Sautoir."

Chef Pardus returned to his desk and said loudly and with finality, *"This is your kitchen for six weeks. Keep it clean."*

It did seem to me a fine kitchen, spacious and bright. It measured thirty-seven-and-a-half feet by twenty-six feet. The two Hobart reach-in coolers—one for the A.M. class, one for the P.M.—at the head of the kitchen included an exterior digital read of the internal temperature. The reach-ins faced one end of a long bank of Garland ranges comprising three sets of four burners alternating with three large flats above six separate ovens. Across the kitchen were the Wolf ranges, seven burners lined side by side, behind which were seven flattops. This side also contained the deep fryer, which remained empty and covered for all but one day of this class. Two industrial extension cords hung from the ceiling. There were three separate sinks, one just for cooling stocks, as well as a giant ice machine. Even the cutting boards were substantial, three inches thick and weighing, I'd guess, twenty-five pounds. You had to use both hands to carry them to your station.

A kitchen like this costs about $330,000 to equip. There were thirty-six others scattered throughout the Culinary.

Chef Pardus instructed us to distribute chairs around the tables and we sat at our stations. "I'm Chef Pardus, but if you see me at Gaffney's or wandering around Woodstock, call me Michael. I graduated from here in 1981. I got my bachelor's in, I don't know what it's called, management and hospitality, something like that, from Johnson Wales—boo hiss, boo hiss." He smiled. Johnson & Wales University, while not devoted solely to the culinary arts, is among the Culinary Institute's biggest competitors. "I began teaching here last July."

Michael Pardus, thirty-seven years old, had spent much of his cooking career in high-end French restaurants and had watched most of them go under as the appeal of French restaurants faded. His last position had been executive chef of the Swiss Hotel in Sonoma. He loved northern California, decided that was where he wanted to end up, but he didn't want to be cooking fourteen hours a day. Not far from him in St. Helena, the Culinary Institute of America's new facility called Greystone would soon be opening. There, he decided, was his future, and he began a long-range plan to earn a teaching position at the Culinary's West Coast campus, built within a nineteenth-century winery and serving only professionals in the food indus-try. The first step was to apply to his alma mater in Hyde Park seventy-five miles north of New York City on the banks of the Hudson River. The school gave him a shot at the chef's practical, then offered him a job; he packed his car and headed east. He intended to show the administrators at the Culinary that he was willing to do anything to earn a position at Greystone.

He sat on the desk and tried to get to know his new students. He pointed to a big guy with thick dark hair, Lou Fusaro, the oldest student in the class at thirty-seven. "Why are you here?"

Lou said, "I don't know, really." There seemed a genuine plaintiveness in his voice, a concern: it wasn't that he hadn't thought about it. Lou was a longtime resident of Poughkeepsie, immediately south of Hyde Park; he was married, had three children, and had for years been a manufacturing operator in the shipping department at IBM, a company that once girded the local economy here. Lou could watch the dynamics of his future changing by the year. Computers kept getting smaller and smaller, requiring fewer people like him to ship them; Lou said while he was there computers that once filled a twelve-foot-by-twelve-foot room had become desktop com-puters. Clearly, IBM would not provide the stability he needed. His father had owned a bar with a kitchen and in the early eighties he'd owned a sand-wich shop; this satisfied the Culinary's entrance requirements, but practi-cally speaking, he had zero kitchen experience. He scarcely knew how to hold a knife. At last Lou said, "I guess to see where I fit in."

Chef Pardus nodded, said that was a good reason to be here. "How about you?" he said, pointing to one of the youngest in the class, Matt, not yet out of his teens. Matt simply said, "I don't know," and that was that. Chef Pardus said there were many reasons to be here; one of them might be to increase your skill level. Happy to have been supplied an answer, Matt nodded and said, "To increase my skill level."

Each of these students had been here for nine weeks already, since shortly before Christmas, in an incoming class of seventy-two. Everyone had begun with fourteen days of Introduction to Gastronomy and Culinary Math. Then they had had seven days of Sanitation and Nutrition, seven days of Product Identification (learning about produce, evaluating quality, buying it, and studying food purchasing)—six-and-a-half hours of class, then two hours of Culinary French in the evening. They moved into Meat Identification next, learning the muscular and skeletal construction of animals, and after seven days they had moved to the basement for Meat Fabrication, where they would practice their subprimal cuts, their boning, their Frenching.

Bob del Grosso, a slender forty-one-year-old with a narrow face and dark features harkening back to his family's roots in Italy, taught Introduction to Gastronomy to everyone who entered the Culinary Institute of America. His résumé was filled with Connecticut restaurants: line cook at the Black Goose Grill in Darien; chef at the Lakeville Cafe; at Le Coq Hardi Restaurant in Stamford, he was, variously, charcutier, first cook, sous chef, and finally executive chef. Del Grosso was also a trained micropaleontologist, with a master's from CUNY at Queens College. A booming oil industry had ensured plenty of jobs in his field, but as he was considering a Ph.D. in micropaleontology in the early 1980s, the oil bubble burst and his future grew cloudy. He gradually became so anxious about what he would do, he couldn't sleep and took to pacing. One morning he fell asleep on the living room floor. When dawn came, he was awakened by a beam of light in his eyes. "I had an epiphany," he told me. "I thought, 'I can *cook*!' "

Del Grosso taught in what appeared to be an old-fashioned lecture classroom—with posters of fish, vegetables, and pasta shapes taped to the wall, an extended blackboard, long curved multileveled rows of permanent seating. When he began teaching the course he was amazed to find out how few people even knew what gastronomy was. "Astronomers know what astronomy is," he said. "Physicists know what physics is. But people who claim to be gastronomers, or gastronomes, don't know what gastronomy is." Del Grosso stood before the rows of seats and talked, questioned the students, paused, squeezing his chin thoughtfully, a near caricature of Ed Sullivan, in what seemed an endless digression on food. The course did have an agenda and schedule, beginning with the notion of etiquette, and moved from there to the history of the chef in French cuisine, into nouvelle cuisine, followed by the contemporary scene, Alice Waters, and the chef-farmer connection. One class was devoted to the question "What is food?" and the final class addressed the ethics of food production.

"Let's identify the process of nouvelle cuisine," he would say to his class. "Not an easy thing to do. My belief is that you must cook to the essence. Think of nouvelle cuisine as Socratic cooking. How many of you have read Plato?" About a half dozen hands rose in a class of thirty-six. Del Grosso briefly mentioned *The Republic*, the allegory of the cave, and the notion of Platonic forms. "There is a perfect form of the salad," he said. "Say you're a Socratic cook and you want to make a hamburger. You would begin the process by posing a question: 'What is a hamburger?' " He posed this to the class. One intrepid student offered, "A round patty of ground beef put between toasted buns." Del Grosso clarified: "Round? Let's call it disc-shaped." A lively discussion of the hamburger followed. The point, del Grosso said, was to get them thinking critically about food. Many of the students had little education beyond high school, and many, whether from the armed services of the United States or having worked only in kitchens, were not used to this sort of thinking. "A chef should be Socratic," del Grosso continued, "questioning everything, including the placement of the silverware. Cooking to the essence," he said with a flourish. " 'What are you, *beef*?!' Cook to your answer. It's a very different way to cook. It requires a lot of thinking. I'm not going to encourage you to cook this way all the time because I don't. Imagine if every time you cooked an egg, you had to ask, 'What is an egg?' But it's useful to do so every now and then."

This course aimed to introduce the students to the culture upon which the school was based—and that culture had its roots in classical French cuisine. But his was a class, by design, of rambling. Del Grosso would expound for fifteen minutes on Celebration, the Walt Disney Company's planned town. And when a student mentioned the word "confit," he stopped the discussion of Gault and Millau, the journalists who coined the term "nouvelle cuisine," to ask if everyone knew the word "confit." Sensing that not everyone did, he began with the meaning of confit, and confitures, the history of confit, its purpose of preservation, and concluded with a small discourse on how he personally prepares *confit de canard*.

After describing his dry marinade and the cooking of the confit, del Grosso explained that he stores the duck legs, submerged in their congealed fat, for at least two weeks, preferably in glass jars, but plastic will do if you're in a restaurant kitchen and don't want glass jars all over the place. After two weeks, he would simply remove the legs from the fat, wipe them off, pass them under a broiler or salamander to crisp up the skin and heat the meat some. He would then serve them with potatoes that had been fried in clarified butter, along with deep-fried parsley. "Have you had deep-fried parsley?" he asked. He closed his eyes and said, "It's a miracle."

Such a class seemed spiritually at odds with Culinary Math, which took up the other half of an incoming student's day.

Homework questions: Convert twelve quarts and twelve tablespoons into a single unit of quarts. How many cups are there in four pounds of honey? You are catering a function of 350 people; you estimate that each person will eat three quarters of a cup of potato chips; how many pounds of chips should you order?

Such things were important to know. A pint is not a pound the world round. A pint of ground cinnamon, for instance, is only half a pound; a pint of honey is a pound and a half.

"You will be doing a lot of conversions when you get to Skill Development One," Julia Hill told her class. "If you're not comfortable with conversions, get comfortable." Hill used to be an accountant. She left that profession to become a restaurant manager. Eleven years ago, she arrived at this school to take a continuing education course and never left. "The moment I set foot on this campus," she said, "I knew this was where I belonged."

Her class, a review of math applications relevant to the food-service industry, was an interesting series of puzzles. When possible, she would have students bring their knife kits, hard black briefcases filled with tools. They would take apart pounds of carrots in problems addressing "as purchased quantity" and "edible portion quantity." The class began with three days of basic math, fractions, decimals and how they behaved, then moved into conversions, cost, costing recipes, ratios, and lastly alcohol measurements.

"The definition of 'cost' in this industry," she told the class, "is: cost is what you use, not how much you bought it for." Cost, therefore, was an idea, not necessarily an absolute. But this was about as close to the world of ideas as the class got, and many were glad for this. Some loathed del Grosso's class, but loved the concreteness of Culinary Math. Others hated both classes and spent nine weeks longing for the kitchen.

This was A Block. The people in it were called A Blockers. Their average age was twenty-six, and 10 percent of them would drop out. Twenty-five percent of them were women, 12 percent were minorities. A Blockers wore street clothes, but were requested to dress in light shirts, dark slacks or skirts, and dark shoes. B Block, which included sanitation and nutrition, followed A Block, and C Block—Meat Identification and Fabrication—came after that. This never varied; every graduate had gone through the school this regimental way since 1976, when the Culinary shifted to what it called a progressive learning year, though the curriculum itself expanded considerably during the following two decades. Each block, fourteen class days spread over three weeks, built upon the previous block.

This idea of building on the knowledge and skills learned in the previous class is the overarching agenda and method at the Culinary. A student doesn't enter the first kitchen until he has a basic understanding of sanitation (including, for instance, why stocks need to be cooled quickly). In Skills, students learn to sauté one chicken breast so that in the next class they can sauté sixteen of them fast. This idea carries the student through thirty weeks and seven different kitchens to Garde Manger, the final class before externship. After externship—a minimum of eighteen weeks' paid work in the industry, at restaurants, hotels, food magazines, or even the TV Food Network—they ease into the cool kitchens of baking and pastry. They then spend six weeks out of their whites in a lecture hall, learning about wines and menus, restaurant planning, and restaurant law, after which they move back into the kitchen for the final chunk of their degree, which concludes with twelve weeks in the school's four public restaurants, half the time as cooks, half the time as waiters.

The curriculum is logical in conception and relentless in practice. Life here is marched out in three-week intervals and there is no stopping. Once every three weeks, the halls fill with parents and relatives of seventy-two graduates of the Culinary Institute of America, and the following week seventy-two new students begin Gastronomy. Every three weeks seventy-two students leave for their externship, and seventy-two return. The school allows itself a two-week break in the summer and winter. There are no classes on Sundays. Other than that, the place never shuts down. The first class, A.M. Pantry, or Breakfast Cookery, begins at three-fifteen in the morning, about four hours after the last class of the previous day ends. There are twenty-one blocks in all, eighty-one weeks including externship, or roughly two years, depending how long one spends on extern. The total cost, including a dormitory room, is about $34 thousand. If a student has more time and money and stamina, he or she can spend two more classroom years here, what will then be considered junior and senior years, and graduate from Culinary Institute of America with a bachelor of professional studies degree.

But there is more to the Culinary Institute of America than these seventy-two students graduating every three weeks no matter what. The Institute has become, in the words of one food journalist, "a paragon of culinary education." When the CIA does something—whether adding a new class, opening a new restaurant, or producing a new book—the $313 billion food service industry watches. While it's never been known for creating legions of cutting-edge chefs, and its graduates are often criticized en masse for thinking they know more than they do and demanding more money than they're worth, the CIA is nevertheless often called the Harvard of cooking schools and boasts many famous graduates: Jasper White, Waldy Malouf, Chris Schlesinger, Dean Fearing, Susan Feniger, Rick Moonen, Charlie Palmer, David Burke, and Todd English, for instance, are CIA alumni. Through its continuing education programs and new California campus, it educates thousands of industry professionals every year. Its several cooking programs outside the United States make its impact international.

Opening in 1946 as the New Haven Restaurant Institute with an enrollment of fifty men, and moving to its current campus in 1972 to accommodate an enrollment of more than a thousand students, the school now enrolls more than two thousand students each year—some just out of high school, others middle-aged and beginning second careers. Tim Ryan, senior vice president of the Culinary, with telling understatement, told me, "We're a food and beverage place." But the Culinary is in fact the oldest, biggest, best-known, and most influential cooking school in America, the only residential college in the United States devoted solely to the study of the culinary arts. It employs more than a hundred chefs from twenty countries. This brick monastery on the verdant banks of the Hudson River contains more food knowledge and experience than any other place on earth.

Chef Pardus slid off the desk and stood. "This class," he said, "is to provide a culinary foundation for the rest of your time at the CIA and for the rest of your culinary careers. If you don't know what mirepoix is, what demi-glace is, what cuisson is, and you go to work in a high-end restaurant, you won't be taken seriously." The school, he said, gave you "a professional language," a standard. "If I ask David"—David Scott was at my table, a tall, clean-cut Californian in his mid-twenties with short dark hair—"to panfry a pork chop, and if I ask Lou to panfry a pork chop, I want to make sure they have the same idea about what a pan-fried pork chop is. It's got to be part of you."

Pardus went over the uniform policy, codes of dress, hygiene, and courtesy. "You know the rules," he said. "I don't want to lecture you."

"We've got quite a few women in this class," he said, five of seventeen. "This is good. A lot of guys here need to learn how to work with a woman on an equal level."

Pardus walked to the steam kettles and ran through homework policy while skimming mats of gray foam off the blanching beef bones. "If you don't have your homework, I don't care why. This is college, this isn't grade school." Four two-page papers would be due during the next three weeks (brown veal stock, derivative sauces, emulsion sauces, and starches); comments on assigned videos and regular costing forms must be completed.

Each student had the chance to earn seventy-five points a day on daily preparation, attitude and teamwork, knife skills, the assigned soups and sauces, timing and sanitation, amounting in the end to half the final grade. You pretty much had to not do your knife cuts to get a zero on these, but if all your food was not finished by six o'clock, points were deducted. If you didn't present your food to Chef Pardus by six-thirty you received zero points because by six-thirty, he said, "your customers have left and your food isn't *worth* anything."

He reminded everyone to carry knives held down and at our side, no horseplay, no throwing things. And a word about side towels. The Culinary imported these sturdy items—gray-and-white-checked cotton cloths that students tuck into their apron strings—from Germany because it couldn't find acceptable ones in the United States, and they were excellent tools. At this stage in a student's career, the towels were crisp and clean, all but new. "Side towels are not for wiping your board," Pardus said. "They are not for wiping your knife, they're not for dabbing your brow. They're for grabbing hot things. Things are going to be hot. Anticipate it, expect it."

"You're going to be lifting a hundred and twenty pounds of bones a day," he said. "I don't want to remind you, bend your knees. If you're going to be in this business, you're gonna need a strong and healthy back."

"I want these floors kept clean. If you see something on the floor, *pick it up*. I don't care if you didn't drop it. It's your *floor*; keep it *clean*."

The chef demoed *everything*. His first demo was peeling a carrot. I didn't think one way or another about this, though I'd heard people complain that the Culinary Institute of America makes everyone learn how to chop an onion, regardless of background, and that this was somehow an onerous circumstance. I knew how to chop an onion, but I honestly didn't mind watching how someone else did it. And there was always something to learn, even about peeling carrots. Pardus didn't hold the carrot in the air to peel it; he rested the fat end on the cutting board, rotating it with his fingertips. This was faster and conserved energy. If you were peeling twenty pounds of carrots, it would make a difference. And you wanted to be fast. If you were paying diswashers five dollars an hour, and they were peeling carrots for you, Pardus said, "you've got to be able to show them how, you've got to be able to beat them in a race."

We stood around the chef, who stood facing us at the head of Table Two, watching him peel a carrot. Somebody asked if it was necessary to peel carrots at all if they were going into the stock.

Pardus stopped peeling and said, "Do you peel a carrot? Some people don't. I like my stock to taste as clean and fresh as possible. My way is not the only way to do things, but I've found that people who don't peel carrots don't do it because they're lazy." He smirked. "Put the peels on their *salad* if they like peels so much. You want to eat this?" He lifted the clump of dirty limp peels from the cutting board.

Everyone would cut two pounds of mirepoix, one part each of celery and carrot, two parts onion. And we would do this every day for the next six weeks. This mirepoix would flavor the stock we made each day.

Next he demoed tomato concassé—chopped tomato. He already had a pot of water on the stove boiling to loosen the tomato's skin. It was the middle of February and the tomatoes were pretty firm so he suggested forty-five seconds in boiling water, then into a bowl of ice water. Every table had a bowl of ice water on it for shocking tomatoes. Chef Pardus peeled the tomato, removed the seeds, chopped it, and told us, "That's tomato con-cassé. That's it." He instructed us, when mincing an onion—every day we would mince half an onion and thin slice the other half—to make the initial cuts as thin as possible, so you didn't have to overwork it later and smash all the juice out of it. The mince should be dry and bright, not gray and soggy. Peeling and mincing garlic and shallots was next, parsley fine-chopped but he didn't want powder, and finally the annoying tourner, a vegetable cut in the shape of a football. We would keep our fine knife cuts in small paper cups and hold these in a hotel pan along with our two pounds of mirepoix. At the end of the day our various cuts would be combined in plastic bags.

On this, our Day One in Skills, Chef Pardus dismissed us to our tables and we began our standard daily mise en place. Even though he had given us a tour of the kitchen I didn't know where anything was, and I circled around looking for a bowl for scraps, a hotel pan (a deep rectangular steam-table insert), a roll of brown paper towel. I asked Paul, who appeared to know exactly where everything was, how he knew and he said, "I don't know. I just do."

For the next couple of hours, as we did our cuts, Chef Pardus would cor-rect our hand position on the knife. We were not to grip the entire handle of the knife like a hammer, we were not to extend an index finger across the top of the blade; we would grip the blade between index finger and thumb and with the rest of the hand grip the knife's handle. There was no other way to do it. If Pardus wasn't showing someone how to grip a knife, he was telling people to clean up the mess at their station or to look at the mess on the floor at their feet. Then he would say, "I do more talking on Day One than on any other day. In a week this kitchen will be humming."

I had been loaned a knife kit by the Institute. It was, I sensed immedi-ately, a powerful possession. The bag contained a twelve-inch chef's knife, a paring knife, a boning knife, and a slicing knife—each with a rosewood handle—a digital thermometer, a pastry brush, some pastry-bag tips, a two-ounce ladle, and a small pepper mill. As we all got to work, the chef, looking a little concerned, said quietly to me, "Are you O.K.? Are you com-fortable in a kitchen?" I told him sure. About two minutes later, having gathered most of the items I needed, I reached for a scrap of cheesecloth to my left. My chef's knife lay flat on my board between my hand and the cheesecloth. As I reached, the tip of my ring finger hit the blade. The knife had been sharpened so well that it didn't move when I hit it; my finger simply slid into it and I had a clean cut. A sharp knife is a safe knife.

To be the only person in the class who had not worked in the industry and to cut yourself almost as soon as you produce your knife is embarrassing. I wanted to avoid calling attention to myself; I also wanted people to think I knew what I was doing. The chef was nice about it, said it was good luck to cut yourself the first day. "Go wash your hands. I'll give you a Band-Aid." He retrieved a bandage from his desk drawer. He also gave me a finger cot, referred to as a finger condom because that's what it looked like and how it worked. It covered the bandaged finger completely, and it did not impede me further as I executed my standard daily mise en place. Bianca Rizzo, twenty-one years old, from Queens, stood beside me doing the same. Greg Lynch, thirty-two, and David Scott and Travis Alberhasky, both in their mid-twenties, stood across from me, their backs to the stoves. All three had worked in kitchens before, and Greg had turned down a promotion to become head chef at a Vermont bed-and-breakfast shortly before he left for the Institute. He was here for one reason: money. A diploma from the Culinary would translate into bigger salaries down the road, and he hoped to get a fairly quick return on his thirty grand.

Each day, then, we would chop our two pounds of mirepoix (named, as so many things are, after an eighteenth-century Frenchman, in this case a field marshal named Duc du Lévis-Mirepoix, whose cook flavored his sauce Espagnol with it). We would slice half an onion, keeping our fingertips tucked in to go fast without bloodying the onion—"Keep your fingers curled back and your thumb tucked behind your fingers," Pardus said. "I'm telling you right now, someone here is going to slice their thumb chopping parsley because they didn't keep it tucked behind their fingers." You could literally lose sight of your thumb squeezing a large bunch of parsley to begin fine-chopping it. We would concassé two plum tomatoes and make a sachet d'épices from a square of cheesecloth in which we enclosed five or six peppercorns, a bay leaf, a thyme sprig, and several parsley stems; garlic is often included in a standard sachet, but Pardus asked us did we know how the stock would be used? Would it be reduced to glace and used for a sauce, and would that sauce want garlic? This is how he wanted us to think in his kitchen. We would give him two turned vegetables. He would also include a couple of special cuts, paysanne and batonnet carrots, for instance. Before six o'clock we would approach the chef like Oliver Twist stepping toward Mr. Brumble for more gruel; the chef, seated at the desk, would glance up through his gold-rimmed spectacles to see your face, then look down, paring knife in hand to flick through the minces. "Your diced onion looks good," he told me on this first day. "Mmmm, your shallots look a little uneven." He was able to produce various sizes of mince on the blade of the knife as evidence. I nodded.

Uniformity, in shallots as in everything, was an indicator of excellence. My sliced onion, for instance, was too thick but the slices were uniform and that was more important. He lifted one of my turned carrots. This was a tough little cut, and the carrot was especially difficult to curve a knife through; you could easily whittle them to nothing looking for that perfect seven-sided football. "Not bad," he said. "They need a little work, but not bad." I took the hotel pan away, and Chef Pardus crimped behind some lifted papers to scratch out my score from a possible fifteen.

The products I brought to him in my two-inch-deep hotel pan were written on the board each day as SMEP, or standard mise en place. After six o'clock, the time by which everyone should have taken his or her hotel pan to Chef Pardus for their daily knife-cuts grade, all would begin dumping their minced onion in the minced onion bag and the sliced onion in the sliced onion bag. The class's combined mise en place would amount to thirty-six pounds of mirepoix, big bags of all the other minces, chops, and dices, and eighteen sachets d'épices.

I was here to learn the basics, and certainly it didn't get more basic than chopping onions and mincing parsley.

Dinner was at six-thirty. We had each been given tickets that told us which kitchen to go to and told the sous chef at the kitchen that we were entitled to eat there. Our kitchen, K-8, ate at K-9, Chef Smith's kitchen next door. Rumor was that Chef Smith had been a marine. He looked like a marine—chin tucked, stone-faced, hands behind his stiff back, moving only to pop a green bean in his mouth to check that it was done—reviewing the troops in his Introduction to Hot Foods class, which immediately followed Skills. This was the first production kitchen, the first time students cooked for their peers. Our Skills class stood at the end of the line and waited in the hallway. Intro meals were classically based: two vegetables, a starch, a protein item, and a sauce, four different plates, one for each station—grill, sauté, roast, braise—along with a vegetarian plate. Roast chicken with a jus lié, for instance, would be served with gaufrette potatoes, sautéed spinach, and glazed carrots; veal blanquette would be served with chive mashed potatoes, batonnet root vegetables, and green beans, and would be called "braise." If you asked for it, the student sous chef would shout, "Fire one braise!" and the student on braise would shout back, "Firing one braise!"

We would then walk our plates down the hall, turn right, and walk through another hall to the dining room, called Alumni Hall, a long room with a high vaulted ceiling, the chapel of this former Jesuit monastery. Large alcoves were used for more tables, and tables lined the altar platform, now called the stage. Stained-glass windows depicting scenes from the life of Christ surrounded you while you ate.

That night I dined with Erica, a youngster of nineteen, from suburban Philadelphia. Erica was short and had abundant thick brown hair that stayed wrapped in a bun and covered with a hair net as the dress code demands. Her face was almost perfectly round, and she had the bluest eyes I had ever seen. They were so blue, with a sort of shimmering, crystalline depth, I thought for sure she wore colored contacts and I asked her as we stood in line in the hall outside K-9. She said she wore contacts but the blue was natural. "Why," she inquired, anxiously, "do you like my eyes?"

"I think your eyes are incredible," I said. "They're the bluest eyes I've ever seen."

She smiled and said, "Do you really? Oh, thank you. I love it when people say nice things about my eyes. David, do you like my eyes?" She batted her lids at him.

"Yes, Erica," David said. "I do like your eyes." He rolled his own, and Erica thanked him and smiled.

We got our plates—I was lucky enough to get one of the last sautés, the veal—and sat down with Erica, Lou, and Greg. Lou told me about IBM, where he worked part-time, from about seven in the morning till eleven. His wife, a nurse, worked nights. Lou would take the kids to his wife's parents' house at around six, where they waited to go to school; Lou would return home at eleven-thirty, have a bite to eat and a quiet moment to study before leaving for the Culinary at around one. Most nights he'd be home before ten. Lou was the oldest in the class and had perhaps the least kitchen experience. He scarcely knew how to chop an onion. Greg Lynch—divorced with two kids; on weekends he'd drive to Vermont to be with them—had done factory work after high school, then moved to kitchen work; he was fast, he could cook, and he made it clear he was putting up with these basics simply for the sake of the degree. Erica had spent half her senior year of high school at a technical school learning kitchen skills, then worked about a year at a bed-and-breakfast on the appetizer station; she'd struggled to convince her parents that kitchen work was a viable career choice. Her eventual goal was to teach.

Dinner was over quickly and we were back in the kitchen before seven-thirty, cleaning bowls and pans, straining the stocks, and shoveling all the steaming bones and cartilage and soggy mirepoix into the big blue bin of compostable waste. The brown veal stock would cook slowly overnight and be strained, cooled, and stored by the students in the A.M. Skills class, which ran from seven to one-thirty.

When the kitchen was clean, when aprons had been untied and rolled up and stuffed in backpacks, paper chefs' hats had been doffed for the evening, and knives were secured in their hard, black CIA-issued briefcases, chairs were once again unstacked from beside the dry-storage cage and set out around the tables. We sat for lecture in the large bright clean kitchen.

Day One lecture concerned stocks. We had already made gallons of stock today—or Greg had; he seemed to be doing all the stock work today, hustling around the kitchen like a scrappy little point guard in a blacktop hoops game—and while the brown stock would simmer all night, the white beef stock we'd made had not had sufficient time to cook. So as Chef Pardus explained how to label the stocks (stored in rectangular two-gallon plastic containers), he noted, "A good white stock should simmer about five hours. Tomorrow we're going to use the weak stock instead of water."

Chef Pardus began his lecture by reading from the paper taped to the wall. Typically, he would carry a wooden spoon while he lectured, spinning it in the air as he talked or using it as a pointer.

"A great stock is judged by," he paused, "its *flavor*." The first bulleted item is, of course, crucial. Does it have a good clean taste, a taste appropriate for the bones and aromatics that have cooked in it? The second item is clarity. You did not want a muddy stock, especially if you were going to use that stock for consommé, as we would soon be doing. Color, too, is to be evaluated; a brown stock should be brown, a white stock white (as opposed to gray), and chicken stock should be a pale yellow. Body: "Texture in the mouth," Pardus explained. "If it feels like water in your mouth, it doesn't have body." And finally, aroma. A brown stock should have a roasted aroma, chicken stock should smell like chicken, and white stock should have a neutral aroma, and the aroma should always be clean and fresh.

"You should judge a good stock by these criteria," Chef Pardus announced. "And if it's not a good stock, you should be able to figure out what went wrong according to each one." If your brown stock lacks color, for instance, perhaps you didn't caramelize your mirepoix well enough. If there's no body, perhaps you used too much water and the gelatin was spread too thin, or you didn't cook your bones long enough to release all their gelatin. Knuckles, bones with abundant connective tissue, release a lot of gelatin but are less flavorful; bones with a lot of marrow have good flavor but the marrow can cloud the stock. A good mix of bones was therefore optimal. With every stock every day, he wanted those in charge to bring a sample of the stock to him and he would evaluate the stock aloud using all these criteria.

Chef Pardus admitted that there were many ways to make stock, many good ways, but said, "We're going to do it the K-8 way." And the K-8 way was the official CIA way—also known as The Party Line—which was spelled out in the Institute's *The New Professional Chef*, a huge cooking textbook.

Pardus used a large flip pad on an easel to lecture from. He performed each lecture once every six weeks, and the reusable flip pad saved a lot of writing on the board. A chart of stock ratios was the first thing on view; I copied it on the inside cover of one of my notebooks. Pardus flipped a page, pointed with his spoon, and said, "Stock is." He paused. "The foundation for all classical French cooking."

*F*ond de cuisine, foundation of cooking. "It is to the production of perfect stocks that the sauce cook should devote himself," wrote Auguste Escoffier, the great French chef and writer, "the sauce cook who is, as the Marquis de Cussy remarked, 'the enlightened chemist, the creative genius and the cornerstone of the edifice of superlative cookery.' " The spirit and name of Auguste Escoffier presides over the Culinary Institute much as Buddha presides over Eastern philosophy. His 1903 book, *Le Guide Culinaire*, eventually translated into English as *The Complete Guide to the Art of Modern Cookery* (known at this school as either *Le Guide*, or the bible), is an extraordinary accomplishment in its thoroughness and philosophy of cooking. Escoffier was born in Nice in 1846 and, after establishing himself as a cook, was invited to work at a hotel in Switzerland in 1884 by a former headwaiter who had moved into hotel management named César Ritz. The two fellows hit it off and went on to open the Ritz in Paris in 1898, and eventually the Carlton in London.

Escoffier, while providing about two thousand recipes, never abandoned his focus on basic culinary preparations, such as stocks. "These culinary preparations," he writes in the second paragraph of his book, "define the fundamentals and the requisite ingredients without which nothing of importance can be attempted." There seemed to be something humble in his hubris—*without which nothing of importance can be attempted*. Furthermore he named these basic preparations, ticked them off like items on a grocery list without which nothing of importance—nothing, mind you—could be attempted. There were thirteen. Of these thirteen he set apart a primary group of eight preparations that were composed of three broad categories: stock, roux, mother sauces. That was it, the basis for the art of modern cookery, and the reason I was here.

I was never one to get all goosey about recipes. Recipes were a dime a dozen. You could follow them for a hundred years and never learn to cook. I was after method; I wanted the physical experience of doing it, knowing what the food should look like, sound like, smell like, feel like while it cooked. I had made my own stocks and had talked to various chefs about their stocks, but at the Culinary Institute of America I would learn the classical preparation of stock, the foundation, the bedrock of classical cookery. If you didn't know how to make a great stock, if you didn't even know what a great stock tasted like, you were doomed to mediocrity in the kitchen, at best, and at worst, ignorant foolishness.

Certain facts concerning one's own behavior and choices in life can only be understood in retrospect. I rented our home in Cleveland, moved virtually everything we owned into my father's house, and transported my wife (a photographer who had paying clients in the city we were leaving), our daughter (not yet ambulatory), and myself five hundred miles to a one-bedroom garret above a garage in Tivoli, New York, a Hudson River Valley town with a one-to-one human-cow ratio. I had done all of this, I eventually realized, in order to learn how to make a superlative brown veal stock.

The physical principles that bring about a brown veal stock are no different from those of other stocks. Water heats bones. The bones (and the meat scraps still connected to them) release protein, vitamins, fat, gelatin, mineral salts, and lactic and amino acids. The vegetables, herbs, and spices release pectin, starches, acids, and sulfur compounds. The younger the bones, the more connective tissue they'll have; connective tissue is made up largely of a protein called collagen, which melts into a substance called gelatin, a gluey protein, and this gives a stock body. When you cook meats, you caramelize the savory juices and meat proteins; their taste becomes liquefied in the stock. The vegetables caramelize, their sugars brown, and this, too, liquefies. Add the mirepoix, throw in some tomato product that is cooked till it becomes a deep rich brown, pour cold water on it, and heat it very, very slowly—till it's just hot enough to release a couple of bubbles to the surface every few seconds, without any other movement—and tend this mixture for hours and hours, skimming frequently, and you'll have a flavorful, brown, nutritious liquid. Degrease it, strain it, degrease it some more. Then it is done.

You would never want to eat this stuff plain, and it doesn't smell very good either. Roasted chicken stock tastes moments away from a tasty soup; beef stock tastes like beef. A perfect brown veal stock has what is referred to as a "neutral" flavor. This is a kind way of saying it doesn't taste like anything you're used to eating or would want to eat.

Neutrality, however, is the key to this stock. You can do a million different things with a great veal stock because it has the remarkable quality of taking on other flavors without imposing a flavor of its own. It offers its own richness and body anonymously. When you reduce it, it becomes its own sauce starter. You can add roux to brown veal stock for an eventual demi-glace and with a demi-glace, you can, in about thirty seconds, create any of a hundred distinct sauces in the manner of Escoffier.

If you are truly insane, take this perfect brown veal stock, this gold, this liquid heaven that you have simmered for hours and hours, and dump it over freshly roasted veal bones, and later add some deeply caramelized mirepoix and browned tomato paste. Simmer it slowly, slowly all over again. If you have made perfect moves throughout, you will have a superlative brown veal stock.

The first day in the kitchen was nearly done. Chef Pardus reviewed the method for making white and brown stocks. When he said the word "pincé" (which is what you're doing to tomato paste when you cook it till it's brown), his gold-rimmed glasses rode up high on the crinkles on the bridge of his nose. Pardus was not even-toned. He italicized words as they left his mouth by making his lips do all sorts of contortions. For instance, when he talked about other stocks and uses for stocks—fumet, court bouillon, bouillon versus broth, essence—and he got to glace, he would say, "Glace is a highly reduced stock. What you do is you take a gallon of brown stock and you reduce it down to a cup, and when it cools it's hard as a *Superball*. That's *glace*." He began the word "Superball" with his lips pursed out beyond his nose, and by the time he got to the *l* sound, his lips had tucked back inside so all you saw was a vague white rim where his lips should have been. This made his consonants really pop. It also made you want to try bouncing some of this glace off one of these stainless-steel tables we'd been chopping mirepoix on all day.

I departed K-8 alone and strode past the former Jesuit chapel-turned-dining room, down the back steps of Roth Hall, through the empty frigid quad, down more steps, and into the vast parking lot on the edge of the four-lane expanse of Route 9. I was in cooking school. Look at my houndstooth-check trousers, my big black heavy-soled shoes, my knife kit in hand, my leather briefcase over my shoulder—the symbolic combination of school and kitchen. I was going to learn how to make a perfect brown veal stock, the reasons it became perfect, and everything that followed from there.

 Routine

Chef Pardus had been right; by Day Three the routine locked in and the kitchen hummed. We typically arrived between one-thirty and ten of two; the food steward, with help, would haul the huge gray tub of food from the storeroom up a flight of stairs and down the hall to K-8; a member of each table would collect cutting boards for the others, another would grab bowls for the table, enough cheesecloth for everyone's sachet d'épices. On this day and for the next two weeks, someone putting together a sachet would call out, "Who's got the thyme?" and Travis would say, "Oooh, about ten after two." He almost never tired of it and when he did, someone would say, "Travis, do you have the thyme?" and Travis would oblige. People found their personal routines. Greg was the unspoken leader of our table. When Chef Pardus needed clarified butter he would have each table clarify five or ten pounds of it, and Greg would be the one from our table to do it. I wanted my onions out of the way first—onions for mirepoix, half an onion sliced, half an onion minced, and move on from there. Bianca, next to me, almost never made a sound moving through her standard mise en place. She had worked five years in a bakery but had no kitchen experience. And David, who set his board between Travis and Greg across from us, worked earnestly and affably—after graduating from the University of Southern California he had begun a career in banking before coming to the Culinary.

Erica had a hard time getting going, her blue eyes notwithstanding. She kept forgetting to put her hair net on and thus lost most of her sanitation points every day. Her uniform was badly soiled, even from Day One, before anyone had cooked a thing.

Erica worked across from Eun-Jung Lee. Eun-Jung, a young nutritionist from Seoul, had worked with one of Korea's best-known chefs who had taken courses at the Culinary and had recommended that Eun-Jung apply. Eun-Jung, who couldn't have been much over five feet tall but whose wavy black hair was always properly constrained by a hair net, first appeared to me as shy, but I soon realized that this trait was more likely an Asian delicacy of spirit combined with a limited understanding of English. To compensate, she took notes like a bandit, always moved her chair smack up front for lecture, and studied continually. She endeared me to her by inviting me on Day Three, before anyone was really talking to me, to a kimchi party in her dorm room, where we would eat various pickled vegetables and she would show off her Korean cookbooks. She missed home.

Ben Grossman, a tall twenty-five-year-old from Rockland County, New York, with short dark hair, was the group leader and thus in charge of making sure everyone had course guides for each class and addressing problems that anyone in the group might have; he made announcements of special meetings, and generally kept school life in order for the group. Ben received his bachelor's from SUNY Albany, then got his C.P.A. from the state of New York and worked for about a year as an accountant, before jumping ship. He can trace his career switch to a 1993 *New York Times* article and recipe for turkey meatloaf. That's when it clicked, he said, and he knew he would go to the Culinary Institute. He worked first for a caterer at the South Street Seaport and then, through a family connection, got a job in the kitchen of the Stanhope Hotel, where for seven months he worked on everything from garde manger to pantry to banquet.

He did not make a good first impression on Chef Pardus. What kind of group is this going to be, Chef Pardus wondered, when the group leader forgets to put his name on his paper? Others failed to hand in initial assignments. Perhaps these were just two of many details—such as Erica's netless hair, Eun-Jung's incomprehension, or the ten thumbs attached to Lou's hands—that gathered in the chef's mind. This was not going to be a good group, he was thinking. But there was Greg, already very proficient, and Adam, tall, skinny, with hair so short and black it looked almost sharp. He rarely smiled and usually seemed angry. When I asked Adam how old he was, he scowled and said, "Twenty-six? Twenty-seven? I don't know, man." But Adam asked a lot of good questions.

Susanne, too, had an intellectual bent. She was a slight twenty-seven-year-old with curly black hair and dark eyes set deep into her narrow face. She had spent three years as an English major at Barnard before dropping out, dissatisfied with her classes, she said, and tired of living in Harlem. She worked in advertising for several years (her husband was still in advertising) before deciding to give culinary school a shot. She had waitressed here and there during school, but she needed more than that to comply with entrance requirements, and she wangled an apprenticeship, or *stage*, at New York's Chanterelle.

On Day Three, my three-by-five prep card read:

Ovens/pans
SMEP (batonnet, sm dc carrot)
Brown Stock
Onion Soup

I had written the first item to remind myself to turn the ovens on first thing and get the pans hot and ready for the veal bones as soon as the students in Meat Fabrication made their daily delivery. You could lose a good half hour if no one turned on the ovens. Each table was assigned one of the three stocks, and the fourth table would set up the chef's demo—today, setting out onion, retrieving sauce and sauté pans, measuring out forty ounces of white stock, filling a white paper cup with a couple of ounces of Blair's Apple Jack so that everything was ready to go when the chef shouted, "Demo in five minutes!" During demo, the entire class would stand around Chef Pardus at the burners by Table Two next to the reach-in coolers. He would talk and perform and we would listen and watch. There would seem little complexity in the subject of onion soup, but it was fun to be cooking anything at all.

Chef Pardus had told us yesterday during lecture that he did not want us to use cheese or crouton. "I'm interested in seeing if you can make a good onion soup." He had gone over the criteria for evaluating the quality of the soup: color, body, temperature ("I want it *hot*; I want it served in a *hot* bowl; I don't want it *boiling* in the bowl"), aroma, and, of course, flavor.

And Day Three he demoed everything, beginning with the sliced onions: uniform; short enough to fit on a spoon. You didn't want a long strand of onion hanging off some lady's spoon, ready to drop onto her four-hundred-dollar dress, the chef said. "Notice how I'm holding my hands," Chef

Pardus said, slicing the onion on the big maple cutting board. He stopped to speak. "My fingertips are *curled*. My thumb's in *back*. I'm not gonna *lose* anything. I'm not going down to the *nurse*. I'm not going to the *hospital*. I got *other* things to *do*."

He turned to the stove, put a sauté pan on the flame, and said, "This is where you play with your flame. The French guys call this your piano. And they say you tune your piano, you want to tune it to make beautiful music. It's up to you. You're the maestro." He lowered the flame to cook the onions slowly.

Pardus regarded the jiggly white beef stock, set out for him in a half-gallon measuring pitcher. "You want to heat a little bit of your stock up and taste it before you spend all the time and effort to waste good soup," he said. "I'm pretty sure this is good. We made it ourselves last night."

"That was the one we used the liquid from the previous day," said Ben Grossman, erstwhile accountant. "Could that be why it's so gelatinous?"

"It could be," Pardus answered. "But also it went for an awful long time. We started it at about three o'clock and it probably went until about—aaw dammit."

We were in darkness. Everyone in the class followed Pardus: "Aaw."

After about thirty seconds the lights came back on. "Go ahead," Chef Pardus said, "turn off all the ovens. Do you have fire over there?" Greg checked, said no. "Turn off all the ovens," Pardus continued. "The pilots went out. It's . . . winter in New York!" When the power at the Culinary goes out, all the gas lines close off and must be manually turned on again. When this happens, the maintenance crew spreads out through the old Jesuit monastery with blowtorches in hand to relight one thousand pilot lights.

"O.K., so the demo's on hold, guys," Pardus said.

"Oh, no!" cried Lola in mock horror. Lola was from Staten Island. When I asked her why she was here, she said, "I wanna learn how to make gumbo." I sensed here a kindred spirit. I'd noticed Lola, her deep brown eyes and long brown hair, mainly because she and Travis, whom I faced daily as I cut and chopped, were often engaged in surreptitious whispering and chuckling. I did not know this then, but they had met for the first time a few weeks earlier in Meat Identification, and all I can guess is that Meat Identification has curious effects on some people.

"Hey," Pardus said, about a half hour later, once the men in Culinary work shirts and brown pants had relit the pilots, and his onions had begun to sizzle. "You guys hear they started a new media branch of the CIA called the Food and Beverage Institute. Really. We're gonna make our own videos, publish our own books, we're gonna maybe do CD-ROMs, stuff like that. So we've got the CIA and the FBI. It's the truth. Isn't that cute.

"O.K., we're starting to get some caramelization here but not quite as much as I want. I want these to be fairly deeply caramelized. I want to build up that complex caramel flavor and aroma we were talking about yesterday. Caramel is a real complex action of sugar. When it starts to caramelize, all kinds of molecular things happen; I can't give you a dissertation on that, but it's complicated."

"What do you mean by complex?" I asked.

There was some talking in the ranks so Pardus piped up a bit and said, "The question is what is complex?" He waited a moment longer, then said, "You guys done? Let me know when you guys are done with your conversation and I'll resume."

Lola apologized.

"Have you taken raw table sugar and put it in your mouth?" he continued. "What's it taste like? It tastes sweet, that's about all you can say for it. You take a piece of *caramel*, a caramel chew? Put that in your mouth. What's that taste like? It's sweet, but there's something else going on in there. It's different, more complicated. Maybe there's vanilla flavors, maybe there's spicy cinnamon flavors; you can get all these different flavors that occur when they start to caramelize and the corresponding aromas that come along with that."

On the back of my prep list for this day, beneath my equipment list, I'd written the name "McGee" and circled it. This was to remind myself to stop at the bookstore and buy *On Food and Cooking: The Science and Lore of the Kitchen*. It's part of the standard issue at the CIA. Pardus had told the class the night before that everyone should read this book straight through— twice—before graduating. The author, Harold McGee, had become shorthand for the title. Throughout the year, whenever there was speculation about what was actually happening to food as it cooked, the response would be, "Read McGee" or "Check McGee."

On page 609 McGee confirms Pardus's comments: "The chemical reactions involved in caramelization are very numerous and not very well understood," he writes. "If glucose, an even simpler sugar than the disaccharide sucrose, is browned, this single species of molecule breaks down and recombines to form at least 100 different reaction products, among them sour organic acids, sweet and bitter derivatives, many fragrant volatile molecules, and brown-colored polymers. It is a remarkable transformation and a fortunate one for the palate."

This browning of food can create such astonishing changes in food that companies have been able to imitate expensive tastes, such as maple, chocolate, coffee, mushroom, bread, and meat, simply by cooking cheap sugar and amino acids. Heating sugar and cereal flours does the same thing. Postum, McGee notes—roasted wheat, bran, and molasses—is an old concoction meant to substitute for coffee, marketed in 1895 by C. W. Post.

"So I've got the fond building up on the bottom of my pan," Chef Pardus continued. He would deglaze the fond, the browned sugar stuck to the pan, with the Apple Jack, then add the white beef stock, and simmer. He would cook it just enough for the flavor he wanted and after it was seasoned exactly to his liking, he would announce that the onion soup was ready and that we should grab a tasting spoon and taste it. This was the mark we were aiming for. As he cooked, we prepared our standard daily mise en place. Mise en place ("put in place") was a term that extended beyond our daily preparations—chefs were often talking about "mental mise en place." Before the onion soup demo, I was in the midst of bringing my parsley to a fine chop, but in the middle I somewhat absentmindedly swiped the parsley off my knife between my thumb and index fingers. My finger caught the blade and I winced. Chef Pardus saw this and said, "I'll get you a Band-Aid."

I said, "That's all right, I brought one."

He did a double take and said, "You brought a Band-Aid because you thought you'd be dumb enough to *cut* yourself?" He chuckled. "Now *that's* mise en place."

When we felt we had brought our soup to caramelized perfection, we would carry our bowl—using our side towels because the bowl had better be hot—to the chef for him to taste and grade. He sat behind the desk like an old-fashioned Latin-school teacher, only with a tall white paper hat on, telling many of us that our onions had been overcaramelized, had gone too dark, past sweet.

After the pots and pans and knives and ladles and china caps and chinois and marmites and bowls were cleaned and put away and the stock had been cooled and labeled and stored, and the floor had been swept, and the stainless-steel tables had been wiped and dried and chairs set around them, Chef Pardus handed back the papers on brown veal stock that had been due on Day One. I usually sat across from Travis, who had been in the army, stationed in Vilseck, Germany, was now in the army reserves, and had a job flipping burgers at Burger King in nearby Kingston; he was a tall, husky fellow from Kansas City, Missouri, had clipped blond hair, and wore glasses. He'd begun his culinary career at age fifteen, washing dishes at Furr's, a cafeteria chain. He gradually worked his way through fry cook, baker, vegetable cook, dinner cook. He then cooked at a Greyhound bus terminal, and after that worked in the bakery of the Kansas City Hyatt. By then he knew he wanted to attend the CIA. He didn't have the money, so he joined the army for two-and-a-half years.

Judging from his expression and the way he shoved his paper immediately into his bag, Travis was not pleased with his grade. No one looked very pleased actually. David Scott, a graduate of the University of Southern California, sat in stunned disbelief. He had gotten a three out of five, and he'd tried hard. Paul Trujillo, from Belport, Long Island, got a four—it took him two hours just to type it.

Pardus seemed to sense people's consternation. With knife cuts, it's clear what's good and what's not. You do them or you don't. If the consommé is cloudy, no one disagrees. But two out of five—Adam's grade—on a paper? This is cooking school, not English, their annoyed faces seemed to say, and we're in a kitchen, not a classroom.

"Hey," Pardus said to the grumblers, "most of you, when you get out of here, are going to be able to get pretty good jobs as line cooks. If you're good, you'll move up quickly to sous chefs. And when you're sous chef, people are going to look to you for *answers*. 'Hey, Chef, why does it do this, why does it do that?' And they're going to *expect* you to have answers. You're training to be managers, not flunkies. When you graduate from this school, you're expected to be *leaders* in the industry. You want to be flunkies? You want to drink generic beer the rest of your life? That's not why you're here. So when I don't think you're *pushing* it, I won't give you the grade." He wanted his students to know how to dig for information. "If someone asks you to do an Escoffier dinner for seventy after you graduate," he said, "you better know how to do it." The next paper would be on emulsified sauces, and he mentioned it now. "If you understand the chemistry of how an emulsion *works*, it's easier to *fix* it when it *breaks*. You have to have the knowledge and skill to fix it. I want you to look deeper into the subject. *Why* is hollandaise considered a mother sauce by some people but not others?"

He relaxed a bit, looked around at the class. Then he spun his spoon in the air.

"O.K.," he said, "you need to pick up the sense of urgency. You can be the best cook in the world but if you can only turn out one plate every two hours, you're never gonna get hired." And then he was off into the evening's lecture, the method for cream soups, which we would be making tomorrow, cream of broccoli specifically, but that was a detail. *Method* was what we would be learning.

What I had expected on this Day Three to be a rather pedestrian lesson in onion soup, more or less still warm-up before the real stuff, became instead an experiment in and discussion of caramelization. The students would be caramelizing their brains out in a hundred different ways, but here was caramelization in a pure form, white broth flavored and brought to a deep rich amber solely with caramelized onions.

That day it began to feel like we were living inside a cooking show. The demos were just like the TV Food Network, only now you could really see things, smell them, hear them, have an actual sense of time. Here you could ask the chef questions. If you thought something was bogus—I was eagerly awaiting the demos on the béchamel and the roux-thickened brown sauce—you could say so and the chef would defend it. Pardus was a fun chef, animated and smart. When he demoed the American Bounty vegetable soup, a soup that calls for ten vegetables, all of which require different cooking times synchronized to the same end, he ladled some clarified butter into his pan and sweated some leeks, then some onions, then added the garlic, saying, "You're cooking with your eyes, you're cooking with your nose, you're cooking with your ears—all your senses." He took the pan off the flame and swept it slowly before us, our heads bobbing one by one to smell the garlic that had only just started to cook. "It smells a little raw now," Pardus said. He cooked it more. "That's almost there," and he swept it again through the crowd of noses, eyes, and ears. The garlic smell had fully developed—a smell I'd inhaled a thousand times, yet I'd never stopped to scrutinize the stages of its cooking. Each stage was distinct and would alter the flavor of the final product accordingly. Pardus shook the celery and carrots, cut to a perfect small dice by Table Two, out of the white paper cup and into the pan. Corn, lima beans, turnips, and potatoes would also be used. "We're trying to time it so that they're all done at the same time, so that you can taste each vegetable," he said. "That's what makes this a great soup." When he added the parsley at the end, he noted that he preferred flat-leaf parsley because it was spicier and not quite as assertive as curly. When I completed my vegetable soup and set it before him on the desk, he told me that it looked good, bright, not overcooked, but the flavor was a little flat. "Take a ladleful out and salt it," he told me. "Then compare the two. It's a big difference. It's a good test. It keys you into the effect of salt." Not the *taste* of salt—a food shouldn't taste of salt—but rather the *effect* of salt.

He made Erica do the salt test as well. She would approach Pardus, her face scarlet and glistening from effort, trying to blow a stray bang that had snuck out her toque and down her forehead, a look approximating terror on her face. Her onion soup had not been hot. Her vegetable soup had been underseasoned. Her cream of broccoli would be too thick, her consommé cloudy. Each day she seemed to return from his desk, hyperventilating and apparently on the verge of tears, her whites becoming less and less so with each class.

You couldn't not like Erica. She tried so hard to no avail, and she did so with such visible effort that one absorbed the pathos of her predicaments. She had the foulest mouth in the class, but she was also sweet-natured and endearingly ingenuous. When we got to the front of the line at K-9 for dinner and Erica was asked if she would like one of the two soups, she responded, "Split pea, please." She turned to me, cranking her head all the way back. She said, "I. *Love.* Split pea soup."

After dinner we'd return to cool the stocks, clean the enormous kettles, wash the pots, wheel three large bins of garbage—compostable garbage, recyclable garbage, and worthless trash—down a flight of stairs, through a hallway, out back doors, and down the drive to the Dumpsters. And then we would sit for lecture. On Friday night, Day Four, everyone was looking forward to the weekend.

"This is nice," Chef Pardus said, pacing before us, spoon spinning in the air. "It's quarter to eight. If we're doing this in three weeks, I'll be real impressed." He went over Monday's products. Roux, first of all, then the soup. "The big one on Day Five, we do consommé. Now keep in mind, six o'clock is still our deadline. All of a sudden you've got extra things to do.

Some of you were right up against the wire today. On Monday, you have to be developing a sense of urgency. You're going to have to be very well organized. You're going to have to have a good equipment list. You're going to have to have a good prep list. Walk yourself through your day. What are you going to do when you come in? Set up your station. Start your bones, whatever you're going to do. Make sure you're going to have enough *time*. Consommé's going to take at least an hour, probably an hour and a half to cook. Might be one of the first things you want to get done as soon as the demo's done."

He paused, picked up his daily grade sheets, and flipped to today's page.

"Today—was a good day. I think. Everybody came in on time, the kitchen was pretty clean." He spotted some low numbers on the page and said, "A few people lost some points on sanitation. Again I want everybody to be clean, I want everybody to *look* clean, I want everybody taking care of their hair, O.K.? *Look* at yourself in the mirror before you get to class. People with long hair and people with pony tails, you need a heavy-duty hair net. People with hair that's getting borderline, make sure that it's under your hat, no stray edges; I don't want to see any bangs coming down the front of your hat. Check your sideburns; they're supposed to be half way, no farther down. Hey, I had to cut my hair and shave off my beard. If I have to give up those things, you guys gotta toe the line too. Make sure your tables are clean and neat. I don't want to see wads of paper towels sitting on cutting boards after you've finished degreasing a consommé. Please. You're going to start losing points as a group, as a table; I'm not going to say, 'Oh, your board is messy. I'm just going to take points off of you.' You're working as a team on that table. You start out with ten sanitation points each day. You can go down to *zero*. It's usually not that severe, unless I see somebody *tasting* with their *fingers*. Then that's an individual case. But watch out for each other. 'Hey, guys, our table's messy. Let's clean it up.' 'I know you're busy, I'll wipe down your area right now, you watch my back later.' Work together. Pots, good job today. Prep list, equipment list, you're getting a good idea of what I'm looking for, that's good; it's gonna come in handy. We're starting to pick up a little speed here. It's still kind of a light load. It's gonna get a lot heavier. Talk to some of the guys in Intro now about what the load's gonna look like by the time you're halfway through Skills Two. They could come in here and knock this out in an hour and a half and go home, something that takes you right up to six o'clock. But that's O.K. You'll learn to become more organized and quicker as the weeks wear on."

To me, this did seem like quite a lot to get done in four hours. We'd made ten gallons of white stock. We'd cut all our standard daily mise en place and turned our carrots. Then we'd done all the additional fine knife cuts on leeks, onions, celery, garlic, tied up a second sachet with butcher's string, small-diced our turnips and potatoes, measured out our lima beans and corn, concasséd more tomato, and chiffonaded our cabbage. And then we made the soup and had everything evaluated. I wasn't out of breath or red in the face, but it seemed to me you could only go so fast.

"Now, American veg soup. Drum roll." He scanned the numbers. "Everyone had a good soup. Nobody had a *bad* soup." He said a lot of them needed salt. He told us how to evaluate the soup, how to think about the tastes. "A little underseasoned, I said? It doesn't taste *bad*. It tastes *good*, right? Good soup, nothing really wrong with it. You add a little more salt, it doesn't *taste* salty. But it *tastes* a little ... *better*. It picks up the flavor, rounds it out a little. That's the balance you try to strike, and that's how you start to develop a palate and be aware of those four dimensions—acid, sour, sweet, and bitter. Knowing how to play off those components and round them out is what makes a well-developed palate."

And if we think he's wrong, he added, "Tell me. I want to talk to you about it. Show me. Show me that I made an error in judgment, or convince me. I'm happy to debate this. I'm not always right. Don't be afraid to challenge me on this stuff. We can both gain something. Any questions on American Bounty soup? I liked it, I thought you guys did a really good job.

"O.K. Let's go first to page four-fifty-four and talk about this consommé recipe, so we get it broken down for you. It's one gallon now; we want to take it down to a quart. So we'll use a small onion brûlé. Mirepoix—we'll need four ounces. Ground-beef-*shank*—we'll use eight ounces. Three egg whites, beaten. Four ounces tomato concassé. Now this will depend if you use fresh tomatoes or canned tomatoes. It depends on the acid content of the tomatoes. This time of year, the hothouse tomatoes, they don't have a great deal of acidity, so I like to use canned tomatoes. Summer, when they're really fresh and ripe and they've got *good acid*, we use *fresh* tomatoes every time. But this time of year we're gonna use canned tomatoes.

"Forty ounces of white beef stock. We want to have some room for reduction and loss and you'll understand why when we talk about the method. A standard *sachet*. For*get* about cloves, and for*get* about allspice. Don't *do* it. You want to try it some other place, some other time, fine. I'd rather concentrate on the flavors of the consommé rather than building a fruitcake.

Kosher salt and white pepper. Careful with the pepper, taste your soup, you may not need it.

"What we're gonna do is make what's called a clarification. A clarification is the mixture of the ground beef, the egg whites, mirepoix, and the *acid* of the tomato product. You could add white wine, you could add lemon juice. You could add hydrochloric acid if you wanted, probably wouldn't be very tasty. It needs *acid* in there. So we mix the beef, the egg whites, the mirepoix, and the tomato together, that's a clarification. It's a noun. It's a thing. It's different from the *process* of clarification. It's gonna look like a too-wet meatloaf." He smiled. "It looks pretty gnarly."

Consommé was clearly going to be the most interesting thing we'd done so far. The idea of making goop that looked like a ground-beef milk shake and dumping it into perfectly good stock offered childish pleasure— like making mud pies or dropping very large melons from very high places or seeing how far apart you and a friend could play catch with a raw egg before it smashed in one of your hands. And yet, despite these crude pleasures—indeed, *because* of them—the end result was one of ultimate refinement.

Over the weekend I read about the method in *The Pro Chef*, our textbook. This had helpful illustrations of what happened to your meat milk shake when you boiled it. It coagulated into a gray, scummy mass, or raft, and floated to the top of your stock, bringing everything that made stock murky with it. The raft was like an organic water filter—and the stock simmered up over it and back down through it. Consommé was not difficult to do, apparently, but it took some care. Sometimes a consommé would get the best of you.

Earlier in the winter, after several months of consommé heaven, K-8 ran into problems. Chef Pardus, who had been teaching since July, suddenly couldn't get a clear soup. The first time he shrugged, said this happened, and apologized to his class; no one else in the class could get a clear one either. And the definition of clear here is *perfectly* clear. Rule of thumb: you can read the date on a dime at the bottom of a gallon.

Pardus went to the books.

Proteins, both in egg whites and in the meat, are actual things, molecules; if you took a twenty-foot metal tape measure and crinkled it up into the shape of a cantaloupe, you would have a replica of a protein. Imagine, further, that at each inch of this crinkled tape measure was a little round magnet. These magnets are sticking to all the other magnets, keeping the protein all balled up. When these bonds are broken, lose their magnetic juice, the tape measure relaxes, loosens up, spreads out. Instead of looking like a tight tape-measure cantaloupe, it looked more like a lazy tapeworm. When you've got millions of these things relaxing all at once in the same pot, they form a net, create the filter that, as the raft rises to the surface, lifts all the muck out of the stock, clarifying it. What breaks those bonds is acid.

When Pardus asked himself what was different between the ingredients he was using in July and the ones he was using in December, it dawned on him that the hard pale tomatoes he was using simply did not have enough acid to break the bonds and unfold the proteins into their salutary net. When he next made consommé, he used canned tomatoes, and voilà: the date on a dime at the bottom of a gallon.

In addition to the consommé demo we would also be learning about roux, flour cooked in clarified butter, and slurries, pure starches such as cornstarch, arrowroot, or potato starch mixed in water to the consistency of heavy cream. Both roux and slurries took something thin as water and made it thick. Greg, doing more than his share (perhaps to keep from becoming bored), prepared the brown roux for Chef Pardus, since this took a long time to cook. Pardus could prepare the pale and blond roux during demo but he wanted the brown roux done at the same time. "Just like the TV shows," he said.

We crowded around Table Two as Chef Pardus dumped three egg whites into a large stainless-steel bowl and took a whip to them "to denature the protein mechanically," that is, break their bonds. "Just a little bit. We're not making lemon meringue pie." He dumped in the mirepoix. A half pound of ground beef shank—because the clarifying process also removes flavor, you must add more flavor. Then the tomato product: "We're using canned, remember," he said, "so we don't have to worry about getting robbed of our acid in the middle of winter." He added the stock, a nice gelatinous white beef stock. And Chef Pardus once again evaluated for quality.

"I've asked Victor to write this down," the chef said. Victor Cardamone, from Table Three, stood by the white sheet of paper taped to the reach-in, marker in hand. "Clarity," Pardus said. "It's perfectly clear. You can read the date on a dime at the bottom of a gallon." Vic noted this on the large piece of paper. "Flaaavor," Pardus continued. "A nice rich flaaavor, the flavor of the main ingredient. What else?"

Greg said, "Full body?"

Pardus concurred: "Full body, nice mouth feel, a rich, full body. Overall appearance?"

Ben said, "Not greasy?"

"Not greasy. *Clean.* Another?"

"Temperature?"

"Temperature," Pardus said. "*Hot.* This is not a jellied consommé." Pardus paused for a moment to look around. And here was what made Pardus a good teacher in my mind. He showed you the classic method, told you why, but then would let some of his own biases show through, broaden the subject to include his own personality. He'd get a little sparkle in his eye and his lips would start their unusual convolutions for popping emphasis. "Though you *could* make a jellied consommé," he said. "It's classical. You see how gelatinous this stock is? We made this clear and poured it into bowls, floated some garnish in it, and chilled it? It gels up. That's very classic, very European summer appetizer—chilled jellied consommé. You don't see it much in this country because people think it's like eating meat-flavored *Jell-O.* But if it's done right, it's very delicate. You wouldn't want a spoon to stand up in it. You couldn't do Jell-O shots with it. *Delicate.* It's very cool, very refreshing in the summertime. Jellied *quail* consommé? Little bits of truffle and foie gras set into the gelatin. *Nice.* Rich, refreshing."

He stirred the consommé with a wooden spoon, released from his reverie. He had put it on a low flame and warned everyone about scorching and the need to stir frequently. "Don't throw your pot away until after I've looked at your consommé." The danger, of course, is that the egg whites will fall to the bottom before they coagulate, then stick there and burn. This gives the consommé a beautiful, deep amber color, but it doesn't do much for the flavor. Pardus knows the color so well, he can take one look at someone's soup and say, "Lemme see your *pot*." And sure enough there will be burnt egg white on the bottom.

Adam, who typically hovered at the back of the crowd and was tall enough to do so, asked, "I was wondering, does the clarification take out the gelatin?" Adam was always asking questions like that.

"No," Pardus said.

"So is consommé a base for, like, aspic?"

"Yes."

"It is?"

"M-hm," Pardus said. "As a matter of fact, a lot of the Garde Manger classes will be coming up here, asking us to save our consommé so they can make their aspic for the Grand Buffet."

There was quite a bit of standing around at this point, since we were all staring at the pot as Pardus stirred, waiting for it to come up to heat and form this so-called raft.

"So why is consommé important to know how to do?" I asked.

"Why is a consommé important to know how to do?" he repeated. He continued to stir with his wooden spoon, thoughtfully, pushing it into the edges of the marmite, making sure he didn't feel any sticking egg white. "It's a technique that requires some finesse," he began. "It's a soup that is popular, that is used quite frequently in good restaurants. And it's something that takes some patience and training to know how to do. You can't just tell somebody to go make a consommé, this is how you do it. It takes some practice."

He stopped stirring, abandoning, for the moment, the party line for his personal thoughts as a cook who had moved through the ranks of several high-end French restaurants. "I would think that it brings together all the aspects of making a good stock and bringing that to the ultimate state of perfection. It's a *perfect* stock." That *p* in perfect really popped. "It teaches you to focus, teaches you to pay attention, to take care of ingredients. There's some chemistry involved and coagulation; there are so many things going on in making it that the beginning cook is made aware of, instead of just making a bowl of soup." He raised his eyebrows. "As a matter of fact, one of my friends had trouble with her consommé in this morning's chef's practical—and consequently probably won't be teaching here."

Chef Pardus's stock came up to heat, and sure enough, there was the raft, gray and scummy and solid, with just a little bit of stock foaming up at the side of the pan. Pardus had stirred almost continuously, even as the meat milk shake congealed. When the raft began to rotate with the spoon he stopped and let the consommé take care of itself. He would slip an onion brûlé down the side of the pot into the stock for more color and flavor, and later a sachet. When it was done we would all evaluate it.

"O.K.," he said, "demo's over. Go to town."

We did, and it worked. The opaque stock became crystal-clear soup, though Eun-Jung created a bit of kitchen drama when she let hers come to a boil, obliterating her raft. She wrote everything down, or appeared to, but certain things she did not understand. It would be very easy for her to miss the modifier "low simmer." Unless she could actually see it, she was never quite sure of herself. Pardus dashed to the rescue. I think he was glad someone's raft had broken. He loved to fix things on the fly, no time to spare. He made a new clarification by dumping the ruined consommé into a steel bowl, adding more ground beef and egg white, and dumping some tomato juice left over from someone's concassé for the acid. (Next time this happened, he spotted half a lemon and squeezed that into the new clarification—he really didn't care what kind of acid it was.) He put it back on the fire and brought it quickly up to a simmer with a beautiful brand-new raft.

Eun-Jung now knew how to ruin a consommé, how to fix a consommé, and how to finish a consommé. When the consommé had simmered properly, she ladled it out of the pot into a second pot through a coffee-filter-lined chinois, a fine mesh strainer. The stock was perfectly clear. She tasted for seasoning, reheated it, poured it into a hot bowl, degreased it by dragging brown paper toweling across its surface, all of which Chef Pardus had demonstrated with his own, and at last brought it to the chef for his inspection. It was a good, good-looking, flavorful consommé.

Making consommé was strangely satisfying. Something happened that you could *see*—an objective improvement. It was sort of like sanding and oiling a piece of wood that had started out pale and rough. After I'd finished my consommé and Pardus tasted it and liked it—"You could be a good cook, Michael," he said, a little surprised—all I wanted to do was taste my consommé and stare at it, remarking on the clarity and color.

I wasn't alone in this feeling. While I was staring at mine, David Scott, who had already finished his consommé, stood across from me, his head bobbing up and down. "That was really cool," he said, grinning.

Pardus even tacked on an elegant little bonus to this consommé class, circling back around to the stock from which the consommé was made. We were going to make the white beef stock and chicken stock a new way, borrowing from the consommé principle.

"I'm going to start with boiling water," the chef said, "and we're going to add some acid. We're going to save all our tomato scraps from today, and we're going to add it to our white stock. We're going to try to make a self-clarifying stock. It's apparently a technique they've been using in Europe for a long time. I never heard of it. I talked with Chef Hestnar and he said,

'Yeah, it's true. We don't teach it here at the CIA, but you can do it and it works pretty well.' Chef Griffiths tried it last week and said it works great, came out nice and clear and took an hour off the cooking time. So you already know the official CIA way, and we're going to go a little beyond that and learn another way. We'll all learn this together. It's a new one on me. This is an experiment. If it doesn't work, then the next time someone tells me, 'Oh, yeah, this works great,' I'll tell 'em, 'No, it *doesn't*. I've *tried* it.' And if it does work, great. Then you guys have two ways of making a good stock."

When lecture was over, I would walk out of the Culinary Institute of America into the cold February night like a kid leaving an amusement park, a kid with an open pass for all the rides for as long as he wanted. Chef Pardus had said today that I could be a good cook. *I* knew that of course I'd be a good cook. But I left the Culinary that night more uplifted than usual because he had recognized it.

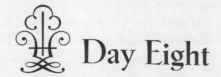 Day Eight

I should have known that Day Eight would be different from all the others preceding it by looking at my own prep list and comparing it to Day Three's:

DAY 8

Consommé
SMEP
Velouté
Béchamel
Clam Chowder
Clarify 5# butter
White Beef Stock

The card hints that I suspected timing would be a factor since I had built into my game plan the order in which I would present the items to the chef—consommé first, béchamel last, and only when that was done would I finish my knife cuts. I'd show him the knife cuts after the six o'clock deadline, which was all right so long as you had them done by six; between five-thirty and six-fifteen a line formed to present pots and bowls to the chef, and he would set out a sheet of legal paper on which to sign our names so we wouldn't waste time standing in line, staring at our reflection in bowls of consommé growing cooler by the instant. At six o'clock, he would draw a line under the last name and anyone below that lost points on their food.

The pace had picked up abruptly the day before. On Day Six we were still at the mise-en-place-and-one-soup level. Day Seven became standard daily mise en place (plus julienne and brunoise carrots, and tourner four pieces of potato), consommé, split pea soup, and béchamel. Béchamel, a mixture of flour and milk, is a mother sauce for many other sauces such as Mornay (béchamel with cheese), Nantua (with crayfish), and soubise (with onion), and it can even be used in various cream soups to good effect, but here for some reason people typically linked it to building material. On the first day, Chef Pardus had told us that he could "build a house" with all the béchamel we'd be making. When I asked Lou what he had done at IBM, he told me he used to ship huge circuit boards that were made by pouring a thick white compound that would harden into a sheet—before it hardened, Lou said, this white compound was just like the béchamel sauce we'd been making. Other mother sauces, though, the velouté (chicken or fish stock thickened with roux) and the brown sauce, were held in somewhat higher regard. The much-maligned béchamel—perhaps soon to be sold at hardware stores—once played a bigger role at the Culinary than it does today.

So Day Seven, rushed and filled with fretting that your béchamel would scorch at any instant, was nevertheless lighthearted busyness. Indeed, the busyness was part of the fun.

I halted once in my endeavors: Erica made her way down the central aisle, passed behind me, her tongue apparently pinned to the left side of her upper lip, so deep in concentration was she, carefully transporting her completed bowl of split pea soup to the chef's desk. She was, as usual, the color crimson, perspiring, and mortified when she approached the stone-faced Pardus, who had very little hope for Erica. She had a sixty-five, barely passing, at the midway point of Skills One. Her soups were mediocre, cold, and cloudy. She was a mess and had lost many points simply by forgetting to put on her hair net.

Pardus sat low in the chair at the desk, typically slouched since he was either scrutinizing food or marking the grade sheets. He glanced up. He didn't actually sigh, but there was a sigh in his expression. He lifted a spoon from the container to his right and said, "O.K., Erica, let's taste your soup." Erica shifted from one foot to another as if she couldn't wait to flee. Pardus felt the bowl to make sure it was hot, said nothing. He dragged the spoon through it, nodded. "Consistency's good, color's good," he said. He lifted a spoonful, blew on it, tasted, and nodded. "Taste is good. This is a good soup, Erica. This is a *very* good soup." Erica returned to her station, bowl in hand, by appearances no less mortified than when she'd left. I went to her and asked her how she did.

She nodded seriously and said, "The chef liked my soup. He said it was very good."

I said, "That's great, Erica," and asked to taste it. Erica's split pea soup was indeed very good soup.

When Vic Cardamone brought his consommé to the chef, Pardus said, "Nice color. Very nice color. I'm not even going to taste it. I can tell by looking at it. It's *scorched.*"

"I scorched it," Vic confessed. Vic, mid-twenties, a former marine from Philly, he would tell you, loved to smoke and drink, liked a loud foul-mouthed chef, and liked to be loud himself in the kitchen; his own baritone carried easily through the noisy kitchen.

"Let me see your pot," Pardus said.

Vic returned with the pot and sure enough, the bottom was coated with scorched egg white. Pardus told Vic to leave his scorched pot and scorched consommé up there and announced to the entire class that anyone inter-ested in knowing what a scorched consommé looked like and tasted like, there was an example on his desk. Vic returned to his station at Table Three shaking his head, evidently not happy to be the model of failure.

Midway through class I saw Susanne sitting down beside the chef's table with her hand in the air, clutching a wad of bloody paper towel. The chef had been right about keeping your thumb tucked when you were chopping.

As we waited in line outside K-9, our plastic trays in hand, people asked Erica if she did O.K. today and she nodded and smiled and said, "I did good, yeah. *Finally.*"

Things had been busy and Adam was grumbling. Maybe he didn't do well on his soup or maybe he was just always mad, I didn't know. He did have that very long narrow face, thin sharp nose, and short spiky black hair; perhaps all those edges and points came from being mad all the time.

Arriving on the tail of one of his comments, I asked, "Isn't that *anything* like a restaurant situation?"

"Not at all, man," he said. "In a real restaurant, you say, 'Get me a pot,' and the dishwasher gets you a pot, *fast,* because if he doesn't, he knows you'll fire him. You don't wash your own pots, you don't do the stupid mise en place every day, and even if you did you'd come in earlier." He continued to grumble as the line began to move and we all chose between broil, sauté, grill, braise, roast, or veg plate.

Day Eight, like Day Seven, quickly became a swirl of activity. Time became impossible to gauge. Forty-five minutes seemed like fifteen minutes sometimes and like forty-five minutes at other times, but you could never be sure which. This was important when you were making consommé. If you didn't note when you got it simmering, you might cook it too long, and the raft would disintegrate; if you didn't cook it enough, it wouldn't have good flavor. This was why you never wanted to rely too much on a clock, but instead on sight, smell, and taste. Clocks were not much good except for saying it was exactly six o'clock and you hadn't turned your potatoes yet. While you stood like a statue in a twister of clanking pots and onion skins, staring at the horizon with glazed eyes trying to remember what time you got your consommé simmering, your béchamel, as if begrudging your lack of attention, began to scorch and you'd have to run and get another pot and dump what was still good into that, hoping you still had enough flour left to thicken it. We were also making chicken velouté for the first time, which is almost the same as béchamel only you use chicken stock instead of milk. This can scorch, too. You wanted to be skimming these things all the time, thus paying attention to them at all times, so there was no excuse for scorching. And if by now you hadn't gotten your chowder going, you were in trouble—because of time and because there weren't any pots left. And if you found a pot—more likely you'd have to clean one yourself—you'd be lucky for a burner or a few inches of flattop to put it on.

At one point early in the day, Chef Pardus said, "I'd like you all to know that you are now using every pot in this kitchen." It was easy to hear him because there seemed to be not a single other voice in the kitchen; everyone was too busy to talk. Chef Pardus added, "That's not good or bad."

I was glad to hear this because the information clarified things for me at the time and I was glad that I hadn't suddenly gone insane or lost my senses. Everyone *was* really busy. Everyone needed three pots each on the stove at the same time—that would be fifty-four pots. Each pot required an array of other pots and pans and bowls. The consommé, for example, required a coffee filter, a chinois, and a pot into which to strain the consommé and, of course, a soup bowl that had better be hot but not too hot. If you left your bowl in a 500-degree oven for a half hour, and poured your consommé into it, your consommé would be glace in about five seconds. The béchamel likewise would need to be strained into another pot. And just about everyone scorched their béchamel so that the sink was stacked high with pots crusted with burnt milk and flour—who had time to clean them?

At one point, a high-ranking chef named Zearfoss—I'd heard him referred to as Captain Sanitation—stuck his head in the door and made a crack to Pardus about all the pots piling up on the floor. Chef Pardus was busy "power tasting," as he called it, and hadn't noticed. "Somebody better get on those pots now!" he shouted when Zearfoss was gone. I pretended not to hear. Someone did get on those pots, probably Greg, since he was always ahead of the game.

At about five-thirty, all was chaos, our table was a disaster with onion peels and paper towels all over the place, steel bowls crammed in between cutting boards and hotel pans and chinois. Compostable scraps, which would be tossed into a huge blue trash can, spilled over onto the table. The whole kitchen was stormy with food scraps and burning sauces, tomato trim slippery on the floor, Pardus's used tasting spoons clinking into a silver bowl at an even four-four beat in the background, and someone yelling "Behind!" or "Hot!" or "Who's got a chinois?!"

Through this chaos emerged something like a mirage or vision: Three students appeared, perfectly clean, uniforms gleaming; each carried two plates. Pardus told the students to set them where they could find space. He asked Travis and me to clear off a spot on our table and, completely uncomprehending and befuddled, but like an obedient soldier, I did. There, beside my cutting board, was set an immaculate white plate with a perfect circle of quail roulade floating atop a delicate mustard sauce. Beside the roulade was a stuffed quail leg, and beside this was a golden brown potato basket, acting as a nest for two tiny, pickled quail eggs. It truly felt like a hallucination. I had no idea why this had happened and at the time I didn't really care. As we chopped and minced and strained and plated on a table that was no longer visible beneath the garbage, the beautiful quail appetizer plate remained on this table beside my cutting board, accusatory, humiliating, but also like a beacon, hope. One day there would be more to life than scorched béchamel and standard daily mise en place.

I barely got my product done by six, and I was too tired to talk to anyone at dinner. Everyone else seemed to be just as tired and discouraged as I was. Susanne asked our entire table—we all sat together, the wounded, sharing bandages—how we were compared to other groups. No one knew, of course, but everyone realized, and seemed to share, her underlying fear: we were no good. We had tried our best and we were no good.

I wondered this myself. All this anxiety and discord because of two soups and two base sauces. People were pretty quiet at dinner, and most returned to the kitchen fairly quickly because it was still the disaster that we'd left it. Twenty gallons of stock needed to be strained. Someone would have to shovel all the bones and vegetables and fat out of each one and dump it in the blue compost bin, which would then have to be rolled down the hall, carried down a flight of stairs, and rolled a quarter mile or so to the compost Dumpster along with recyclables and worthless trash. We also kept a fat bucket; all the fat skimmed from stock went into yet another giant receptacle outside, eventually to wind up as soap. Meanwhile someone else would have to cool all this stock in giant ice baths. Travis was the first man on the pots crusty with burnt milk and flour. He was an awesome pot man, probably from spending so much time in the army. We didn't begin lecture till after nine o'clock. Chef Pardus, who had been staying late working on vegetarian recipes for an unrelated project, was tired himself and not chipper.

"Brown sauce, sauce Espagnol," Chef Pardus began, going over tomorrow's recipes from the *Pro Chef*. "Do one quarter of this recipe. Hot oil as needed. Tomato paste, one ounce. Brown veal stock, forty ounces. It says pale roux here—we're gonna use *brown roux*. It says twelve ounces per gallon—we're gonna use thirty-*two* ounces for a gallon, or eight ounces for a quart."

Pardus was subdued. He sat on the desk instead of pacing and spinning the wooden spoon in the air. He lacked the typical mischievous glimmer. When the recipes were done, he moved into his evaluation of today. I believe I sensed, and participated in, a sort of cumulative class slouch.

"Um, today," Chef Pardus said, taking a breath. "The béchamel. *Problems* with that sauce. Several people burnt the bottom of their pan and consequently lost a lot of their thickening power because their roux stuck to the bottom of their pot; so you were ending up with thin béchamel and/or the béchamel tasted scorched. All of this is a matter of paying attention and being careful. I *know* you were all rushing today, I *know* you had a lot to do. This was an overwhelming day for most of you." He paused, momentarily sympathetic. Then: "*It doesn't matter.* You still have to pay attention to your *products*. Serving them in cool bowls or pots is unacceptable. You all *know* that. *Don't . . . do* it. It's too thick? You've made this once before—if it's too thick you know how to fix it. *Do* it! A couple of people are still not cooking it out long enough, it's a little gritty on the mouth. Tastes thick; rub your tongue against the roof of your mouth. If it doesn't taste *perfectly smooth*, if it tastes a little bit gritty . . . *cook it a little while longer*! You think it's too thick already, and it'll get way too thick if you cook it more, heat up a little milk and add more milk into it, *then* cook it a little longer. You gotta cook that starch out so that it's not gritty; it's gotta be a perfectly smooth sauce.

"This is an inexact science, this is where the art comes in. You've got standard ratios that work up to a point. There are always variables, as far as: Did you cook all the roux out? How high was your cooking temperature? How much evaporation did you have? How much did it reduce? You have to take all those things into account, see what your final product is, and figure out how to *fix* it. I think all of you now know how to fix it; you just have to be not so stressed out or under pressure that you can say, 'I know it's not right and I need to fix it.'

"You can't *ever* send out a product if it's not right," he continued. He was standing now. "It doesn't matter how busy you are. Your reputation is on the line every time you put a plate out. If you get into the mind-set that 'I don't care what it looks like, I'm too busy, just take it out, maybe they won't know the difference,' then that's the kind of restaurant you'll work in the rest of your life. You'll never work in a really great restaurant and you'll never be a really great chef. You'll work in a mediocre restaurant and you'll be a mediocre chef. Because that's the mind-set of a mediocre chef: 'I'm too *busy* to do it right; get it out of my *face*!'

"*So. Start. Good habits. Early!* Do it right. Take your time."

He evaluated the velouté—gritty, not cooked out enough, or a little too thin—then the chowder—some pork cut too big, others cooked it so long it became oatmeal—then the consommé, the one bright spot apparently.

"Very good consommés, by and large," he said. "All the way down the line they came out nice and clear. Some were very pale and a little light in flavor, some were very deeply colored and flavored. The difference generally between pale and light and deep and rich was cooking time. Consommés, small amounts like this, can stand up to about an hour and a half, an hour and forty-five minutes before the raft starts to deteriorate. I would suggest tasting it at about an hour, take a spoon, look at the clarity, look at the color, taste it, feel the body, feel the flavor in your mouth, and say, 'Well, what do I have here? Could it be richer, could it be darker?' "

He stopped, looked at his legal pad, a list of notes.

"I'm not going to beat this drum too hard because we don't have a lot of time, but you guys gotta work harder on keeping those pots clean. I was not aware until Chef Zearfoss poked his head in and asked how bad it was. It was a *disaster*. You guys have to take it a lot more seriously. There were a lot of things over there that could have been cleaned by the people who put them over there, like *that*." He snapped his fingers. "Bowls that clams have been stored in, all you have to do is dip it and wipe it, dip it and sanitize it, it's done, takes you three seconds. This is a big issue, O.K.? If you get to the point where I am humiliated by the amount of pots, I'll shut this kitchen down. I'll say, 'O.K., stop, shut off everything, everybody get over here and wash pots. When all the pots are washed and put away, then we'll open the kitchen back up.' You've *still* got a six o'clock deadline. But I'm *not* going to let you work like *pigs*.

"Recyclables, you gotta watch that. You get under pressure, you're pushing hard to get your product done in time and have quality, that's admirable, but you can't throw all caution to the wind. You still have to keep the pots up, you still have to make sure the right things go in the recyclable. We're not throwing cheesecloth, we're not throwing dirty towels in there; we're not throwing in coffee filters that are soaked with clarified butter.

"Standard daily mise en place. You are responsible for this. And this is a reasonable amount of time to get it all done, and if you come up at the end of the day and say, 'This is all I got, I didn't have time to do my brunoise, I didn't have time to do my batonnet, I didn't have time to do my chopped parsley,' you're going to lose serious points, because you're only doing half the job.

"Stock teams, you've got stock to do; make that a priority, get it started, get it started fast so we don't have to be making stocks at eight-thirty at night.

"Demo team. We had a fifteen-minute lag time today. We could have started earlier, but the demos weren't set up on time. You guys pay for it. When the demo's fifteen minutes late, that means you don't start your production. Demo team, that's the only thing you should be concentrating on; set up your stations and start setting up your demo; when that's done, *then* you worry about cutting vegetables and making your mirepoix. You're not being team players; you're being *selfish*.

"I don't know if this will help. I'm not reading this laundry list of things you guys need a little work on to be a tyrant. I'm not comparing you to anybody else and I'm not telling you that you're not trying hard. I'm just trying to get you to push.

"And one more thing. This monitor cost several hundred dollars."

I'd spotted a heavy-duty digital instant-read thermometer sitting in a puddle of ice water on the stock sink. I'd told Victor, who was cooling stock, that I didn't think it was a good idea to leave it there. I didn't move it myself. "The digital thermometer," Pardus continued, holding it up. "Someone left it lying on the side of the sink in a puddle. All the electric circuitry in there is soaked. It's probably not going to work for a few days, if ever. I'm assuming it will dry out and be O.K., provided there wasn't too much *salt* in the water it was sitting in, and it's not going to corrode it to hell. *Guys. Come on.* This is an expensive piece of equipment. If it's your restaurant, you would be well within reason to severely reprimand or discipline or fire someone who mistreated such an expensive piece of equipment."

Pardus stopped. He looked around. He grimaced. Then he said, "O.K. *Dad* lecture is over. Emulsified sauce lecture begins. You can read about all this stuff. It's getting late and you're going to fall asleep if I get too detailed on the chemistry of emulsions. But you can read about it and it would *behoove* you to do so."

I was glad he didn't go into the chemistry of emulsions and very glad when he said, "O.K., see ya tomorrow." I slunk to the parking lot. I thought about home twenty-five icy miles away and how good it would be to see my wife, who would still be up, reading the newspaper or checking E-mail. We'd tiptoe into the next room to look at our tiny daughter sleeping silently. This was what I looked forward to, but it was later than usual and I had a lot of homework to do for the next day. The emulsified-sauces paper was due. I had my prep and equipment lists to write out and more reading in McGee. Before I knew it I'd be back in uniform, unzipping my knife bag, tying the apron at my waist, and hefting a cutting board to my station.

 # Brown Sauce

I know of no more infelicitous name for a standard ingredient or item than brown sauce. The French name, sauce Espagnole, sounds drab, even leaden to my ears, an attempt to cover up what is obviously sauce brown. Like the gravy you can buy in jars at Shoprite. Veal stock thickened with roux. More paste. *Old* paste. Who used it anymore? Fine reduced stocks and nothing else for meat-based sauces, that's how American chefs work today. But at the Culinary Institute of America, on Day Nine of Skill Development One, you learn to make brown sauce, the mother sauce first classified by Marie-Antoine Carême in the early nineteenth century. Carême's recipe calls for a Bayonne ham and partridges and about three days of cooking, but we have since reduced the simmering time and dispensed with partridges and ham.

We, of course, meaning the students, were following the textbook, *The New Professional Chef*, for our recipe: four ounces of mirepoix well caramelized, an ounce of tomato paste deeply pincé, five cups of brown stock, eight ounces of brown roux, and a sachet. We would simmer this slowly for at least an hour, skimming, skimming, skimming, and making sure to stir up the flour sticking to the bottom. We would taste it, shrug—"Tastes like brown sauce"—and strain it into another pot or bowl. Some would strain it through cheesecloth. As far as I could see at the time, there was only one pleasurable aspect of the brown sauce: Chef Pardus had to eat eighteen spoonfuls of it each time he assigned it.

Despite the dated and pedestrian nature of the brown sauce, a few contradictions kept the sauce lively in my mind. Nobody noticed that first brown-sauce day Pardus's willful variance of the recipe—he directed us to use a brown roux when the recipe called for a pale roux, running outside the baseline, as it were. Or was he? The recipe called for a pale roux but twice on the same page of my *Pro Chef*, the fifth of six editions, under "Method" a *brown* roux is added to the stock.

The second was that, while brown sauce was not used much anymore and was widely looked down upon as dated, it nevertheless had a legion of articulate supporters. After all, the brown sauce, refined through further cooking to a demi-glace, was the base for hundreds of small or compound classical French sauces. Espagnole was thus the cornerstone sauce when the edifice of French cuisine was built and proceeded to dominate the Western world.

Listen to Julia Child. In her classic text *The Art of Mastering French Cooking*, one of a few books that permanently altered the home cook's culinary landscape, her falsetto and invisible exclamation points intact, she writes: "Sauces are the splendor and glory of French cooking." And yet she too seems slightly dismissive of demi-glace, making brief reference to it in her book, then writing, "But as we are concerned with less formal cooking, we shall discuss it no further."

The poor *Pro Chef* is almost apologetic in tone about classical sauces: "Although they may not be relied upon as heavily as in years past, the grand sauces are still important in a contemporary kitchen." *The Pro Chef* fails to say why, as if hoping people will assume it's self-evident and get to work on the old dowagers.

The great British food writer, Elizabeth David, discoursing more than thirty years ago, sounds almost nouvelle nineties: "The result of all this sauce mystique, evolved in the eighteenth and nineteenth centuries, when conditions were so utterly different from our own, is that today, sauces have become horribly debased." She even derides the concept of grand sauces and their derivatives: "The inevitable result is that every dish has the same basic flavor, and because the sauces are stale, not a very good one."

But the redoubtable McGee is almost wily in his discussion of sauces. He calls the process "quirky," "forbidding," "fickle," owing much of the success or failure, he says, "to the particular action of a cook's arm." Sauces, he concludes, "are by nature very tricky physical and chemical systems." This, clearly, is respect based on facts.

One of the best books I've read on classical sauces is *The Saucier's Apprentice*, by the journalist and food writer Raymond Sokolov. In reminding the reader of Brillat-Savarin's oft-quoted aphorism about a great meal without a sauce being like a beautiful woman without clothes, Sokolov explains the truth of this statement, that such a woman or meal lacks "the coating of civilization that would arouse our fullest interest." You know immediately that Mr. Sokolov reveres, with almost chivalric protectiveness, the brown sauce. "French sauces," he writes, "are the height of culinary technique," noting further that demi-glace, a reduction of brown sauce and brown stock, is "the highest refinement of brown sauce."

The man credited with propelling sauce out of the Middle Ages (a time marked by heavily spiced sauces, often thickened with bread, that overpowered food) was François Pierre de La Varenne. He used a "flour liaison," now known as a roux; his "fragrant sauce" for asparagus suggests, in its resemblance to hollandaise, that he may have been the inventor of the egg-based emulsified sauce; and one of his creations, "sauce Robert," is alive and well today, as would soon become obvious. Over the next hundred years, many of the classic French sauces were invented and named (béchamel, for example, and its derivatives soubise and Mornay). The cooks who did the inventing rarely got credit; their employers took the credit as the various sauces became associated with particular noblemen's tables. It was not, for instance, the writer and statesman Chateaubriand, but rather his cook, Montmireil, who created the famous sauce.

In the new library at the Culinary—a fireplace glows and sputters on the cold bright afternoons of February—a Tiffany-style glass panel above a trophy case quotes Fannie Farmer: "Progress in civilization has been accompanied by progress in cookery."

This seems to have been borne out after the French Revolution and the ensuing Reign of Terror, which scared all the remaining noblemen—many noblemen had already lost their heads—out of the country. This resulted in many unemployed cooks. It seems more than coincidence, then, that the first restaurateur hung his shingle in Paris at this time (a movement apparently begun by a Monsieur Boulanger, who in 1765 advertised sheep's feet in white sauce). A public restaurant, now here was an idea. What else might an unemployed cook do, given that consulting had yet to come into its own? With the blossoming of the restaurant scene came a new interest in food cost—cooks no longer had enormous sums of money to spend on food—and efficiency. Then as now, the more people you fed, the more money you stood to make.

During this time, a vain and strident cook, who was a mere five years old when the Revolution began, became the first renowned chef of France. Sokolov says Marie-Antoine Carême is "the towering figure of the entire history of the *grande cuisine* of France." It was Carême who, according to Sokolov, "articulated for the first time the concept of mother sauces" and was the man who chose roux as a universal thickener. The man went on at length to demolish verbally anyone who turned their nose up at roux. "They," Carême wrote ("they" being roux denigrators), "do not know that our roux, prepared according to the principles enunciated above, have a nutty taste that is pleasing to the palate. . . ." A roux thickens a sauce, he argued, and then is separated from it. For one hundred years, chefs followed Carême and roux became the universal thickener in the West.

By articulating the concept of mother sauce, by classifying numerous small sauces according to one of four mother sauces, Carême created a "scheme" that fit the new post-Revolution needs: big vats of the mother sauce could be made economically and stored and the small sauces could be conveniently prepared *à la minute* moments after the diner placed an order. McGee and Sokolov are both excellent on this sauce business, as McGee recognizes by quoting Sokolov, who called this new idea of a base sauce "convenience food at the highest level." One might even go so far as to suggest that haute cuisine was in fact history's first fast food.

Carême was fairly proud of himself, claimed his books carried an "indelible mark." But he was also generous and humble: You too could cook like Carême, he suggested, if you followed his mother sauce scheme, used your common sense, and occupied yourself "without relaxation."

Escoffier would further refine and advance the work of the man who is really the first celebrity chef. Escoffier himself believed in the value of a good sauce. He put nearly two hundred of them in his first book—not including dessert sauces. "It is they," he wrote of the French sauces, "that have created and maintained to this day the universal preponderance of French cuisine."

Escoffier believed—nay, predicted and hoped—that roux would be replaced by pure starches such as arrowroot and cornstarch. Roux took too long and didn't add anything, he believed; once pure starches became economically feasible, they would become de rigueur.

He was wrong. In February 1996, Chef Pardus's Skills class, and the seven other Skills classes, would be making bucketfuls of roux into which they would dump their fine stocks.

Adam Shepard stood out from the very first day because of his questions. During a lecture on hollandaise, Chef Pardus criticized many people for serving it cold. "You cannot serve a cold hollandaise sauce. Learn how to serve it warm." The problem was, of course, that if it were too warm the egg would coagulate, and people would rather have a cool sauce than a broken one.

Adam raised his hand and asked, "Since acid raises the temperature of coagulation for proteins, couldn't you add the lemon juice first, and then you could add butter that was maybe a hundred and fifty degrees?"

I remember being sort of mystified by this, mainly by the fact that Adam even knew what 150 degrees felt like and what butter that hot might do to some frothy egg yolks.

"That's an excellent point," Pardus said. "Did everybody understand Adam's question?" Responding to the blank faces, he reconstructed Adam's question, concluding, "You could make your hollandaise *hotter* by adding the lemon juice first. You want to try that, you have my blessing. That's a great idea. I'm surprised I didn't think of that." Pardus smiled as if to say, That's right, you heard me. "That's the way I try to approach a problem. That's excellent thinking, Adam." Pardus believed that good cooking was simply a series of problems solved.

Getting to know Adam wasn't easy, nor was squeezing out a clear or complete answer. This was the general rule at the Culinary; it was not a verbal place. But there was something more to it with Adam—I couldn't even get a clear answer on how old he was. His questions, on the other hand, were complex and articulate, suggesting he'd spent plenty of time reading and thinking; moreover, he never seemed to want to conceal anything. He just always looked angry; he glared at you. And at certain angles, you would notice that one of his eyes drifted a little higher than the other. The force of his gaze, I think, and also his speed and skill in the kitchen, were likely why two weeks passed before I realized that Adam's right hand, his knife hand, was maimed.

This was not something one brought up out of the blue, but when Adam mentioned it I asked. It was after class on a Friday night; we'd made our first brown sauce and hollandaise sauce, and two white *à la minute* sauces, supreme and cream (the former, based on a chicken velouté and flavored with mushroom, was a dead ringer for Campbell's cream of mushroom soup, but the latter, béchamel-based, was, to my great surprise, beautifully delicate and light). Adam had a dorm room, but he was headed home to Brooklyn to be with Jessica, his wife of two-and-a-half years. We were walking down the dimmed and mainly deserted hallway, past the dining hall, and I asked him why he was here, why cooking.

"An accident made the choice for me," he said, lifting his right hand. Index finger and thumb appeared to be fine, but the middle finger was gone and the last two fingers were pinched together and cemented at a permanent right angle to his palm.

Adam, who said he was from all over New England, had worked in Maine fish houses. He enrolled at Marlboro College in Vermont but dropped out after one year, got a job in the kitchen there, and for three years audited classes in photography, woodworking, philosophy, art history, religion, and linguistics. But book work, in the end, didn't appeal to him. "I'm a trade-school guy," he said.

I told him the strength of his questions in class seemed to suggest otherwise.

"Trade school, not by necessity, but by, by—I don't know . . . ," he mumbled.

"By disposition."

"Yeah, by disposition."

He left school without a degree with two career options: kitchens or wood shops. He chose wood shops, building commercial furniture and cabinets. At night, he would craft instruments. Adam's friend played music at his and Jessica's wedding on a guitar that Adam himself had made. Adam also made the wedding cakes himself—thirteen of them, the centerpiece for each table.

I asked him how the accident happened.

"I don't know, man," he said.

"What do you mean you don't know?" I asked.

"I don't *know*," he said. "I don't remember how it happened or why it happened. I thought everything was fine." He made a quick suggestive motion with his hands, pushing a three-quarter-inch plank of plywood through a table saw. "But I chopped off half the fingers on my right hand."

Adam had liked cooking and restaurant work and had been curious about the Culinary Institute of America. In November 1993, he and Jessica, then living in western Massachusetts, visited the Culinary. They had dinner at St. Andrew's Cafe, a restaurant (one of four at the CIA) devoted to nutritional cuisine; for this reason, it is not the Institute's most popular restaurant, but it happened to be the only place Adam and Jessica could get a last-minute reservation. Adam would remember it as one of the best meals he would have at the Culinary.

Three weeks later, on November 30, he cut his hand. "He said to me the day he was injured," Jessica recalled during one of the weekends she spent in Hyde Park, "that as long as he could hold a knife to cut vegetables, he would be O.K. He said it to me as soon as they'd given him the injection of morphine."

Adam corrected her: "I was saying that as soon as I left the wood shop."

For two years Adam underwent reconstructive surgery and physical therapy. They'd been married for two months when the saw redirected Adam's career, and the recovery was hard on them both. For someone who worked with his hands, who was most fulfilled when crafting something, Adam had to learn how to spend time not making anything. He watched cooking shows on the Discovery channel. When he regained, gradually, some use of his right hand, he began to cook for Jessica. Eventually, he would cook two elaborate meals a day for her. When his right hand was strong and he felt sure he could wield a French knife, he applied to the Culinary and began Culinary Math and Introduction to Gastronomy in December 1995.

The injury scarcely seemed to affect him now—"I have trouble tournéing, that's about all," he said—though I wondered if this might be the source of his anger. Our conversation the night of the brown sauce was not long. He had a two-and-a-half-hour drive south ahead of him and it was after nine-thirty. I too looked forward to being home.

"These are *à la minute* sauces," Chef Pardus said, as we clustered around him for the day's demo. "Derivative sauces, you make them at the last minute." Chef Pardus checked the mise en place neatly arranged in a hotel pan by Table Three. "You can make them in quantity, but they're best if finished at the last minute. You make the brown sauce or the demi-glace and finish the sauce *à la minute*, at the moment, in the pan that the item was cooked in: sautéed cutlets, sautéed pork chop, or a piece of pork loin that was pan-roasted. Sauce Robert is traditionally served with pork."

We had done just what he'd said, made our brown sauce and from that made our demi-glace, equal parts veal stock and brown stock, the veal stock first reduced by one third, then all of it simmered and skimmed—the highest refinement of the brown sauce. To me it didn't taste so good. Didn't taste much like anything except brown. Brown sauce actually tasted brown, and that was about it. The demi-glace simply tasted more brown.

Chef Pardus sweated some minced onion, then, lifting a bottle of white wine, said, "You add the wine." He stopped. "You add the wine off the fire. We talked about this. Why?" He had taken his sauté pan off the flame but had not yet poured. "Because you don't want that flame to jump back up into the bottle, blow the back of the bottle off, and cut the guy *next* to you. It's really scary. Has that happened to anybody in this class? I saw it happen once. It's pretty much of a disaster. First of all it frightens every-body; somebody can get *hurt*. Second, you've got to shut the *line* down because there's broken *glass* in everybody's *mise* en place. And in the middle of Saturday night, that's a real drag. That's when you start comping dinners, buying lots of drinks, giving away lots of wine." He paused. He still hadn't poured. "One person's carelessness cost your restaurant a thou-sand dollars, or more."

Paul Trujillo asked, "How do people avoid that? By using plastic containers?"

"*No!*" Pardus said. "You avoid it by taking it off the fire and adding your volatile liquid *off* the *fire*." Paul nodded quickly. Pardus returned the pan to the flame till the onion began to sizzle, removed it, and poured out a couple of ounces. "Reduce your white wine—not all the way down, by about half. You want to retain some of the liquid there. You can adjust it down if you want to adjust it down." Four ounces of demi-glace had been put in a white paper cup. Pardus had to squeeze the cup and shake it hard to snap the congealed sauce into the pan. It quickly thinned and began to bubble. "We don't want to reduce it much more. It's a light-sauce consistency, it just barely coats the spoon. It's liquid, it flows, you can't draw a line in the bottom of your pan at all."

He passed the pan around so everyone could see the consistency. He drew a line down the middle of the pan with a wooden spoon and the line vanished immediately.

"At this point we're going to add our reconstituted mustard. Do we have a whisk?" Adam handed Pardus a whisk.

Almost there, just needed a little pat of butter for flavor and texture and what is often called mouth feel, though some people wince at that phrase.

"Monté au beurre," Pardus said. "Bring up the temperature a little bit more to swirl it in." As the butter became first a bright swirl in the dark brown sauce, Pardus left K-8 in his mind and said, "I would do smoke roasted pork loin in my pizza oven in California—I'm gonna add a little bit of salt and pepper—a slow-roasted pork loin." He swirled the pan some more to incorporate the salt and pepper. "And I would do a sauce very similar to this and finish it with a whole-grain mustard. I would make a brown pork stock and reduce it, monté au beurre, and finish it with whole-grain mustard." Silence, then, as we all reflected.

"This is the proper consistency," he said, removing the pan from the heat. He strained the sauce to remove the chunks of onion, needing only their infusion. "You might choose to leave the onions in there, if you wanted a more rustic presentation. I wouldn't see a problem with that. In a very refined restaurant—someone was talking about La Caravelle last night, a very refined classical French restaurant in New York—they would certainly strain it. Escoffier room, they would certainly strain it. Across the hall here at Caterina, if they were making a sauce like this—Italian cuisine is a little more rustic than classical French—maybe they wouldn't strain it, leave the onions in for a little textural interest and a little more flavor."

He passed the sauté pan around and our silver spoons descended like a fleet of little dive-bombers.

I can only say that what happened in my mouth was a revelation. No heaviness, no pastiness, but instead the opposite: lightness. The mustard was sharp and distinct, the wine rounded it out, the butter had made it rich and velvety. This would go very well with pork, I thought. Suddenly, there was nothing at all brown about this sauce. It was like magic.

"This is about what this would taste like," Pardus said, himself pleased. "You see how this would go well with pork? This would complement pork well. It's a nice sauce, it's got a nice flavor, a nice texture, it's got some depth to it. It's a nice sauce primarily because you started with a good demi-glace. If we had not cooked the brown sauce properly, if we had not cooked the demi-glace out properly, it would be a bit gloppy, it would have a kind of starchy feel in the mouth. But we don't have any of those bad characteristics because we took care of making a *good* demi-glace, from a *good* brown sauce. That's why we have to be particular all the way down the line. If you make a lousy stock, you're not gonna have a good Espagnole. You don't have a good Espagnole, you can't make a good demi. If you don't make a good demi, you're not gonna have a *good* finished *product*.

"O.K., the next one—this is like falling off a *log*." He took a clean sauté pan and set it on the flame. "Sauce Madeira, all you need to do is start with a good demi-glace, heat that demi-glace up, and finish it with, what's it call for, two ounces of Madeira? One ounce? Yeah, this looks like a little bit much."

As the wine sauce bubbled, Pardus turned to us. "The recipe says don't reduce. If you have a high-quality Madeira, it's a good idea not to. And if you have a *bad*-quality Madeira, it's a good idea *not* to. If you have a poor-quality Madeira, why wouldn't you want to reduce it?"

Adam's voice rang out immediately: "You reduce the poor-quality flavor. It's really concentrated poor quality."

"*Exactly*, Adam."

That day, Day Eleven, I had experienced another revelation—one beyond the sauce Robert, though that in itself was a kind of high, like finding the key to a hidden room. Knowing that a sauce that tasted brown one minute could be refined to the point of flavorful, exquisite delicacy in thirty or forty seconds, well, if this were true—and I had seen and tasted it—what more was there to learn? Part of the elation, a balance and counterpoint to it, was shame. I could never be smug again about food as I had been about the roux-based sauce. If I didn't know how sauce Robert worked— perhaps the oldest sauce still in use—if I didn't know the qualities and behavior of a demi-glace, the queen mother of French sauces, then truly I knew nothing.

 # The Storm

A friend of mine once described what it would be like for mortals like us to take a single blow from a world-class heavyweight boxer: "It would be like a ceiling beam falling on your head." This, I believe, is an accurate way of describing how snow hit the northeast that winter. And the blows kept falling. They began a couple days after the new year. A week later the Blizzard of '96 struck. After the Eastern seaboard dug out of that one, another storm would blow in about once every third week. The block before Skills had ended with a winter storm watch. Exactly three weeks later, Day Thirteen of this block, another storm began.

As I watched the snow fall that March morning, I thought twice about heading down to the Culinary at all. My little Nissan Sentra was not much heavier than a pie tin. I decided to leave an hour early to make sure I arrived on time, and out into the whiteness I went, toting my knife kit and shoulder briefcase. By the time I arrived at the Culinary, an hour and a half later, my main concern was not the knife cuts practical but just getting home. I devised my plan as I hustled to class. The knife cuts practical happened first. Afterward there was just a dry run through tomorrow's sauce practical. I could miss this practice.

Shortly before two-fifteen, Chef Pardus said, "Begin." We had twenty minutes to mince one onion, slice one onion, concassé a tomato, and chop one bunch of parsley. You had to hustle but timing wasn't meant to be the issue. No one cut themselves and everyone did about the same as I did.

Minced onion, good but a little too big, the sliced onion a little uneven. Three points off on each. The chef found two tomato seeds in my concassé, a point off for each seed. Parsley was good, but the chef was skeptical that I'd done a full bunch. It did look a little shy. He picked through my trim to make sure I didn't throw away too much onion. I finished on time and my hand positions were good, so my grade came to the equivalent of 97.5 out of a hundred. Chef Pardus admitted that it was an easy test.

I packed up my knives as he finished grading the final hotel pans of onion, tomato, parsley, and trim. He stood behind his desk, back straight, eyes wide behind his gold-rimmed glasses, expressionless.

"Chef," I said.

"Yes!" he said.

"I'm worried about the snow. I'm gonna bolt."

"Fine," he said.

I think he knew I was going to say what I did, and I suspected, from his posture and lack of expression that he was thinking something. When he didn't speak, I said, "See ya tomorrow."

He said, "See ya tomorrow."

And I was gone. I actually jogged through the snow to my car because I knew that every second that passed more snow was piling up on the roads from here to Tivoli. It was mid-afternoon but the sky was so heavy with clouds that there was a crepuscular winter grayness to the light and the heavy snow further reduced visibility. I waited at the stoplight hanging at the exit of the Culinary parking lot; my wheels spun before catching and I turned left onto Route 9, my back end swinging out slightly more than it ought to have, but the car righted itself easily and I was on my way.

The road through Hyde Park is one lane and a steady stream of cars motored along at about twenty-five miles an hour. Just beyond the next town, Staatsburg, Route 9 becomes a divided highway, two lanes on each side. Normally this was your lucky chance to pass the Sunday drivers, but today, no one was passing. The roads were completely white, not even tire tracks visible, and everyone stayed in one lane, snow beginning to drift in either passing lane. I felt the Nissan drop slightly as I veered off the lip of the road invisible beneath the snow. I slowed to below twenty, gripping the wheel tightly. I turned the wheel just a bit to get back on the road, and I felt the back tire catch on the lip. I gave a small jerk to the steering wheel to get this back wheel onto the road. I overcompensated, and the back end of the car faded into the passing lane. I turned the wheel counterclockwise and the back end straightened but then kept going. I turned the wheel again. There seemed to be no friction at all and I had the experience of an astronaut floating through space. But part of me knew I was on a four-lane highway as I slid across the passing lane and over the rough brick divide, smoothed with snow, into the southbound lanes, and eventually came to a halt facing the opposite direction. I managed to maneuver perpendicular to traffic and someone actually dared stopping, a hazard itself given that you'd be relying on all the other cars behind you to stop as well. But all did. I pulled into the traffic and crept prayerfully toward Tivoli, thinking only then that I was fortunate to have fishtailed into the oncoming traffic at a moment when no traffic happened to be coming on to halt, with a muffled thunk, my graceful spin.

In earlier years, a little drive like that would have been more fun than anything else. But this sort of fun ended when I became a parent. Kids change the way you behave; new instincts engage. One of them is self-preservation. A friend of mine who lives in Manhattan, for instance, remembers he began walking closer to the insides of the sidewalk, farther away from the curb, once he became a father. When I spun out on Route 9, floating backward into who knows what, I didn't think of myself but rather of my daughter's face. That's what gets you back in the right direction. Then I thought how mad my wife, Donna, would be if she knew what had happened. I'd have hated to have been injured or even killed on account of a desire to make brown veal stock. I told Donna how glad I was to be home; I hugged her, hugged my beautiful daughter, then snuggled up to the warm glow of my computer to catch up on a backlog of notes.

The next morning snow fell. It hadn't stopped so far as I knew. I paced the room. I stared out the window—one blanket of snow all the way down to the Hudson River. Through the pattern of ice crystals on the window the scene looked like a Currier & Ives print. I couldn't believe it was still snowing.

Had it been any other day, I wouldn't have been so angry at the weather. But today was the final day of Skills One. I needed to be there to record this. There was a cooking practical. I wanted to take it. I'd already missed the written test yesterday. How could I miss the last two days of Skills One? But there was even more snow now than there had been yesterday afternoon when my car did its ballet on Route 9. Attempting the journey would have been foolhardy.

I had a small hope. I called the main switchboard at the Culinary. "Yes, we're open," the voice told me with what I sensed was bemusement.

At 12:30, with the snow still falling, I called Chef Pardus.

He answered his phone. He sounded quiet and subdued, as though he were very tired.

"Hi, Chef, this is Michael Ruhlman."

"Hi, Michael, what's up?"

"It's still snowing up here. I don't think I'll be able to make it in."

"That's up to you," he said softly.

"I'm sorry," I said.

"Hey, that's O.K.," he said, almost a whisper.

I paused. I needed him to know I wasn't blowing this off lightly. I said, "I am sorry. I really want to be there."

Silence on the line. Then, still quiet and weary, he said, "Michael, I don't want you to take offense at this." He searched for words. "I was going to say this yesterday. Maybe I should have. I don't want you to take offense at this."

When I hung up, I wasn't sure exactly what had happened or why I was feeling so strongly. I paced. Then I sat down and tried to think about the conversation.

"Part of what we're training students to be here is chefs—and when chefs have to be somewhere, they get there," Pardus had said calmly and evenly, not as judgment but as fact.

"Chefs are the people who are working on Thanksgiving and Christmas, when everyone else is partying," he said. "Or at home with their family."

He didn't stop there: "You're cut from a different cloth," he told me. At that moment, I believe, I stopped thinking as a writer and just listened to what he had to say. There was a hint of snobbishness in his voice. I knew every now and then during class he would look at me trying to figure me out, when I argued with him about whether or not my hollandaise had too much lemon juice. He would grow pensive and just stare. He had told me he watched the way I carried myself. He never said this, but I could see it in his eyes and hear it now over the phone: College boy. White collar. Smooth.

Writer. I sensed that part of him envied this and part of him was amused by it. He was a smart, articulate man. But he was a cook through and through. We *were* different. But I resented his saying that we—and it was a cumulative we, meaning himself and everyone in that class but me—were cut from different material. As if I were satin gown or Oxford cloth. As he went on, he seemed to grow less tired. He was getting worked up, too.

"We're different," he said. "We *get* there. It's part of what makes us a chef." I was quiet. "We *like* it that way. That's why this place never shuts down. And we're teaching the students this."

He knew I was doing a different job, he said. This wasn't meant to be a criticism. He just wanted me to understand. He had his job to do, and I had mine, he said. I said I understood. I asked him, if I were a student and was making this call, didn't make it in, what would happen? He told me if I were a student and didn't show for Day Fourteen, I'd fail.

This is a physical world. The food is either finished at six o'clock, or it's not. You're either in the kitchen or you're not. Much of what one learned here was why food behaved as it did. But sometimes there was no room for why. Sometimes *why* didn't matter. It wasn't simply that excuses were not accepted here—excuses had no meaning at all. The physical facts in any given moment—that was all.

When I entered K-8—the cooking practical in full swing—Chef Pardus's eyebrows rose above the frame of his glasses and he strode immediately toward me, shaking his head. "I didn't mean to *shame* you into coming," he said.

I said, "I know." I told him what he'd said had angered me. Then I said, "Can I still take the practical?"

"You happen to be in group two," he said. "Group two starts in a half hour."

On Day Fourteen of Skills One, Chef Pardus divides the class. Half do their practical, the other half cleans pots, cleans the kitchen—no jockeying for burner space, no running to the sink to wash a pot because your béchamel sauce was scorching and the pot room was empty. The school simply wanted to see that each student knew how to make a consommé, a stable emulsion. After an hour and a half, the groups switched.

My name was on the board in the second group. It was significant, I think, that he'd written it down at all.

I was an hour and forty-five minutes late but had made it in time not only for the practical, but I also had an extra half hour to take the written test I'd missed yesterday. I stowed my knives and briefcase beneath my station, my heart still racing, and accepted the test. I sat outside in the hall between K-8 and K-9. I forgot to write my name on the test. I had gone from my warm room in Tivoli twenty-five miles away to the Culinary; I was not certain why I had done it or why I was here, and I was not certain why I was so furious. But again, this was not a place that concerned itself at such times with *why*. I read the first question on the test: "Describe the procedure for making brown veal stock. List ingredients in sequential order."

I paused and thought. "First, you rent your house in Cleveland and move your family hundreds of miles east to the Hudson Valley. . . ."

Clearly, something had changed but I had no time to reflect. Twenty-five questions to answer in that many minutes, occasionally interrupted by a student giving a tour—the Culinary receives about two hundred thousand visitors a year—who would move down the hall ("And this is a Skills kitchen, students' first kitchen experience at the CIA, and behind you is the kitchen for the Caterina de Medici restaurant . . ."). The moment I finished, I hustled into the kitchen.

David and Bianca had prepped their stations and gathered their mise en place. Their consommés were already at a simmer beneath sturdy rafts of ground meat, egg white, tomato, and mirepoix. They nodded, said hello. I asked them if we were going to have enough room here—feeling a complete outsider now, I didn't want to screw up their practical. I wasn't a real student, after all. David was confident and welcoming. "No problem," he said, "plenty."

I was a little behind because of the test and because I hadn't prepared to be doing this at all. We'd done everything—a quart of consommé, a quart of béchamel, a three-yolk hollandaise, and a one-yolk mayonnaise (we used an ounce of a pasteurized yolk out of a carton)—in class many times, so much of it felt like rote. I grabbed three bowls from the cage and on my way to my station picked up a healthy ten ounces of meat—Pardus would be looking for flavor, no time to skimp—whipped three egg whites, dumped in the meat, cut up some mirepoix, and carefully measured the tomato paste—

short that and you've got a cloudy broth—poured in the beef stock, whipped it some more, then got it heating. Slowly. Plenty of time now that the consommé was on the flame. As soon as the raft had formed, a perfect thick flesh-colored disc, I got the béchamel started, first cooking the flour in clarified butter till it had a nice pastry-crust smell, added the milk and seasoned it, and put it on the flattop on a ring of aluminum foil to keep it from burning. The foil wasn't enough and I scorched it three times, each time dumping it into a new pot, bringing the scorched one to Travis; Travis was at the helm of the sink, so I knew there would be plenty of pots.

"How ya doin'?" Travis asked as I passed him.

"I'm a little disoriented," I said.

The two emulsions were simple, though the mayonnaise could take time; one of the big problems with the mayonnaise was that we had to whip the heck out of it, and if you whipped too much, the mayonnaise would turn gray because of the old steel bowls we used. I liked the hollandaise best, so in the middle of the practical I relaxed a bit with that, took my time, cooking my eggs over water till they were a nice sabayon consistency. Pardus said he'd seen people cook eggs on a flattop and once seen a hollandaise cooked in a deep fryer. The double boiler was safest so long as you didn't let the water boil. I added some lemon juice first, then whipped in warm clarified butter. It took more than eight ounces and I had to reheat it before I brought it to Pardus.

Chef Pardus, behind his desk, regarded my sauce. "It's got a nice color," he said. "It looks a little flat, though. It could be more fluffy." He was right; I didn't argue. He lifted a spoonful and let it fall in a thick slow ribbon. "Good consistency." He tasted it, didn't move. Then he nodded. "This is a good hollandaise sauce." He squinted at me and said, "It's just a little light on acid. You could have added a little more lemon juice."

"All week I've been adding too much lemon juice," I cried.

He shrugged and said it was a minor point. He took off a point for the flat appearance. It would be the only point I would lose during the entire practical. Everything else was perfect, and the mayonnaise was best of all, a perfect body, "exactly what I'm trying to teach them to do to make it a great base," Pardus said, and it had a perfect balance of salt and acid that gave it "a real brightness." With fifteen minutes remaining, I'd gotten a 199 of 200 points. My head was now clear. I'd crushed the test. Cut from a different cloth? I'd absolutely crushed it.

The question that now pressed on me: Had I gotten out of hand? Had something snapped?

I don't know. A few days later, having mentioned in an E-mail to a friend what had happened, he sent a chuckling response: "I can't wait to read about how, leaving wife and daughter on the hearth, you drove twenty-five miles through a snowstorm to make a béchamel sauce." I could understand, from a distance, that the situation had comic possibilities, but at the time it wasn't funny to me. Something had happened.

After the phone call with Pardus, and having reflected on the situation, I'd gone into the other room to talk to Donna.

"So he basically called you a wimp," she said, deftly assessing the situation.

I started, then said, "Yeah, I guess you're right."

"This is really upsetting you," she said.

"I guess it is." I paced the room awhile, hyperventilating.

Then Donna, who watched me as one would a tennis game, said something that upset me more. "Michael, you're *not* a cook, you're a writer." I ignored the angry subtext of her statement (*Don't even* think *about going out in this weather*), and said, "I *know* that, I *know* that."

This, of course, was a lie. I didn't know that at all. In fact, and it wasn't until that day and that snowstorm that I fully understood what had gradually taken hold of me since the moment I pushed through the door of the stall, dressed not in jeans and sweater, but in white chef's jacket and houndstooth-check trousers.

I wanted to be a cook. *I wanted to* be *a cook*. That's why I was angry beyond reason. Pardus's I'm-tougher-than-you got to me. His snobbishness ran so deep it was blasé. *I seethed.* I would show him.

The second problem—what lent confusion to my anger—was that I *was* a writer, and I had certain obligations in telling a factual story. Pardus had thrown my entire modus operandi into question, had revealed me as a kind of double imposter. I was not solely an observer, a recorder dressed in student gear, to learn what it was *like* to learn to cook. I now intended to play, too. I wasn't here for recipes. I was no longer here to learn how to make a great veal stock. I knew that now, and that wasn't the end. I needed to know what it took to be a professional cook. But in order to know this, I had to relinquish what made me a credible reporter—my objectivity, my serene writerly distance. And yet it became clear to me that day that I could not know what it meant to be a cook from a distance, simply by watching. Pardus had upped the ante by saying I could neither learn to be a cook nor write completely about what it took to be one. Pardus had told me I couldn't know, because I wasn't one of them. Cooks *git* there.

And if I couldn't know, didn't live up to it, wasn't tough enough, *didn't git* there, then I was failing as a student and as a reporter simultaneously.

I had promised my wife that I would turn back if the road grew too dangerous, and headed out into the snow. That day changed me: I *would be* a cook. I didn't have the experience, I wouldn't have the time, and I would be forced to jump around in the curriculum and stay true to my reportorial obligations, but somehow, someway, I was going to prove myself as a cook.

The Making of Chef Pardus

Following the catharsis of the cooking practical and still unsure why I had behaved as I did, I suggested to Chef Pardus that we talk, preferably before he began his three weeks of doubles next week.

With no lecture on Day Fourteen, with the kitchen cleaned, and with no failures, class ended shortly after seven o'clock. As we pushed out the doors of K-8, I told Pardus how furious I'd been earlier. This interested him. I said I didn't know if I could explain, but I told him what Donna had said. Pardus chuckled. "I guess she was right," he said. "I kind of was calling you a wimp."

Now, as we headed through the dining hall, down a flight of stairs into the mailroom—Pardus checked his box—and into the chefs' locker room, a narrow, carpeted chamber with seventy-six slim green lockers, I asked *why*?

"Wow," Pardus said. "This brings up a lot of stuff for me." He began to unbutton his chef's jacket, then stopped. "It's sort of like therapy for me. I get goose bumps thinking of it." I expected him to smile, but he didn't.

"I think part of it is protection." He tossed his chef's jacket into a hamper. "Protection against feeling like you don't have a normal life. To protect you against all the things you give up because of this work." I nodded but he stopped changing and turned to me to say, "I haven't had a Thanksgiving since I was a *kid*. Till *this* year. This was the first. Mother's Day? I didn't *spend* it with my *mother*. Busiest day of the year. I've lost a lot for this work. And I'm not happy about it."

He put on jeans, a green sweater, tied the laces of his shoes. I hadn't really thought of it while he was changing but the transformation was startling. He looked like a grad-school student in his jeans-and-cable-knit attire, trim, clean-shaven, short wavy brown hair, preppy wire-rimmed glasses. It was only then that I realized how powerful a uniform can be. Then I suggested that life as a cook must be like a cross between life in the military and life in a traveling carnival.

Pardus laughed, said the analogy wasn't off the mark, and we headed into the cold. The storm had passed; the roads had been salted and appeared dry. The night was frigid but clear. Pardus said he might be a little behind me, he'd have to dig his car out of the snow. He'd slept at the Culinary last night to ensure the storm didn't waylay him in Germantown. Susanne, who lived an hour south of Hyde Park, had stayed the night in Eun-Jung's room. Everyone had gotten there.

We met at Starr Cantina in Rhinebeck, a cozy little town midway between Hyde Park and Tivoli, populated on summer weekends by New Yorkers but, in cold early March, happily unfashionable. The bar, too, was slow on this Friday night, though a couple at the next table called out "Hi, Michael" to Chef Pardus when he sat down; he introduced me to former students heading into Garde Manger.

This was the first time Chef Pardus and I had talked outside class. I knew he'd worked in New Orleans because our bad posture, hunched as we were over our SMEP at Table One, led him to tell us about working garde manger station at a hotel in the French Quarter, cutting all day. "I blew out my sciatic nerve," he told us, which had caused him to collapse to the floor. Weeks of tai chi got him back in shape, he said.

I knew that he had traveled in France, eating. "You know that moment in *Amadeus*," he told us, a memory sparked by the bright green germ of a garlic clove on my cutting board, "when Salieri says God speaks through Mozart? That's how I felt when I left Robuchon's restaurant." He had said that attention to detail, such as removing the germ from the garlic if you weren't going to cook it well, was what distinguished a good restaurant from an excellent one. And Jamin, the three-star restaurant of Joël Robuchon, a chef known for almost machinelike perfection, had proven to be Pardus's own private mecca, food holiness he had never before encountered.

And I knew that he had an abiding love for northern California, where he could forage for wild mushrooms, where farmers' markets were so abundant he would sometimes drum up business at his restaurant in Sonoma simply by walking out the front door to the market across the street and buying a few unusual ingredients. Shoppers, attracted by his uniform, inquired what he would do with this or that and he would create some daily specials on the spot that they might try for lunch or dinner if they cared to stop by the restaurant.

I knew that he worked hard, was ambitious, focused, thoughtful, an occasional braggart, that he kept McGee, *Le Guide Culinaire*, and the latest issue of *U.S. News & World Report* on his bedside table, and that he was intensely competitive—he got there.

Still throbbing slightly from the unusual events of the day, I tried, at his request, to explain why I'd gotten so mad. Because I was responding to something he had started, though, I returned the focus to him and a particular sense of loss: namely, Vicky, his former wife, who had begun A Block at the Culinary just as Pardus was about to graduate. She too became a cook. The marriage lasted eleven years. It ended in part, he believed, because in a line of work requiring such long hours from two people who were by nature perfectionists, and who therefore worked even longer hours, lines of communication broke down. About a half year later, he fell in love with a woman several years older than himself, the mother of a ten-year-old boy. They discussed children of their own, she was getting old ("Now or never," she said), but Pardus didn't feel stable in his career at the time; later, when he did, she said he'd waited too long, that she was too old. Not long after that he began to feel that he had "topped out" in the chef world, would never hit the ranks of celebrity that would make the long hours and work worthwhile, and he felt he'd burn out if he continued to cook. At the same time, the Culinary's Greystone campus neared completion, a spectacular state-of-the-art facility in a nineteenth-century winery built of volcanic rock in the Napa Valley, for the continuing education of professional cooks. This, he knew, was where he wanted to be. So he began a long-range plan to get there, the first step being to apply to the Hyde Park campus for a job.

Feeling he'd grow bitter if he did not make this career move, he packed his car and left the woman he loved and her son, whom he had all but adopted, and returned east, realizing, he told me, "I had nothing to show for thirteen years of my life." Not his former wife, nor his current love, only, as is true of many cooks, a long résumé of restaurants scattered from the East Coast to the South Coast to the West Coast. The work of a cook can be almost medieval in its itinerancy, and this has its repercussions. "A big chunk of me is still back there," he said.

We drank beer, I ordered a basket of fries because I hadn't eaten dinner, and Pardus explained how and why he came to be where he was. There is no typical chain of events that leads an ordinary human to become a chef, but Pardus's path and personality contained elements similar to many chefs'.

Michael Pardus was born in Wilimantic, Connecticut, in 1957 to an elementary-school teacher and an employee of the local telephone company, and he grew up in Storrs, Connecticut. Most chefs I had met had some sort of formative kitchen experiences with a woman in the family. In Pardus's case, it was his father's mother. Pardus described her as the sort of woman who would bake 140 dozen cookies at Christmastime. "She knew *exactly* how many there were," he said. She taught him about the care of food. His grandfather, who had cut the grass flanking highways for a living, tended a beautiful garden, and from him Pardus learned the pleasures of fresh produce.

Pardus grew up to be a rebellious teenager not atypical in the mid 1970s. "I looked like Ted Nugent when I was fifteen," he said, referring to the rock musician who would leap about on top of giant speakers during performances, brown frizzy hair trailing like a banner behind him. He took a job as a dishwasher at an old-age home to support his skiing habit and found that he got along in kitchens.

Michael Pardus hated high school and avoided it whenever possible. During his junior year he took courses at a branch of the University of Connecticut and managed to accrue enough credits to satisfy his high school's graduation requirements. Thus, on the day when his fellow classmates were beginning their senior year of high school, Pardus filled his backpack, actually watched his school bus pass by, then said, "Hey, Mom. I'm going to Boston. I'll see ya later."

He hitchhiked there, he told me, found a nineteen-dollar-per-week room with a hot plate and a kettle-washer job at Massachusetts General Hospital. He still felt an affinity for kitchens. "It wasn't that I had a love of food," he said. "I had a love of chaos." He was soon joined in Boston by his girlfriend and another friend. "It was a gas," he said, but eventually their lives turned rather dissolute and "weird" and as he moved into his twenties, it dawned on him that washing steam kettles was not satisfactory long-term employment. He knew about the Culinary Institute of America, found out how much it cost, and asked his parents for tuition money. His father, who had already paid for a year at Boston University that his son didn't show up for, said no. But, his father continued, he could have his room back if he wanted; this would allow him to save money. So Pardus returned home and worked till he could apply to cooking school. When the CIA had no openings, he began a small campaign to get in.

"I badgered them," Pardus recalled. "Every week I'd call them up and say, 'This is Michael Pardus. Do you have any openings?' It got so they expected my call. 'No, Michael, we don't have any openings yet.' " Late in the summer of 1979, when he had just turned twenty-two, the Culinary called to say they had an opening if he could get to Hyde Park in late October. Pardus sold everything he owned, including his stamp collection, and moved to Hyde Park. It became a new home.

"It was the first time in my life where I found a whole lot of people like me," he said. "They were brothers and sisters. We'd get up and talk about food. We'd go to class and *study* food. We'd eat lunch together and talk about food. At night, we'd drink beer and talk about *food*."

And yet it wasn't the food he was hooked on. He learned what the chefs taught at the Culinary in the early eighties, classical French cuisine (he never butchered a fish here, never used a fresh herb, he said), wondering to himself, *Why would people eat this?* "But I followed the party line," he said. Pardus admitted that he was still the sort of person who thought Long John Silver's was a fancy restaurant.

He did his externship at a resort in Sun Valley, Idaho, which among other things offered a gigantic buffet every Saturday that served a thousand people at twenty-five dollars a head. When the cook in charge of the buffet quit, Pardus, in the middle of his cooking-school career, took over. "I'm a sucker for responsibility," he told me.

Here he learned organization. He had one job: feed one thousand people each Saturday. He would roast forty or fifty prime ribs, forty or fifty pork loins, clean and cook thousands of shrimp. "American continental crap," he said. "Food was still not the thing. It was a vehicle for being organized." He loved being organized. His prep list ran pages. Other people wouldn't and couldn't do what he did. And each week, when it was over, Saturday night, it was time to unwind. Or as Pardus put it, "Fifth of gin, fall asleep in some bathtub with a waitress."

He returned to the CIA and graduated in 1981, taking a job as a line cook in New Orleans at the Royal Sonesta Hotel on Bourbon Street. He moved quickly to garde manger. It was here that he filled an eight-foot-long ice canoe with ten thousand shrimp and blew out his sciatic nerve.

When Vicky graduated from the Culinary, they married. "You can't do much in New Orleans without a drink in your hand," they agreed. "Maybe we should think about somewhere else." Eventually, that place was Dallas, where Vicky had landed a job at the Four Seasons. She helped her husband find work at a new country club called Las Colinas Sports Club ("same old American continental crap," Pardus said). She arrived in Dallas first and began work; he followed a few days later, arriving at the hotel where Vicky had been put up while searching for a place to live.

That first night, they decided to order room service. Room service was a turning point in his culinary career.

"That first meal blew me away," he said. "It was room service from the grand dining room. I realized, 'This is food.' It was incredible." Genuine nouvelle by a good French chef. Not bullshit nouvelle, he said, but the real thing. He had no idea food could *be* like this. It was the early eighties when nouvelle *was* nouvelle, and good, and Pardus was twenty-four years old. "This was really cool stuff. I knew how to make a *mousse*. It never occurred to me to make a mousse with *lobster* and wrap it in a cabbage leaf and steam it and serve it with basil sauce and a beurre blanc. Basically you've got lobster and butter, which is a classical combination, and playing around with it." He and Vicky sat on the bed staring at the plates, picking apart the food, examining it, scrutinizing it, verbally dismantling it, and putting it back together again. "It was beautiful," Pardus told me, "and I said to myself, 'Hey. I know how to make all these components. I never knew they could be put *together* this way.' It never occurred to me that you could *do* this."

With that meal, his education began.

He bought books, scrutinized photographs, read recipes, and thought, What can I do? He began experimenting on his own. "The wheels were turning and turning and turning," he told me. He still put out country-club food, but every now and then the chef would give him some leeway to make the kind of food he and Vicky talked about late at night after work. She'd return from the Four Seasons, her hands cramped and knotted from cutting bas-relief roses out of potatoes, and tell her husband what the chef there was doing. Now, instead of putting out the standard smoked salmon for the Sunday buffet at the sports club, he'd do a salmon mousseline roulade filled with spinach and chunks of lobster, sliced and served warm with a light beurre blanc.

But he knew this wasn't enough. He needed a teacher. He asked associates who was doing the most interesting work in the city. He was told of a Frenchman named Roland Passot who was opening his own restaurant. Pardus went to Passot and asked for a job. Passot said he couldn't pay anyone, forget it.

Pardus said, "I'll work for free."

"When can you work?"

"I work from two till ten; other than that, I'm free," Pardus said.

"Can you come in at seven A.M.?"

"Yes," Pardus said.

"How many days a week?"

"How many do you need?"

"Four."

Pardus said, "Fine."

Pardus worked for ten mouths for free for Passot. Passot had worked in some of the great kitchens of France and under great chefs and what Pardus remembered most, the first thing he said he learned from Passot, was how to make a good brown stock. He had made brown stock at the CIA but the way he had been taught had been in a classroom situation, not cooking it long enough and then not reducing it to the proper flavor and consistency. Passot's brown stock—cooked long and then reduced to a tasty brothlike liquid—now here was something he could use. Passot and his partner spoke French all day, but Pardus asked enough questions to learn how a true French chef worked, and how the classical methods at the CIA could be put to use beyond what he'd learned in school.

The second turning point came after his next job; he and Vicky had moved to California and he began cooking at Miramonte Restaurant in St. Helena under a man named Udo. Udo himself had worked under Bocuse and Michel Guérard and it was here that Pardus came into his own as a chef. He began a daily journal of the specials they created at Miramonte ("Quail stuffed with foie gras," one entry read, for instance, "poached in quail stock served cold with grapes and pickled cherry, clarified jellied poaching liquid"); his descriptions were often accompanied by a diagram of how the dish was plated, where the pickled cherry was placed, where the aspic was spooned. He still had this notebook, jammed with food entries, and he still referred back to it as a reference. In 1985, Udo closed the restaurant to take his staff on a tour of France provided they paid their own airfare; the last entry in Pardus's notebook records the revelatory twelve-course meal he had in Paris at Jamin by Joël Robuchon, the cook through whom God spoke.

The journal, containing hundreds of entries, ends here as if, after that meal, he concluded one phase of his education and career and began a new one.

You Understand What I Am Saying?

"**A**l dente vegetables don't fly here at the CIA, I'll tell you right now," Chef Pardus said to start his demo on Day Fifteen, the beginning of Culinary Skill Development Two.

We'd had the customary three-day weekend, typically scheduled after the end of each block unless a holiday fell in the middle of the block. I'd only completed one fourteen-day block, but so much had been packed into those days that I was glad for a Monday off. Furthermore, we were heading into vegetable cookery, far from the intriguing intricacies of the consommé and sauce Robert. We began Skills Two with glazed carrots, creamed corn, and Mexican-style corn. As if to heap further insult upon us, Pardus had added a quart of béchamel to each person's production for the day.

It wasn't business as usual. Pardus had called out new table assignments. I had been moved to Table Three, the back of the room. No more listening in on Pardus's evaluations of veloutés. I grabbed a spot near the stove, which would save traveling time. The new dynamics seemed to set instantly. Adam had taken a spot nearest the stove also and would work beside me. Eun-Jung had tried to sneak into my spot by the stove when I'd gone off to get a cutting board, but I muscled her out upon my return. She would work across from Adam, having least direct access to the stove of any of us. I reasoned that because much of our production required group efforts (clarifying butter, say, or reducing stocks), I would be of more use near the stove than Eun-Jung, whose linguistic challenges continued; in fact, she seemed to understand less and less as we went on, though this may simply have been that she no longer tried to hide her difficulties. But the real reason I stayed where I was—to be perfectly honest—was that I was looking out for Number One. I admit it. I was in the game here and saw no reason to be kicking into the wind if I didn't have to.

Across from me was Leonard Mormondo, a stocky youngster from Queens. Len was a workhorse, rarely spoke, and had large blue eyes and downturned features that gave him a perpetually sullen look. He had worked a year and a half each in a restaurant (front of the house), a bakery, and a butcher shop. I could see him as a butcher, hefting a side of veal to the board and dismantling it, effortlessly, into saleable components. Something about his demeanor, his silence, the efficiency of his short, compact frame echoed *honesty* and *work ethic*. When a smile reversed his dour aspect, as would happen only occasionally, it was because he was genuinely pleased.

Adam, of course, would be the angry leader, if only by default (Eun-Jung followed by necessity, Leonard by disposition, I by profession).

"I know that people are looking for al dente where you've worked and where I've worked," Pardus continued, standing before his customary burner. He had begun three weeks of doubles, which meant he was now repeating the demo he'd performed seven hours earlier in K-2. "However. There are an equal number of people who are looking for *cooked* vegetables." Not mush, he said, but a good bite with no discernible crunch, bright color, and fresh flavor. Temperature control was critical, he said. Uniformity of cuts was critical. Jumping the veg in your pan was critical—learn now, don't fry it. Vegetables here are to be cooked and not overcooked. "It's a lot easier to learn how to do that up front," he said, "and then if you go someplace where they want al dente vegetables, you back off a little, rather than say, 'Oh, yeah, well I just cook my vegetables al dente.' That's a lame excuse that a lot of people use for undercooked vegetables. 'Oh they're *supposed* to be that way, they're al *dente*.' Yeah, *right*." Pardus paused and scanned our faces. "They're *salad*! Raw vegetables are *salad*."

Occasionally an unusual man would appear in our $330,000 classroom to observe. He would exchange a few words with Chef Pardus, and when we looked up from our board he would be gone. We first saw him as Chef Pardus demoed American Bounty vegetable soup. He, too, was dressed in chef's attire. The green nameplate pinned above the pocket of his jacket read "Uwe Hestnar." He was tall, graying, and solidly built. A forceful figure. He wandered the kitchen as Pardus sautéed leeks and onion and carrot. He stopped by the steam kettles, dipped a bowl into the veal stock, let the stock fall from the bowl back into the kettle, and regarded the bowl thoughtfully. Then he disappeared.

Chef Hestnar had been at the Culinary for more than twenty years and was now a team leader, the name the Culinary gave to its managers. Eight team leaders managed 120 faculty. Hestnar presided over a team of twenty chef-instructors running the formative kitchens: Skills, Intro, American Regional, Fish Kitchen, Oriental, and Charcuterie. Chef-instructors agree to a three-year probationary period when they begin at the Culinary. During this time they can be sacked with no questions asked, no reasons given. Part of Hestnar's job was to evaluate each instructor regularly during this period. When a Skills instructor complained to him that all the consommés were coming out cloudy, he dropped in and saw (to his silent amazement) that every single consommé was at a vigorous boil; he methodically passed each burner, reducing the boil to a simmer. He sat in the back of the class-room after dinner as Pardus lectured on cream soups, and Pardus, while he didn't alter his style or his lecture, realized that he was going out on a limb in answering a question from Ben, that he might improve on the onion soup by adding a drop or two of sherry vinegar. Hestnar would depart without a word.

On Day Sixteen, Skills Two—represented on my prep card as glace de volaille, SMEP, bread crumbs, spinach, peas, green beans almondine, broc-coli hollandaise—Hestnar appeared as I was readying my peas and spinach. Chef Pardus preferred at this point that we bring up the veg items two at a time. The peas were sautéed with blanched pearl onions in a little beef stock, beurre manié swirled in at the end to thicken the stock. The spinach, a ubiquitous item at the Culinary, was to be sautéed in clarified butter with shallots and seasoned with salt, pepper, and, curiously, a dash of nutmeg, which added an apt and intriguing flavor to the greens. I put them both on a warm plate and approached Chef Pardus's desk. He and Chef Hestnar had been talking but stopped when I arrived.

I stayed one step back, but Hestnar ushered me forward with a sweep of his hand. Pardus lifted a small forkful of peas, then praised the sauce. He tasted an onion. "These are just a bit crunchy," he said. With Hestnar there, I didn't want to argue. To my surprise, and I was suddenly not so comfortable or sure of myself, Hestnar drew a fork from the container and tasted some peas and an onion. I'd been, I realized only then, more cavalier than I'd wished; I cursed myself for not tasting the peas and onions again for seasoning and doneness. If it was perfect, it would have been luck. I hadn't put 100 percent into the damned peas; had I known Hestnar would taste, I would have.

"Crunchy?" I asked him.

Hestnar was from Hamburg, Germany, and still had an accent thick as molasses. "He's the chef," he said, not looking at me. He had thin eyes and a thin wide mouth and square features. He didn't smile.

I nodded, feeling rebuked. I was not to talk to him.

Pardus tasted my spinach. "Good cooking time, excellent flavor," he said. I knew this. I'd done the spinach perfectly, mainly because I loved spinach cooked this way. Hestnar lifted another fork and tasted my spinach. He said nothing.

When Hestnar was gone Pardus reminded me about Hestnar's he's-the-chef remark and said, "I could have told you those onions were asparagus and he would have said the same thing." Pardus also told me that Hestnar had been favorably impressed by my vegetable cookery, and somehow this made vegetable cookery seem more worthwhile at that moment. Pardus was happy, too, because it made him look good, particularly since I wasn't even a real cook but rather a more lowly life-form.

The next time I saw Hestnar happened to be in K-2 downstairs, a long, gloomy Skills kitchen where Pardus taught A.M. Skills, the class normally presided over by Chef Le Roux, who had been a cook in various capacities at Manhattan's Le Pavillon, Le Cygne, and La Côte Basque. I'd asked Pardus if I could hang out, observe a different Skills class, watch what happened unencumbered by the need to crank out the daily mise en place. Also I wanted a sense of what doubles were like. I enjoyed sitting back and watching. I could talk with Pardus here. Like my class, this one had five women; Pardus stood staring down the narrow kitchen, and said softly to me, "A lot of them"—male students—"still think it's a boys' club. I can take them into the field and introduce them to some women who will *cook* them into the *dirt*. It's a matter of stamina and skill, not upper body mass."

Also I gained a new appreciation of Chef Pardus. At eight-thirty in the morning an hour and a half into class he was power-tasting fish veloutés, fish stock thickened with roux. People lined up with their quarts of fish velouté and he would evaluate each one for flavor and mouth feel. Mmmmm. Nothing like starch-thickened fish stock in the morning. I watched him and he looked at me once, smiled with mean hunger, and said, "Breakfast of champions."

When Chef Hestnar stopped by to check in on Pardus, Pardus introduced us. I told him about why I was here and noted some of the questions I hoped to examine. He offered a comment on the nature of teaching cooking. We stood side by side in front of the reach-ins (here some refrigerators come equipped with movie screens). "A balance of training and education," he said. Then he dipped slightly, squinted, and held his hands out flat, side by side, and rubbed his index fingers together to create an image of equilibrium.

"What's the difference?" I asked.

"Training is I show you how to do something and you do it." He looked at me and lifted his eyebrows.

"What is education, then?" I pressed.

He thought but a moment, then said, "Education is, you figure it out for yourself."

At first I thought he was saying I should come to my own conclusions, but he was giving me a knowing nod.

"I see," I said. Then I asked, "Isn't it important in cooking to know why something happens and why something doesn't happen?" Pardus was always talking about *why* and most people said they liked Skills because now they knew why things happened.

Hestnar did not answer me. Either that or he responded with a gesture or expression that did not translate into English.

I found something interesting, something cryptic about the guy, and told him I'd like to talk to him more. He produced a pocket calendar and a pencil. "Where is your calendar?" he demanded.

I did not say that it was on my wall at home, only that I didn't have it with me. He showed me his and we agreed on a date and time. He wrote this down in his calendar and regarded me skeptically, I believe, as though privately laying odds on my showing up at the right time on the right day. Apparently another way chefs got there was by using pocket calendars.

Hestnar departed. I mentioned our exchange to Pardus and he weighed in with his own thoughts: "Training is I show you how to do it, you do it.

Education is I show you how to do it, you do it, then we discuss why it did what it did, why mine is better than yours."

I moved through two shifts of Skills Two, feeling tired by the end of the day but not wiped out. One day, of course, was not three weeks, and the fatigue mounted in Pardus. He began writing his increasingly involved demos on yellow Post-Its, affixing them to the top left corner of his cutting board to ensure he didn't leave anything out. Part of the reason a chef could put in fourteen- and fifteen-hour days (not including grading papers) was because so much of the work was physical; psychological focus and clarity of mind were what became difficult to maintain.

By doubting me, Chef Hestnar had ensured that I would arrive on time at his modest office—team leaders had offices; all other instructors shared cubicles formed by gray partitions on the fourth floor of Roth Hall. I did not know if he truly understood what I was here for and I explained that I hoped to write about the basics of cooking.

He nodded approvingly, saying, "The fundamentals of cookery don't change."

When I mentioned to Chef Pardus that I would be meeting with Hestnar, Pardus said, "I love that guy," and his smile stopped just short of a laugh. He had noted that Hestnar was extremely knowledgeable, always referring back to the texts. And I did sense an immediate gravity anchoring his simple-sounding words. With his first statement—the fundamentals of cookery don't change—he seemed somehow to extend his meaning all the way back in time to remind me that water has always behaved as it does now, the physical properties of heat work the same way now as they did ten thousand years ago. Cooking, now as ever, meant learning the physical forces of the world and applying them to eggs, to flour, to bones and meat.

When I asked him how he became a chef, he wagged a finger in the air and said, "I am a cook." I had heard this sort of talk before. The term "chef" was double-edged. Today, being a chef—now laden with the trappings of celebrity—often had little to do with cooking. Here at the Culinary, chef was a title, and Hestnar wanted me to know that he was not a chef in the way we have come to think of chefs. He was a cook: that's what he did, that's what he *was*, and that's what he had been, beginning at age fourteen, when he accepted the job of bellboy at the Hotel Reichshof in Hamburg, Germany.

Bellboy was the mandatory starting position for all those who intended to apprentice in the kitchen of Hotel Reichshof. One had to be a bellboy for exactly two years by order of the chef-owner of the hotel, who maintained that before one could understand cooking, one had first, Hestnar said, "to understand the meaning of customer service and hospitality." From October 1950 until October 1952, Uwe (pronounced Ou-vay) carried bags. It was believed that cooking was about hospitality first, and then about food. Without hospitality there would be no guests to serve food *to*. If you were not willing to be a bellboy, you were not chef material. "You better live it," Hestnar told me. "Nobody forces you." He shrugged. "Become an electrician."

After two years, the frightened Uwe moved for the first time into the grand professional kitchen of Hotel Reichshof, with its huge "piano range" and bright skylights and vast ovens. "I was allowed to hold a bowl for two years, with the chef's mise en place," he recalled.

This was the apprentice system and it was how chefs traditionally trained in Europe, and still do, though the programs are slipping in some countries, Hestnar said. In the apprentice model you learned one-on-one. I asked which he thought was better, the apprentice system or a formal culinary education. He said that one-on-one meant you learned one person's training, only one person's ways.

Then he said, "Culinary arts is vast, so for a person to learn one method . . ."

Hestnar would often trail off like that, raise his eyebrows, shrug—you figure it out for yourself. The main thing the apprentice system lacked, he affirmed, was theory. The whys of cooking. For instance, Chef Hestnar did not recall learning how to make a hollandaise, meaning that he was never taught. More likely he was told to make one, and by asking and watching he figured out what one did to achieve the final result. But no one ever told him, as Chef Pardus and Harold McGee had told me and Adam, and Greg and Ben and Erica and Susanne, that you had to break up the oil into infinitesimal bubbles that would be separated by water, mainly via the lecithin in egg yolks, to form a stable and tasty oil-in-water emulsion, which happens to go very nicely with asparagus.

Here, Hestnar said, "we do both at the same time." Theory and training. And, he said, "There is a certain standard attached to it." Again, he was somewhat cryptic on this point—he used Beethoven as the metaphor when I asked him to elaborate—but I believe he meant that when we consider a Beethoven sonata, there is a certain standard we share in our expectations of how it sounds. And yet interpretations vary, how long certain notes hung in the air, how heavily one hit each particular note. This finally determined its quality, its artfulness. The same with cooking—first you learned a standard, then you refined it. He said he could make a thousand hollandaise sauces and each would be different.

"Depending on what?" I asked.

The corners of his mouth turned down; his hand swept at the air as if dismissing the view out his window. "How I feel that day."

I moved to my favorite subject: stock. Why did the Culinary Institute of America teach two different ways of making stock—the standard way and the self-clarifying method? He had already explained that instructors have a certain amount of freedom to teach as they will, that they discuss methods, address problems among themselves. But the CIA had a party line, as Chef Pardus often referred to it. The Powers determined one method as standard, and that standard was taught. Wasn't teaching Skills students two methods of making stock contradictory, potentially confusing? Shouldn't there be only one? I was trying to bait him a little, which he must have sensed, because he didn't answer.

I tried a more direct route. "Is one way better than the other?" I asked. "Which do you prefer and why?"

He was quiet for a moment and then answered: "It's very interesting."

He smiled. And it was here that it occurred to me that Chef Hestnar had a vaguely reptilian look. There was something hard and wily and mischievous, the way his eyes would narrow to slits and his mouth likewise would spread thinly across his broad square face. His accent also enhanced his elusiveness. I grew accustomed to his style and I waited. Eventually he said, "Let's see what Escoffier says, the bible." He scanned the index and flipped the pages for white stock, dragged his finger down the page as I followed along. "It says bones and water. It doesn't say begin with cold water or boiling water," Hestnar said. "Zo."

He paused again, then checked *Hering's Dictionary of Classical and Modern Cookery*. This recommended blanching the bones. Hestnar's copy of *La Repertoire de la Cuisine* called for bones, mirepoix, and salt. Last, he pulled from his tightly packed shelves a book held together by a rubber band. It was a German book by Ernst Pauli, the title of which Hestnar translated for me as "Book of Learning of the Kitchen." Removing the rubber band, Chef Hestnar said, "My schoolbook." Pauli suggested one begin with cold water.

Hestnar closed this last book, sat back in his chair, and shrugged.

All right, there are many ways of making a stock, I thought. But he was still avoiding my question. "What about adding tomato?" I asked him.

He said, "Tomato, bay leaf—that's art."

"But using the tomato to denature proteins in order to create a clearer stock in less time?"

He smiled and said, "That's applied theory."

Yes. Excellent! I thought. He didn't miss a beat.

Such was the nature of our conversation. It rambled; he sprinted, strolled, cut left, cut right. I wondered aloud why we were taught the dated cauliflower polonaise, a bread-crumb-and-egg mixture sprinkled on cauliflower and baked. He responded that he supposed they could do cauliflower with cheese sauce instead. I told him my question remained, why teach something so old-fashioned as that, so infrequently used, polonaise or cheese sauce?

He agreed that cauliflower was not often used anymore. "People don't want to pay five dollars for two ingredients." And yet a more complex dish, one with twenty ingredients, he said, was in fact simpler because it was much easier to cover a mistake; with two ingredients a cook had no room for error. Therefore, cauliflower with bread crumbs or with cheese sauce was a true test of a cook.

This led him to the proliferation of cookbooks, a situation he scorns. "The shelves are bulging with cookbooks," he said dismissively.

"You don't like that," I responded.

He said that everything any cook could possibly need to know was contained in five books: Escoffier, *Larousse Gastronomique, Hering's Dictionary, La Repertoire.* I told him that was only four. "And Carême," he said. Then he said, "No one wants."

Another long pause before he tacked again: "What makes culinary arts tick?"

I didn't know if he was actually directing this to me or offering it rhetorically. He had more or less lofted it into the air. He lifted his index finger, then spun in his chair to a file behind him, as if quickly reaching for a bat to knock this question into the bleachers. He riffled manila folders and turned to me with two sheets of paper. He handed them to me. They contained a chart or grid covering a page and a half. This, he said, was all one truly needed. Here were the fundamentals of culinary arts—all of Escoffier, Larousse, Câreme, as well as Julia Child, James Beard, *The Joy of Cooking,* and the TV Food Network—in their entirety, distilled to a page and a half. "I would like to sell this for fifty dollars," he said, "but no one would buy them." Then he chuckled heartily.

I examined the sheets—a list of twenty-six items and their ratios. Along the top ran the numbers one, two, four, six, eight, and sixteen; these columns were divided by base products, such as aspic, pâté à choux, sabayon, court bouillon ordinaire. Here, on this sheet, was his answer to an earlier question: one quart of water, two pounds of bones, four ounces of mirepoix equaled stock. "For a quart of stock, you must use two pounds of bones," he said. "Will it be stock if you use three pounds of bones?" He shrugged: *You see what I'm trying to say? Understand?*

I found the sheets mysteriously thrilling. For hollandaise sauce, the sheet listed six egg yolks and one pound of butter, nothing more. We had learned to make hollandaise by reducing cider vinegar with cracked pepper and adding this, strained and with lemon juice, to yolks whipped with clarified butter to make a hollandaise. But on Chef Hestnar's grid of ratios, he had reduced everything to its essence. Take away vinegar, pepper, and lemon, and you still had a hollandaise. Take away yolks or butter and it was no longer hollandaise. I found the ratio sheet beautiful. Like a poet chipping away at his words, polishing until his idea was diamond, Hestnar had removed every extraneous element of cooking.

I asked Chef Hestnar if I could hang on to the ratios and thanked him for his time. As I stood at his door, feeling as though I had worked up some sort of cautious rapport with him, I asked, "Of the two methods of making stock that we discussed earlier, which do you, personally, prefer?"

He took a breath. I honestly didn't know if he would answer. He seemed absolutely unwilling to make judgments or answer questions directly. But he knew cooking. He was a cook. He had been a cook in Hamburg and in Pennsylvania, in Washington, D.C., São Paolo and Rio de Janeiro, Zurich, Geneva, England, and the Canary Islands. In his throaty German accent, he said, "In my experience, I have one hour too few and one day too few." He smiled. "You understand what I am saying?"

Indeed—there were many facts to consider when preparing a stock.

"Why, *Erica*," I exclaimed. "Do you have *mascara* on?" Class had not yet begun and those who were here had begun to set their stations. Adam stood beside me steeling his knife. He would steel for many minutes and, with great care, he would feel the edge with his thumb while holding it very close to his face. Eun-Jung was here, too, "shopping" as she called it—that is, gathering all the carrots and parsley and shallots not just for her own mise en place but for the entire table (we had coalesced into a team by this point). Erica happened to be passing our table close enough for me to notice that, unusually, she wore makeup.

"Yeaaaah," she said, "and eyeliner, too."

"Why?" I asked. "Why wear makeup in a kitchen?"

"I think I have nice features," she said. "Do you think I have nice features?" She turned her head slightly to the right then left.

Adam lowered steel and knife, chuckled with disbelief, and said, "Nothing like fishing for *compliments*."

"I think I've got nice features," she told us both, "and I wanted to . . . *accentuate* them." She moved closer to me and said, "So I dolled myself up, yeah."

Again, I asked her, genuinely curious, why one would where makeup in a greasy, sweaty kitchen.

Suddenly—and Erica, I knew by then, could turn on a dime—she grew defensive. "Eun-Jung wears lipstick," she said. Eun-Jung, hearing her name, looked up. Indeed, as always she had on her bright but unobtrusive lipstick. Erica said, "Look at that pink-ass shit."

Adam rolled his eyes and, addressing the ceiling said, "Pink-ass shit."

Hearing her own words, Erica took a breath, smiled wide with her teeth clamped shut, covered her mouth with her hand, and laughed. She turned bright red. Then she scurried off to her table.

We had grown familylike. I had been completely welcomed. At first, Ben, the group leader, wouldn't look me in the eye. He was cordial and answered my questions when I asked, but he was brief. Now, when I asked him about the events of his weekend he all but gushed. He had walked cold into the Gotham Bar and Grill on Saturday afternoon and asked to see the chef, Alfred Portale. "He's one of my idols," Ben told me. He was hoping to extern there and had written Portale letters that remained unanswered. He was told Portale was in a meeting but that he could wait. Eventually, Portale, a former jewelry designer and now popularizer of vertical cuisine, spoke with Ben, who managed not to embarrass himself.

"I was like, 'Holy shit, I can't believe I'm *talking* to this guy,' " Ben recalled.

Portale said he had just hired a CIA graduate and that there would be no room for externs when Ben was looking, but he would be welcome to trail next Saturday night if he wished, that is, watch and work for one evening. Ben said he would be honored.

Ben cut himself before he'd been in the Gotham kitchen a half hour. "Sliced the tip of my thumb," he said. "It bled a lot. I was *so nervous*." He peeled pearl onions. "Same way we do here," he said with surprise. He eventually calmed and proved proficient enough that the cooks let him on the line where he sautéed duck breasts.

"I cooked," Ben said the following Monday. "I cooked *duck*."

Adam, sounding jealous, said, "I can't believe they let you cook."

"The food's no different than what we do here," Ben went on. "The sauce, they do a Madeira sauce that's a little different, but the food's not any different from what we're doing. But the presentation is *incredible*." He described the tuna dish, which included pasta ingeniously raveled into a tube around a stem of rosemary that stands about a foot off the plate. "It's about this high," Ben said gesturing. "It's just an awesome dish."

On Day Eighteen of Skills we had begun to make single completed plates that would be our dinner. "If you blow it," Pardus had said, "you go hungry."

We had begun with the most common and most commonly overcooked protein item in America: the chicken breast.

"Sauté," Chef Pardus said to begin his lecture, "is a *blast*. Sauté is where the action is on Saturday night. Sauté is where you guys all want to *be* in about three years, right? Sauté is the next step to *sous* chef. Sauté is the guy who's juggling eight or ten pans at a time, makin' flames, makin' things jump. Sauté is the *hot* seat." He paused, his little riff at an end, and turned to the easel with his spoon. "Sauté *is*: a rapid, *à la minute* cooking technique. It has no tenderizing effect, so the product has to be tender. You cannot sauté a *lamb* shank. The cooking is fast. That's why it's so much fun. Bing bang boom, it goes out the door. In a small amount of oil. Over high heat."

Pardus still lectured with energy but he had begun to look a little sautéed himself. He arrived at seven A.M. and rarely left before ten P.M. for his forty-five-minute drive home. His sauté lecture concluded a day during which he had tasted thirty-six brown sauces, thirty-six spoonfuls of duchess potatoes, thirty-six mouthfuls of cauliflower polonaise, thirty-six bites each of glazed zucchini and summer squash. He had assigned a numerical grade to each of those 180 mouthfuls.

The following day, Pardus demoed our assignment: whipped potatoes, steamed Brussels sprouts, pan-steamed carrots cut in batonnets, and chicken breast sautéed and served with a reduction of stock, wine, and fresh herbs. One portion each, plated and hot at the same time. Nothing most of us hadn't done at home in some form at one time or another. But here it was even easier. First, the chicken arrived in a suprême cut, bone-less with one wing joint attached, a particularly elegant cut. Moreover, we had all the equipment, the heat, the steel sauté pans, plenty of clarified butter, plenty of stove space, and plenty of time. No one was late and many were as much as an hour early. And yet only one person so far as I knew had presented a perfect plate.

I had not put enough clarified butter in my pan when I went to cook my chicken, and I had not ensured that the surface of the meat was dry (Pardus didn't believe in dusting with flour), so my chicken stuck to the pan imme-diately. I frantically pried it off, but a few strands of chicken, which I had obediently started service-side down for the cleanest appearance, remained stuck to the pan. I managed to cover the error by browning the surface to a dark gold that looked excellent to me. I plated the other items as my sauce reduced; I swirled in chopped parsley, chervil, and tarragon at the last moment, then plated the chicken and brought it to Pardus.

My Brussels sprouts were very good, he said, as were my whipped pota-toes. "You like whipped potatoes, I can tell," he said. And then he bent close to scrutinize my chicken. "It looks like you overcooked the outside just a little bit. See this stringy, caramelized—" and he picked at it with the point of his knife, wincing. I stooped for a closer look and saw the strings he was talking about. I'd never noticed that chicken meat had such defined strings; thinking back on it, then, the chicken stuck to my pan in strings. Pardus then pressed the breast to check cooking time—he wasn't tasting chicken—as I explained what happened. "Maybe your pan wasn't hot enough," he said. "Just a minute or two overcooked." He cut into it. "See that grainy appearance in the meat?"

I was flustered and agreed. I'd thought I'd done a good job. Pardus tasted my sauce, liked it, said a few more words I didn't hear because I was mad about the chicken. As he bent pen in hand over his grade sheets, I regained my composure and said, "Wait a minute. Look how juicy it is. How can you say it's overcooked?"

He looked. "That's true, it does look juicy." He tasted the chicken for my benefit. "It's juicy but the texture is still a little grainy."

His verdict stood, as I admitted to myself, it should. We were looking for perfection here, after all. This was where perfection began. My meat had cooked too long on the surface, having stuck to the pan; it had taken on more crunch and toughness to the bite than I had intended. It wasn't perfect. It was my dinner, and with the elegant sauce, I thought it quite tasty. But not perfect. Acceptable, absolutely. Good, even. But not perfect.

Perfection had come that day from Erica. Pardus had approached me a little after five o'clock, pulled me aside, and began to speak in quiet tones. Erica had just brought him an almost incredible plate. Sweating, terrified, and red in the face as always. Everything, he said, was perfect, perfectly and simply presented ("I don't want you guys getting creative on me," he would say. "I don't want froufrou—concentrate on the food"), and *perfectly* cooked. "It was the kind of plate I'd expect from Greg or Adam," he told me. "If I didn't see her bring it up to me, if I didn't *know* everyone in this *class* so well, I'd swear someone else did it. Blew me away. I would never have expected it."

Erica, who had scrambled the eggs meant for sauce hollandaise, clouded her consommé, served onion soup in a cold bowl, Erica, whose roux had caught fire, was improving.

Each night at 6:30 most of us would eat together. I often asked people about what they were learning, how they were liking Skills. Len, my tablemate, said, "Now I know *why* things happen," echoing a sentiment voiced by almost every student I encountered. Len said he could troubleshoot, think problems through. When he saw an emulsion beginning to look greasy on the surface, he said, he knew he needed to add more water and he knew why.

Ben said he'd read about such mysterious concoctions as béchamel, had been curious about them, and was glad now to have done them himself.

Adam likewise had never worked with the mother sauces. Now he had and he liked them. "*I'd* use a demi-glace," he said, imagining a restaurant of his own. I asked him what he thought of the cauliflower polonaise. To my amazement, he liked this too. "I'd maybe change it though," he added, "so that the cauliflower laid flat and somehow I'd make the breading stick."

Erica had found the polonaise pleasing as well, shyly noting, "I really like hard-boiled eggs." Then she frowned and said, "Some people call me simpleminded." This appeared to hurt her, this recognition, though she showed no compunction about offering it aloud as we all sat eating our trout à la meuniére with steamed new potatoes, green beans, and braised endive.

I asked Erica what she'd learned so far in this class.

We were all quiet as Erica mulled the question over. Then she chuckled and said, "Just about everything. I didn't know *any* of this."

What could one say about Adam Shepard, beside whom I worked daily? I found him compelling because he seemed to be the one person who was solely interested in food. Almost everyone else said they had chosen this school mainly for the brighter financial prospects it promised. Adam never talked about money; money was simply something he would never have much of and that was fine by him. I had sat next to him in one of the front rows of the Danny Kaye Theater, where visiting chefs demoed their work for an audience and two video cameras. Chef Pardus had given us a break from class on Day Twenty-One to see Chef Michael Lomonaco, who had resuscitated a wheezy "21" Club and brought it to the forefront of New York restaurants serving American regional fare. Adam sat with his camera (he shot for the school newspaper, *La Papillotte*), slouched, propped on his left hand, waiting.

I asked him what his ultimate goals were. He said, "To be the best possible chef I can be." This was not a dumb, Miss America response; he really meant it. But I knew this already. In the best of all possible worlds, I asked him, what would he be doing?

"If I had fifteen million dollars?"

I nodded.

"I'd open a space that had a restaurant, a gallery, and a performance theater."

I stared at him and said, "You're not a tradesman."

He said, "I told you I was an artist, too."

He had mumbled it, perhaps, but here he offered it plainly, with a self-protective shrug. Here was one student who hoped to aspire to the level of artist.

After the lively performance by Lomonaco who, unlike many chefs, was enormously articulate and spoke well that day about the importance of regional fare and quality ingredients, I said, "Good demo."

"I guess," Adam said.

It had been better than "I guess" for me on a number of counts, not least of which was that Lomonaco had given some perspective to our daily classes. Watching him sauté whitefish—a Great Lakes fish served with morels and asparagus—was itself instructive: he first placed the filet in the pan, heard very little sizzle, and pulled it immediately. His pan wasn't hot enough. He checked the flame, waited a moment longer, then lay the fish in the pan and a loud crackling began. This was just as Pardus had taught us.

Adam, however, remained unimpressed with Lomonaco. Adam's standard was never less than perfection. And it remained so in class I found, when he and I teamed up for the roasted chicken with pan gravy—one chicken for every two people. When Pardus called us over for the second part of the demo, I pulled our chicken out of the oven. It was nearly done and I didn't want to overcook it. Adam was furious when he found the chicken. He thought I'd thrown everything off. He'd had everything under control. And he pretty much remained furious all the way up until he made the pan gravy—there was no discussion who would make it—though it wound up with little black specks in it. I told him to settle down, the six-o'clock deadline was not in effect today because of the Lomonaco demo. "Yeah?" he said.

Adam was a loner, didn't depend on anyone, and didn't want anyone depending on him. He used his own equipment, never borrowed. When Eun-Jung grabbed his tongs from their customary spot on the handle of the oven, and he needed them, he would say, "Eun-Jung, I thought you had your own tongs." Eun-Jung would look at the tongs in her hand and look back at the tongs on her cutting board, and say, "I am sorry, Adam." Later, Adam had set his braised lamb shank on the flattop to keep it hot as he strained and degreased his sauce. When he turned around again, the pot his shank was in had begun to smoke. Quickly, he reached for his tongs to get his pot off the heat. His tongs were not there. Eun-Jung was at the stove an arm's length away holding her own lamb shank in the air with his tongs, casually watching sauce drip off of it into her pot.

"Eun-Jung!" Adam cried, gritting his teeth. Eun-Jung glanced at Adam.

Adam looked for anything to pull his smoking marmite off the heat, found a fork to drag it to a cool spot. The shank was stuck to the bottom. While he tried to pry it loose, cursing, the sauce he had so carefully strained and degreased boiled to almost nothing. He had just enough to reconstitute it with water. Finally, in the mad rush to get his plate to Pardus on time—at last sprinkling his gremolata just so over the plated shank and rushing it to the desk where Bianca's food was presently under scrutiny—only then did I tell him that he must sign his name. And wait. "Aw, *man*," he said. I took some pleasure in this. My shank was, according to Pardus, "very good"; then, the complex flavors continuing to open on his palate, he changed his verdict: "Excellent." Adam's, by the time he presented, was less so, but Pardus took the waiting time into account.

It had been a tricky day. Chef Pardus continued to stress the building of flavors; teaching palate was one of his chief aims as a Skills instructor; what good were skills if you couldn't taste for proper seasoning, proper balance. Shank day, we worked on sweet-sour-salty combinations with glazed beets and braised cabbage with Granny Smith apples, seasoned with vinegar, juniper berries, clove, bay leaf, and cinnamon. I had been looking forward to the juniper berries because I'd never used them before and they smelled wonderfully like gin. But did I taste the cabbage to try to distinguish the effects of the juniper berries? No time. No time to even think about sweet-sour-salty. The demo hadn't ended till quarter to four. The shanks, once you seared them, would take an hour and a half to cook to fork-tender, then you'd have to put the sauce together and the rest of the plate. We were serving the shank with turned steamed artichoke hearts and buttered fettuccine; this took planning because the pasta dough had to rest at various stages. A few people wrote their name down at six o'clock even though they weren't finished. Ben finished before six but didn't write his name down in time and was therefore late and he was furious.

Back at the table, after deadline had come and gone and the kitchen calmed, Adam said, "I'm sorry, Eun-Jung."

Eun-Jung said, "Yes, yes," not looking at him.

"I'm sorry I got so mad at you."

"Yes, yes."

Adam looked at me with frustration and said, "She doesn't even understand what I'm *saying*."

"Yes, yes," she said, "I am *sorry*, Adam."

Every now and then, despite my own underlying competitiveness with Adam, we would share a moment of sympathy. Fennel big as cabbage had arrived from the storeroom (we would eventually braise it), and its size got us talking about vegetable gardens. I said to Adam, as I could not say to

Erica or Len or Eun-Jung, "Cooking food you have grown is an almost unequaled pleasure."

Adam nodded immediately. Then he said, "Lettuce. Everyone knows what a good fresh tomato tastes like. Whether you grew it yourself or got it from a market. The freshness holds. But lettuce pulled straight out of the garden—there's nothing like it. It is so tasty if you can pull it out of the ground and have it on the table in ten minutes."

Pardus had picked up on Adam's sensibilities as well. When he lectured on potatoes, the various starch-to-water ratios of baking, chef's and new potatoes, new potatoes having high water content resulting in their creaminess, he noted that new potatoes just dug from the ground and cooked right away were a genuine treat. "Has anyone—I bet you have, Adam—has anyone eaten freshly dug new potatoes?" he asked. "Just steamed and with a little butter. It's a really wonderful thing." I looked back at Adam, who nodded *Sure have*.

And it was Adam who explained to the class during Chef Pardus's lecture on deep frying that you could run a diesel engine on a mixture of equal parts kerosene and Fry-Max, the deep-frying oil used at the school.

Adam was a cook, I began to think, in the very best and most unusual ways. It wasn't a matter of desire alone, or ability, I began to realize, but rather something in one's chemical makeup and psychological wiring that made this so. In my notebooks I wrote down something Adam said that revealed an elemental part of himself. He said, "I can be having a bad day, a *really lousy* day. But as soon as I get into this kitchen I get a boost; it all changes."

There had been in our group a young guy named Matt from a small coal town in the middle of Pennsylvania. He was the one who had told Pardus on the first day of Skills that he didn't know why he was here. Matt, a friendly, wiry fellow, was always the last to finish. When he broke his consommé raft, he wouldn't do it just once. It would take him forever, it seemed, to emulsify his mayonnaise, even though he whipped it like a madman. Midway through Skills Two, Matt didn't show up for class and the rumor spread that he was moving to Hawaii. The next day I called his room. There was loud music in the background. Yes, he said, it was true.

Matt was simply uncomfortable in a kitchen. The physics didn't come naturally to him.

Adam, on the other hand was apparently more at home in a kitchen than anywhere else. I grew to suspect that some people, maybe most people, who became good professional cooks didn't *choose* to be that way. They were simply fulfilling something that was in their nature to begin with.

The night of the lamb shanks ended a long week. Adam headed off to Vassar down the road to hear a band called Morphine. Ben and others were off to drink anywhere but Gaffney's, the local CIA watering hole. I headed up icy Route 9 toward Tivoli, wondering about my own chemistry, my own choices.

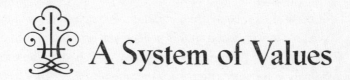 A System of Values

Culinary Skill Development Two rarely veered from the basics. Vegetables, Chef Pardus instructed us, once an afterthought, now contributed
nutritional balance to a plate, added flavor, provided color and textural con-
trasts. "Sort of like a *sauce*, huh," he said. "It's part of the whole picture
now. It's not just a garnish, it's part of the meal."

We had braised shank to learn the technique of braising, and we had
roasted chicken to learn the technique of roasting.

"What is the difference between baking and roasting?" Pardus asked.
"Today, roasting is done in an oven. So is baking. What's the difference?"
Various answers were shouted out simultaneously.

Adam said, "Essentially, they're the same except they're different
products."

"Essentially the same, just different products?" Pardus said and stopped
to consider this. The class nodded, thinking Adam had got it right. "Nope,"
Pardus said. "There *is* no difference. It's a semantic difference."

Adam, peeved, said, "I thought you were talking about bread and meat."

"There's no difference," Pardus continued. "We *bake* bread. We *roast*
meat. Right?" Pause. "What do you do to a *ham?* You *bake* a ham. So it
doesn't always follow."

And when we learned to braise and sauté, one question seemed to occur
to all.

"Now what about searage?" Pardus asked, his back to the range as we circled around him.

"That's what I wanted to know," Adam said.

Ben said, "To give it color and flavor."

"You sear meat," Pardus said, "to give it color and flavor and aroma. All of those things come from caramelization. It does *not* seal in juices. There are people who teach in this school who will tell you that it does. I thought that for a long time. I'm sure most of you thought that for a long time. Sounds good, sure. Seizes up the outside, makes a crust, must seal in the juices. *It doesn't happen that way.* If you don't believe me, read McGee."

We learned deep poaching and shallow poaching; we learned how to use a court bouillon and how to use a cuisson. We even learned how to boil pasta.

"We're going to fit some pasta into this little routine today," Pardus called out on Day Nineteen. "Ratio. How do you cook dried pasta? A lot of boiling water, right? The boiling water should be *salted*. It should be salted to the point where it tastes like a seasoned consommé." This was news to me. I had never tasted the water before I dumped the pasta in. But this is what Pardus wanted us to do. "I've got two pots over here. One is properly seasoned. One tastes like a mouthful of the Atlantic Ocean. You want the water to be salted properly; if it's salted properly you're going to have properly seasoned pasta." Pardus told us when he was chef at the Swiss Hotel, teaching his cooks to properly season their pasta water was a constant battle. He used to walk down the line saying, "More salt, more salt, more salt, not enough salt, more salt."

After that class I occasionally added aromatics, such as bay or sage leaves, to my pasta water as well as salt. We poached salmon in a court bouillon—most commonly, acidulated water seasoned with mirepoix. Escoffier listed salted water as his sixth court bouillon, which he recommended for poaching sea perch and mullet. Why not, then, cook pasta in a similarly seasoned liquid? Why not infuse the pasta with specific flavors that might complement or add to the final dish? I had never given much thought to how my pasta water tasted but now it concerned me, and I would always have a spoonful or two to ensure that was how I wanted the final pasta to taste.

Chef Pardus focused on mind and method. "You cook with your senses," he said when someone did something stupid. "And one of those senses is *common* sense."

B ut something happened to you in Skills class that was greater than learning how to season pasta water or braise shank. It was more than technique, more than ratios, and more than knowledge. Something was slowly being woven into one's very fiber, something that extended out and into everything one touched. I couldn't name it. I'm not sure it had a name. I could only point to parts of it.

Efficiency: no wasted movement. This idea, this will, bore not only on one's actions in the kitchen; it extended to one's life outside that kitchen. It changed how I packed for a trip—I tried to diminish the number of times I moved from closet to bureau to suitcase just as I learned to minimize my trips to the pot room or dry storage. I didn't make two trips to the hardware store because I forgot something or failed to have foreseen a potential problem. I didn't go from the bedroom to the living room, stop before I got there, and go back to the bedroom because I *forgot* something. And if I did, it made me mad. I solved problems differently. When we awoke one morning with no electricity and therefore no way to run the coffee machine, for instance, I thought immediately to put a pot of water on the grill on the deck out back for coffee. I am certain this wouldn't have occurred to me before Skills, because I had been in identical situations before Skills and didn't think, "No electricity for coffee? I'll just get a fire going out back." Certainly not at seven A.M. And the coffee had a nice campfire flavor to it, too. With efficiency of action, one also wanted speed, efficiency's ultimate goal. I tried to do everything faster. The faster you worked—in the kitchen, in life—the more you could do. Whoever did the most the best, won—no matter who you were or what you were doing, even if you were just playing against yourself.

The physical world grew more friendly because we were learning to harness and manipulate it. Look what we could do with heat and water and a steel surface. This created a sense of strength that I had not felt before. Control over properties—hot, cold, wet, dry—became a metaphor for control over oneself, one's actions and thoughts.

Embedded in this control was a sort of anger and fierceness that I saw move very close to the surface of Adam as I worked beside him every day. This fierceness was necessary for the perfection he sought. You cannot be blasé and achieve perfection. You must be in relentless pursuit of it. You can never stop. If you stop, you lose. We know that the physical world tends toward disorder and that energy is required to create and maintain order. Perfection was the highest degree of order there was, and if you didn't bring a ferocity to your pursuit of perfection, you simply wouldn't have the energy to finish the job at hand well; you'd be too tired because this was hard work and a lot of it. The work in a kitchen, the perfection, we learned, began with the even roasting of veal bones and a good caramelization of the mirepoix and a long, slow simmer—just the occasional bubble rising to the surface—until your roasted veal stock had perfect flavor and body, and then in the color and flavor of your roux, and skimming all the time till your brown sauce felt perfectly smooth on the palate, and skimming again till the demi-glace was rich and free of impurities. That was the beginning and you never let up. Not if you intended to be a good cook. You couldn't *not* do this. It was like driving a car. Once you pulled onto the road, you didn't just some-times drive and sometimes stop paying attention, or fail to make a turn when you knew in order to reach your destination you had to make that turn; you didn't simply ignore things like red lights because you were too tired or you didn't feel like it or you'd *do* it *later*.

Many potential metaphors orbit what there really aren't words for. I have no doubt that people felt the effects I'm trying to describe in various degrees, and those who did not, or did not like the effect, such as Matt, left the school. Skills differed according to the instructor, whose personality inevitably set the kitchen zeitgeist, but in order to be successful in a Skills kitchen, you had to engage these ineffable forces. Once you did, you couldn't simply turn them on at two o'clock when class started, and turn them off when you left. They became permanent structures in your mind. They became, finally, all of them together, an ethic, and something more: a system of values—a morality.

"Of course!" Susanne cried, stomping into the kitchen wearing a winter overcoat over her uniform. "Of course. We can't end a block without a winter *storm* watch!" The snow fell heavily, and I had left early to make sure I had plenty of time. Up to ten more inches were expected. The snow was wet, the roads icy. Every block since January had ended with a winter storm. With April three days off, we were all getting fairly tired of winter storms. Susanne—former Barnard student and advertising marketer—seemed to be having a tougher time of it than most with weather and kitchens. Her face appeared small within a dark orb of loose black curls; her eyes were large and dark, worthy of a Hirshfeld drawing. She was the sort of person who somehow attracted accidents. She now carried four stitches in her left hand. She had been at home and a knife fell, point down, into and through the meaty flesh between thumb and forefinger. Her husband wasn't home; driving was out of the question, blood gushing as it was, so she had to call 911. When she cut herself in class, it wasn't just a Band-Aid-and-finger-condom nick; it was a cut that forced her to stop work, sit down, and wait out the bleeding, hand in the air, clamping a wad of towels to the wounded digit.

Though the block was ending, the usual kitchen chores such as making stock still needed to be done. The entire school depended on Skills' stocks, and we made them on test days. Susanne, having driven an hour and a half through another winter storm, had stuck a pot in an oven that was also being used to roast veal bones. Midway through class we heard a quick, piercing shriek loud enough to halt everybody. People could hurt themselves badly in a kitchen, so you never ignored such outbursts. The shriek had come from Susanne, who had been burned.

"I don't know!" she said angrily. "Something just spit out at me!" She walked swiftly to the stock-cooling sink and held her right hand, the one without the stitches, beneath cold water.

Pardus, like a private eye hot on a trail, was already squatting at the open oven. "I know exactly what happened," he said. "One of the joints exploded. It filled with steam and popped. You can see it." He pointed, and there, in the back, was a bright white cartilaginous veal-bone joint. This knowledge did not seem to comfort Susanne. With the burn apparently growing worse beneath the water, she left for the nurse's office and would soon return, her hand and wrist slathered with cream beneath a gauze bandage.

Later in the day, when production was over, Susanne and Erica compared burns, talked ointment. Erica's entire left arm was bandaged. Veal bones once again had been the culprit, but this time the victim could assign blame. It was David Scott.

"Erica," I said when I saw her bandages, "what happened?"

She said, "Stupid-ass Dave did it."

I got slightly different stories from both of them, but what was not in dispute was that Dave was transferring browned veal bones from one really hot pan to another. These bones and scraps have fat on them, so there's a lot of rendered grease in these pans. As Erica helped prod twenty pounds of bones out of the pan Dave was tilting—some had stuck to the pan—they all fell at once and Erica was splashed with boiling oil. Huge deep welts covered her arm; the scars would be permanent. Dave said he had warned Erica away. Erica said that Dave had been careless. Every time I saw Dave after that, I shouted out, "Stupid-ass Dave!" And for a while, everyone started calling him that. Erica would cover her mouth and giggle, teeth clamped. Dave would always chuckle, a good sport, but plead that he'd *warned* Erica to be *careful*.

One tended to believe Dave, of course. Erica was still not a master of efficient action. And sweet as she could be, her mouth remained the foulest in the class. "I take a lot of shit around here," she would say, with her customary delicacy.

But the next minute she'd disarm you.

"Michael," she asked me once, just as class was beginning, "am I lovable?"

"Of course you are, Erica," I said.

She was immediately suspicious of my response and said, "Is *everybody* lovable?"

"Well, uh—"

"I don't think so. But I think I'm lovable."

I concurred and she walked off to gather her daily mise en place.

The day of the winter storm would see us all attempting to mince two onions and slice two onions in less than five minutes. This was the knife practical and it didn't sound hard until you realized it took two or three minutes just to *peel* four onions. Strategy was required. The task would be almost impossible unless you halved the onions *before* peeling, then ripped their skins off, not worrying too much about trim, and got cutting. Slice first; then mince like crazy till time ran out.

"This is a serious speed drill," Pardus told us. "It's ten percent of the final." If you finish, he said, "you're really wailing, you're working at production speed."

When he was asked what happened if you cut yourself—does your time stop, can you get a Band-Aid, what happens?—he responded, "Please, *don't* cut yourself. It is a *knife skills* practical. If you *cut* yourself, it means you didn't *do* it right!"

Paul would cut himself, and lose too much time to finish, and Eun-Jung continued to chop when Pardus called "Time!" but then looked at Adam, who had put his knife down. She chopped a little more, then saw that Len and I had put our knives down, and as she turned to scan the room, only then, reluctantly and with evident disappointment in herself, did she relinquish her own. Erica finished. And big Lou, who had arrived not knowing even how to *hold* a knife, had finished, too.

Pardus was particularly proud of Lou. "He's an ex-*shipping* clerk," Pardus had said to me. "You should see the quality of work he's bringing me now. His cards, he sweats over those cards." Lou, a husband, father of three, worked hard and it was paying off. Pardus wanted me to know this, in part, because he knew he was a main reason for Lou's success; he was openly proud. Proud, I think, not only of Lou, but of the whole class. He had not held much hope for this class six weeks earlier. But as Skills Two wound down, he said, "I train you and then you go to another kitchen. Just like in the restaurant business. I train someone and that person leaves to be sous chef at another restaurant." He paused again. "You guys are going to do great in Intro. I think you guys are really going to do well."

And we liked Chef Pardus, all except for Erica. I could never figure out why. After dinner that night, before the written test, Chef Pardus passed around evaluation sheets that were filled out and sealed until after he'd turned in his grades; he left the kitchen while we filled them out. He would eventually read the anonymous evaluations, as would CIA administrators. Erica could hardly wait to get at hers.

She was making noise as Ben collected the forms and I asked her what she'd written.

"I coulda been a lot worse," she said.

"Why?"

"He treated me like shit in here."

Erica seemed to think Pardus was harder on her than anyone else, that he made fun of her (scrambled eggs, burning roux), and that he was a lousy teacher. I had witnessed none of this but Erica could not be convinced otherwise.

"When it says 'What could the instructor do to improve?' I was gonna put 'Quit.' " She paused. "But that woulda been too mean."

When Len heard what she was saying, he shook his head and said to no one, "They'll never believe her, not when they look at her grades and the other comments." Len said he thought Pardus had been a great instructor.

Susanne would remember Pardus's class as the best she had. Travis, who was still working mornings at Burger King, had wondered openly on his evaluation if Pardus deserved a raise.

Adam was mad. While most people couldn't wait to get out of Skills, to leave the monotony of the standard daily mise en place and brown sauce and start cooking for real, Adam wanted the class to be longer. "We only panfry once," he said. "Sautéeing or shallow poaching once is not enough." And the daily grading annoyed him. It was far too woolly, he said. While he admired Pardus for his teaching, Pardus was, Adam felt, too subjective; from one plate to another, from the first plate graded to the last, the grading of food had been inconsistent.

Pardus returned after Ben had sealed the evaluations and distributed an easy test. We departed as we finished and the next day were back again for the final day of Skill Development—the cooking practical (brown sauce, béchamel, rice pilaf, and duchess potatoes). The mood was festive. Erica brought a camera. So did Dave. Dave asked me to take a picture of him with the chef, "for my CIA scrapbook," he said happily.

Big Lou smiled from ear to ear. "I really feel like I'm getting somewhere," he said. This was exciting; I could see it in his eyes.

Erica was hugging people, camera in hand. She said to me, grinning unself-consciously, "I know it's high schoolish, but it's the last time were gonna be together as a group."

This was true. The group was to be split in half, each half rejoining with half of its sister group, which had been in a separate Skills kitchen, boiling the heck out of their consommés. That something significant happened, not just to me, but to everybody in a good Skills class, is supported by the reluctance of the students to split up afterward. Almost everyone dreads it. Some groups appeal directly to President Metz and Senior Vice President Tim Ryan, claiming that they are different, they are special, they have formed a unique bond, and it would be criminal to break it. "They all feel that way," Ryan said, and the Culinary never altered this rule.

No one looked forward to joining a new group partly because friendships had solidified here, but also because you wouldn't know how good the other people were, how fast they were, whether or not you could depend on them. And this was precisely why the Culinary re-formed groups after Skills. It's in the nature of the work to move around, to work with people one doesn't know. Learning to work with strangers was part of the education. The group that they became beginning next block would be the group they remained until they left for their externships in July.

I would not be joining either group. The entire program lasted about twenty-one months, including a four-and-a-half-month externship—four years for those who move straight into the bachelor's program. I had deadlines of a different nature than my Skills comrades. I hoped to rejoin them later, just before they left for their externships; I would move through the courses at the Culinary at an accelerated rate, working with many other groups, but I would feel an affinity with none more than the people I'd gone through Skills with. Something significant happened to most everyone in Skills, not unlike that which happens to strangers who endure a catastrophe together—a plane crash, say, or a shipwreck. There is a common and permanent bond that will remain no matter where they go.

Roux Decree

The last product I made in Skills was brown sauce. I happened to be the last person to finish the practical that ended Culinary Skill Development, bringing my bowl to Chef Pardus after Bianca handed in her duchess potatoes (doomed from the start by her failure to make them big enough to hold enough steam to keep them fluffy inside). Bianca shrugged and left the kitchen. I presented the final bowl. Pardus lifted a spoon and tasted; mine was a good brown sauce, made from a good brown roux; he could not find fault with it. There was, however, just a touch of bitterness, he said.

"Sometimes you *want* a hint of bitterness," he continued. I agreed. Bitter was a flavor component that could be used well.

Rudy Smith entered the kitchen, surprised to find it empty. Pardus apologized for letting everyone leave. Chef Smith normally used this day to talk to his new class to prepare them for Day One of Introduction to Hot Foods, the first production kitchen, the students' first chance to cook for people other than themselves. Most people were nervous moving into Chef Smith's class. Travis, who was scheduled to be sous chef on Day One, was, he said, "scared shitless." Chef Smith's demeanor did not help matters. Smith never smiled. He lacked that mischievous streak you saw in Pardus. We all saw him every day, presiding like a drill sergeant over K-9 as we passed through, picking up our broil, our roast, our sauté; he stood militarily at ease, head cocked slightly back; his eyes were lidded, almost sleepy, but

ready to attack in a flash, and his nose in profile seemed to me incongru-
ously aristocratic. He was young, tall, fit, a no-nonsense corn-fed boy from
the flatlands of Ohio.

Pardus introduced us and told him what we were talking about. I asked
him if he used a blond or a brown roux for his brown sauce.

Pardus had told him I was a writer, and he stared at me suspiciously. "I
teach what I'm asked to teach," he said.

"Personally," I said. This was usually the word to use when trying to
draw a chef away from the party line to their own beliefs, which most were
happy to offer.

"I'm old-fashioned. That's all I'll say."

He would not admit what we all knew. He was a brown roux guy.

A squall had struck the Culinary Institute of America. I first got wind
of it from Pardus, who told me about a dinner conversation he had had
with a few other chefs. The chefs eat separately from the students, typically
in the first alcove of Alumni Hall. On Day Twenty-Three of Skills, as our
class gnawed away at our own braised lamb shank, Chefs Pardus, Smith,
and Reilly, all of them CIA graduates, all of them relatively young, and
Chef Almquist, a senior chef-instructor, sat discussing brown sauce. Chefs
at the Culinary Institute of America did not talk foie gras and truffles at
dinner, I was happy to know; instead, they talked brown sauce, specifically,
what kind of roux one used. Chef Almquist, the ranking chef at the table
whose girth suggested he had known many a brown sauce in his time, said,
according to Pardus, "No one has made brown sauce with brown roux since
Escoffier died!" This sort of definitive comment was common at the Culinary. Passions ran high on such matters.

Chef Reilly, twenty-eight years old and a 1988 graduate, who had been a
sous chef at the Hotel Metropole in Moscow, taught his Skills students to
make brown sauce with a blond roux. Reilly's contention, according to
Pardus, was that one could make an excellent, richly colored brown sauce
through deep caramelization of mirepoix and tomato and by using a richly
colored stock. (Reilly stopped by Pardus's kitchen after Chef Smith and I'd
asked him for his own words on the subject; he shook his head.) A brown
roux is difficult to make properly, takes much more time, and more care; a
brown roux can turn from nutty to bitter in an instant, and thus required

patience and finesse. Why use precious time to make a brown roux and, further, risk bitterness, when you could make a perfectly good brown sauce with blond roux? So said blond roux advocates.

This was a reasonable response. Pardus himself liked the idea and intended to taste Reilly's brown sauce to compare. Pardus was open-minded. There's more than one way to make stock, more than one way to make brown sauce. This was what a culinary education was all about.

Two days after the brown roux discussion at dinner, matters became serious. A computer terminal stood beside Pardus's desk; every kitchen had one, and Pardus spent time at this terminal daily, sending his food orders to the storeroom. He also picked up E-mail and announcements here. On Day Twenty-Five of Skills Two, he found this message in his mailbox:

> Chefs,
>
> According to our skills guide, professional cooking knowledge and the New Pro Chef, 6th edit., a brown sauce (sc. espagnole) is NOT made with a brown roux.
>
> Please refrain from teaching our students THIS incorrect method.

The message was signed "Uwe" and added that if anyone had any questions, please see him.

Pardus got really mad. He asked me to check my *Pro Chef*. I had the fifth edition. Sure enough the debate was evident even here. The recipe for "Sauce Espagnole (Brown Sauce)" in my edition of the *Pro Chef* called for six ounces of pale roux to thicken five pints of brown stock. But step two under "Method" reads, "Add brown roux to the mirepoix and gradually incorporate the veal stock or estouffade," a crucial and revealing error.

When I asked Chef Hestnar about this, he more or less evaded me in his Raymond Carveresque way; I asked why they didn't teach a brown roux for a brown sauce and he rejoined with spare oblique stories: "Escoffier predicted that eventually roux would no longer be necessary. . . ." When I continued to press the issue he pushed his hand through the air and said, "Oh, forget the brown roux!"

I couldn't help it. Something fundamental was to be found in the question of brown or blond roux, something revealing in people's preference for one or the other, how the school reacted to it, and the chefs' response to Hestnar's Roux Decree.

"You can tell me that we have to teach a blond roux instead of a brown roux," Pardus exclaimed, "but don't tell me it's an *incorrect method*." This really burned him up.

Pardus and Smith continued to discuss it that last night of Skills, my own brown sauce steaming on the table in a steel bowl. Pardus tried to make a case in favor of a slight amount of bitterness.

Smith said it needn't be bitter at all and doubted that you would ever want bitterness.

Pardus handed Chef Smith a spoon and said, "This is Michael's brown sauce. I think it's pretty good."

Chef Smith tasted it. Chef Smith had eyes set so close together they seemed almost to touch. He squinted hard. He gave the impression of wanting either to spit or to hit me. Then he said, "Could be sweeter."

Chef Smith was cause for me to step back and take stock of the situation and the people I'd met here. First there had been the unusual Mr. del Grosso, a micropaleontologist who became a cook on the strength of an epiphany upon waking one morning on his living room floor. The sanitation instructor, Richard Vergili, was the sort of man who could have his students rolling on the floor with laughter during his lecture on *e-coli* bacteria; when I told people he did Atlantic City on the weekends, as Mr. Virgili himself had joked, they said "Really?" with admiration. The Product Identification man, Jay Stein, a former caterer, would go to the grocery store, buy seven kinds of lettuce, and rush home to lay them on the dining room table for a taste test; his teeth appeared to be ground on a slant, and I imagined this was an indication of his intensity. One of the Meat Fabrication instructors had been for years a baseball umpire in the minor leagues, had gotten his degree in English, and acted in community theaters; his name was Ligouri and he taught people to butcher meat for a living. Chef Pardus almost paled beside this hale cast.

Shortly after Adam began Rudy Smith's Introduction to Hot Foods, I asked him how he liked the chef.

"The chef is great," Adam said. "He's a really smart chef." Then Adam told me that Chef Smith used to live in a teepee.

"Pardon?" I said.

Rudy Smith, a 1986 graduate of the Culinary, was, for a time, executive chef of a restaurant called Krabloonik, in Snowmass Village, Colorado.

Krabloonik was on a mountain. A single road wound up the mountain and dead-ended at the restaurant. One day Chef Smith walked uphill away from the restaurant, beyond any roads, for about thirty minutes, and pitched a teepee. He lived in this teepee for three years. Every workday he'd walk down the mountain to the top of the dead-end road and the restaurant. After work, he would fill water bottles and climb back up.

I asked him why he quit living in a teepee.

"Skiing," he said. "I broke my leg in two places. My fourth time on skis."

A cast, of course, made it difficult to climb, especially through the snow of an Aspen winter. I asked him how it felt to return to civilization.

He squinted at me and, without a trace of humor, said, "It was really hard to write that rent check."

He had lived for free on the mountain. His site was remote, and nobody bothered him. He dug a hole in the ground that, in the summer, served as a cooler. He had a battery-operated light and CD player. He joined a health club in town where he could shower. Chef Smith's goal at the Culinary was to become a certified master chef. At the time there were forty-nine cooks in the country who had passed the grueling ten-day, 140-hour exam. Chef Smith believed this was the highest achievement in his profession. I figured someone who could live three years on a mountain in a teepee probably had the self-discipline to pass such a test.

I wondered aloud what winters in the mountains of Colorado were like. This was ski country, snow measured not in inches but in feet. It must have been freezing, I said. Chef Smith narrowed his eyes at me.

"It's important to have a really good sleeping bag," he said.

Part II

The Formative Kitchens

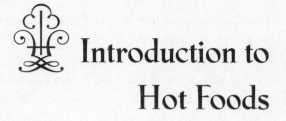

Introduction to Hot Foods

"**M**y name's Rudy Smith, and I'll be your chef for the next three weeks. It'll be an interesting three weeks."

Day One, Smith said privately, is like running into a brick wall. By the first week he has the kitchen running smoothly; by Day Fourteen it runs itself; then the next day, boom—take two steps sideways and start again with eighteen new students.

"Here we're serving customers," he said. "If we're late, we're penalizing them. . . . Speed needs to be much greater here. In the last class, you were learning skills, now you're producing. This is a really big transition.

"I need you guys to respond," he said. "You need to challenge me. 'Hey Chef, Escoffier says to do it this way, but you say to do it a different way. Why?'

"I must taste everything before it goes out that door," he said. "Everything goes through me. Think of me as a funnel.

"Today is a day of following directions. It's not a day I want you guys making decisions. If I say I want you to have a two-ounce ladle and you have a four-ounce ladle, that won't be acceptable."

He stood in front of his desk and scarcely moved from there. His clean crisp chef's hat made him seem seven feet tall.

"I'm not here to teach you to season your soup," he said. "I expect you to do it. When it's perfect, bring it to me. Green beans, when they're cooked, bring one to me so I can taste it. If I'm talking to someone, stick it in my face. I'll know what you're doing. I'll say they're done, you'll run back and shock 'em. I want you to do that with every batch, every day, through Day Fourteen. That's how you learn."

"I thrive on the classics. I live in the present," he told his new class on Day One. "I'm very into the idea of giving attention to food. It's like a child. The more attention you give it, the better it will be. Smell it, touch it, listen to it. You gotta give it everything you got. If you're uptight and nervous, your food will come out that way."

Ben and Adam liked Chef Smith because, in Ben's words, "he gets excited about food." And to everyone's relief, he turned out not to be the ex-marine that everyone expected. Travis's fears were unfounded. Even Erica would grow to appreciate Chef Smith because she said she learned from him. The reconfigured group seemed to be a good one. Greg, Bianca, Paul, and Travis also remained, and so did Lola from Staten Island, and Travis and Lola remained as one.

"I'll marry ya, but I'll never work with ya," Travis would say.

"Oh, *Trav*," Lola would say.

Gone, however, were Lou and Eun-Jung and Len and Stupid-Ass Dave, Susanne and the rest, to a different Intro kitchen. There were an equal number of faces (and personalities and skill levels) to get used to, but the main thing to learn now was the chef and the demands of a new kitchen, a new classroom. Each chef had his or her own personality and this dominated the kitchen and could affect your grade if you didn't abide. Some chefs liked a heavy use of salt. Some didn't want you using black pepper or garlic. Some wanted you to flour meats that were to be sautéed (Smith); others wanted it patted dry but no flour (Pardus). Some did not want you to make decisions; others encouraged experiment and autonomy.

In Chef Smith's class, prep lists were elaborate and were to display a clear sequence of movements and times. If you were on braise, your prep card had better read "2:45 Roll, tie, season, sear meat" and "3:30 Pot roast in the oven." One might also remind oneself "3:00 Check mise en place" since the supplemental order is placed at 3:15 and if you didn't have everything you needed at service, it was your own fault; you either had it or you didn't—no excuses, didn't matter why. If you were on starch, your card should include "4:50 Start pilaf." And everyone's card read "6:05 Service." Sometimes prep lists would go on for several cards. These cards were not checked, but if Chef Smith saw you in the weeds, he'd ask to see your cards.

He could usually point to the spot on the card, the error or omission, that put you in the weeds.

Chef Smith also wanted a card with your station setup; if you were on sauté, he wanted you to plan before class where your veal would be, where your bain-marie insert would be, and what utensils would be in it, where every item of your mise en place would be, from salt and pepper to clarified butter to the sliced mushrooms for your sauce champignon to the rack you'd hold your veal on while you made the sauce.

Also you were to write on three-by-five cards all the recipes you would need for the day. On Day One the soups were puree of broccoli and chicken broth. The broil station would do lamb chops (Smith wanted them Frenched to the eye), which would be served with a cabernet-rosemary butter, orzo, ratatouille, and sautéed spinach. Sauté station prepped for veal scallopini champignon served with a lemon-almond rice pilaf, green beans, and ratatouille. Everyone would be responsible for the entire menu and should be able to answer questions regarding any station. Everyone would know the method, recipe, and history of each item without referring to notes.

The breast pocket of a student in Chef Smith's kitchen bulged with three-by-five index cards, along with a pen and an instant-read thermometer. And on Day One, Chef Smith could spend ten minutes at the roast station explaining how to use that thermometer.

"It's only as accurate as you are," he would say, then ask if the thermometer were calibrated; you should calibrate your thermometer regularly. He explained what part of the metal bar read the temperature. When the roast station was ready to check the strip loin, he said, "You try to get to the coolest part of the meat there is. That will be the center of the thickest part of the roast." He eased the thermometer into the meat. "How do you know you've got the center?" He waited, then said, "If you push it farther in, the temperature should *rise*."

Chef Smith generally would float through the kitchen, demonstrating how he wanted the broccoli florettes (wedged apart for a natural break rather than cut and small enough to fit on a spoon), tasting the vinaigrettes, tasting sauces, checking doneness, calling out, "It's four-twenty. Are my potatoes on the stove?"

"Yes, Chef!"

"Is my roast in the oven?"

"Yes, Chef!"

The meals on Day One were clear and not altogether complicated. Everyone was usually frightened into overpreparing. Chef Smith would walk the hot line and explain to each student how to set that station. He was a stickler for perfect setup. "I'm a true minimalist," he said. He wanted nothing extraneous, not even an errant grain of kosher salt.

"Sauté, let's talk about station setup," Chef Smith said. "I want you to have a full hotel pan with ice, I want a half sheet pan here; I want your flour here, salt and pepper, spoons." He turned to the range and, pointing, said, "Bain-marie here, clarified butter here, sauce here, white wine, stock, all of them with two-ounce ladles." The veal would be pounded and rolled in three-piece portions. Why? "Because in service you don't even have to look," he said. "You're doing two hundred fifty covers a night, the orders are coming, you just grab 'em, boom boom boom, they're in!"

In a restaurant situation, that is. Here, eighteen people would be preparing about eighty plates. The sauté station would do sixteen of them. Many people deride the kitchen experience at the Culinary as not being like a real restaurant. True, a third of the people would be needed were this an actual restaurant kitchen; on the other hand, a restaurant doesn't change every item on its menu daily, start with nothing daily, not even cracked pepper. In Chef Smith's class, you cracked your own pepper, minced it with your chef's knife to the consistency you desired. You did everything the long way here.

Chef Smith would cruise the long bank of ranges, beginning with broil and ending at roast, which had the use of a convection oven with glass doors. Learning how to set a station was a primary objective of this class. Chef Smith also wanted students to understand the types of meat on the menu and how they were cooked; they must be able to identify their total mise en place, have their mental mise en place in order, and be able to do all this in any kitchen in which they might find themselves. The transition from cooking one plate of food to sixteen plates required a shift of gears and deeper focus on execution. If they didn't learn all these basics here, Smith said, they would not be able to focus on the new tasks coming their way in future kitchens.

By five-thirty all were ready for Chef Smith to demo plates, and again he'd walk the line, preparing one plate at each station. He would begin at broil and demonstrate the quadrants of the grill for perfect cross-hatching during service. He explained that one should check doneness by touch, then by cutting into the meat to check your touch judgment. "This is the one kitchen where you can actually cut into each one to check doneness," he said. "Take advantage of that." To make sure no one misunderstood him, he reiterated that this would *not* be considered an acceptable way of determining doneness in a restaurant kitchen. He would then demo how he wanted the item plated and move on to the next station as service approached.

During our Skills Two a change in service had occurred. Instead of receiving meal tickets and waiting in line outside K-9 for dinner, Skills One and other classes would be seated in Alumni Hall and waiters would take their orders. This meant that instead of having "customers" passing through your open kitchen, Intro students cooked with the doors closed and filled a hot box that would be wheeled to the dining room. While this made for a more orderly and refined dining experience, Chef Smith didn't like it for his kitchen; it took the urgency away. You didn't see the faces of people you served. He tried nevertheless to keep everyone working at production speed, telling the sous chef when to fire what orders, and the sous chef, standing between the hot box and the steam table that had been set up to hold the veg and starch, would shout, "Fire two sautés! Fire two roasts. Fire two broils!" or "Pick up two veg entrées! Pick up two braise!"

And each station would respond—"Firing two sautés!" "Picking up two braise!"—in turn. Other than those calls, Chef Smith, who all the while would be checking each plate, sending inferior platings back, wanted the kitchen silent.

After the first week, the kitchen hummed rhythmically. Each day at one-forty-five the group would gather their physical mise en place, which would happen quickly if they had good mental mise en place before they arrived. By two o'clock, chairs would be spread around the huge stainless-steel tables and lecture would get under way.

Lola was on soup station today, corn chowder. Chef Smith said, "Tell us about chowder."

"Whaddaya wanna *know*?" said the affable Lola.

"What is it? What makes it chowder?"

"It's a thick soup," she began and fumbled thereafter for a precise description.

Smith squinted and said, "Sounds like a puree."

"Main ingredient is part of the thickener?" she suggested.

"I wouldn't say that." Chef Smith paused and said, "It can be red or white, it can be cream- or broth-based." He stopped there. "Come on, you should have had this in skills. You probably *did* have this in skills."

Ben said, "It should have the flavor of the main ingredient."

"Well, *yeah*. That goes without saying. But yeah." Smith chuckled and shook his head. "How about pork?"

"Classically, you have pork," a voice called out.

"Classical chowders always have pork," Smith continued, customarily salt pork. "It's going to be *packed* with ingredients. It's almost going to be a stew." He turned to the board and wrote *Chowdière*. "Anyone know what this is?"

Ben said, "A small chowder?"

Smith chuckled again. He described the type of pot often used for chowders over open fires, said sometimes chowder was meant to be a one-course meal, then moved into the specifics of today's chowder, which would use bacon, roux, potatoes, a mixture of milk and cream.

Following discussion of the next soup, cock-a-leekie soup (a Scottish specialty using chicken, leeks, and classically thickened with barley), Chef Smith said, "Roast pork, pan gravy, who's got it?" then on to broil, a strip loin with sauce fine herbs. "Make the reduction with stems, add chopped herbs at the end," Chef Smith instructed Melissa, a student from the other Skills class.

"Can I make it in one batch?" she asked

"Absolutely," Smith said, adding, "don't monté au beurre."

"Should I start that at five-thirty?"

"Start it now."

Greg was on stew today and asked how much liquid for the stew.

"It depends on the size of the braising vessel," Smith answered.

"Can I caramelize the mirepoix separately?" he asked.

"Because you're washing your own pots you can, yes," Smith said. "In a restaurant, I'd be nicer to the dishwasher. Any other questions? O.K., starch!"

Bianca and Travis would be making potato pancakes, potato chips cut into gaufrettes, and basmati rice pilaf. All clear.

Chef Smith asked sauté what can be done to save time on the sauce.

Several people shouted out, "Reduce the cream."

"Do *crème double* to save time," Smith said. He wrote it on the board behind his desk. "Or, if you're from Ohio like me, double cream." He wrote this, too. "If you're doing two hundred covers a night and you're in charge of twelve burners, you don't have time to spend ten minutes reducing the sauce. With double cream, service comes up like *that*." He snapped his fingers.

"Does the cream keep as long once you've done that?"

"It keeps better," Smith said. "More fat, less water. Vegetable entrée!"

Ben asked, "How many peppers should I roast?" He and Adam were on vegetarian entrée and had come up with the idea of a quesadilla pizza, flour tortillas with a smear of goat cheese, roasted garlic, rosemary, and black olives topped with roasted red, yellow, and poblano peppers, and cheese with a sundried- and roasted-tomato sauce.

"You're making sixteen portions? You're using poblanos?" Smith asked.

"Yellow, poblanos, and red."

"I'd use about three peppers each."

And after veg entrée, they were off, the kitchen aclatter with activity.

E rica was on veg, a high-volume station making all the vegetable side dishes for every plate. Though she was taught in Skills how to prep asparagus, she called the chef over. "I want to make sure I do it right," she said. Smith grabbed each end of the asparagus, bent them together, and the asparagus snapped in two. Erica said, "O.K., yeah."

Chef Smith attended to the broil station, explaining to Melissa how to butcher the strip loin. "At a family restaurant that's selling a strip for twelve-ninety-five—with a vegetable, baked potato, a slice of pecan pie, and coffee for dessert—we'd leave this on." He pointed to the gristly fatty tail of the strip steak he'd cut from the loin. "White-tablecloth restaurant, twenty-two-fifty for the same steak, we wouldn't leave this on." Nor should Melissa; the scraps would go to Greg on braise, who would trim what he could and add it to his beef stew.

Smith returned to Erica's station to show her how he wanted the roasted beets cut. When he tried to slice one, it mashed in his hands. He glared at the paring knife he'd picked up and said, "Whose knife is this?"

"Mine," said Erica, looking down.

"Go sharpen it," Smith said. "Don't ever come to class with a knife like that again." He walked away.

Erica retrieved her steel, gave the paring knife a few desultory swipes. Disheartened, she dug a stone out of her kit and used the time she needed for prep to try to get an edge on her knife, something she had yet to master.

Meanwhile, Bianca overcooked the potatoes. She showed Chef Smith. He could tell by looking, shook his head, and said, "Will everyone now stop what they're doing and take a few minutes to tourner three new potatoes? Use the largest ones you can find. Do a good job with them." And everyone did, immediately.

Smith stopped by Erica's station again. She had a potato in her hands. He took her knife, slid it through a potato. He felt the blade. Then he ran a finger along the potato. He sliced the potato again and felt the potato. He put the knife on her board and said, "Tomorrow, I want this sharp. This is not sharp. Feel how rough this is." He offered the freshly cut side of the potato to Erica. "It should be smooth as glass."

Smith walked away, glanced at the clock, which read seven minutes after five. "In eight minutes, I want this set for service," he said, slapping the steam table.

The sous chef hustled the steam table into place, plugged it in, retrieved the hotel pans. He called out, "It's five-fifteen. Everything should be set for service."

"We are late!" Smith shouted. "Get that line set up!"

And so it went until three minutes after six, when the kitchen quieted and everyone readied their stations to start cooking. Soon they were off.

"Fire two broils!"

"Firing two broils!"

"Fire two sautés."

"Firing two sautés."

"Fire two roasts!"

"Firing two roasts!"

Smith tasted vegetables as they were cooked or reheated to check doneness and seasoning. He watched for errors in plating and sent them back. Otherwise he stood beside the sous chef like a marine, his expression one of concrete, eyes bloodshot and narrow in his face.

After service, the class had a half hour to eat, then return to the kitchen to clean before lecture. Lecture began with an evaluation of the day's work and product. "The end result was good but the way we got there wasn't," Chef Smith said. "I don't think it was the worst day. The plates *looked* wonderful. What's disappointing is the types of mistakes that were made, methods you learned at the beginning. The energy wasn't positive; it wasn't negative but it wasn't positive and focused as it should be."

Then he moved into specifics, beginning with sauce fine herbs. "The sauce was a little thick and pasty. That means it wasn't skimmed"—Melissa tried to interject in her own defense, but Smith simply raised his voice— "and that started with the *stock*. If you've got a perfect stock, you can make a perfect sauce. If you've got a mediocre stock the *best* sauce you can make is a mediocre sauce. Skimming is the key to a good brown sauce, and finally to a good derivative." Smith paused. "You know how with wine the flavor stays in your mouth? With sauce you don't *want* hang time. You want it to dance around in your mouth." There had been no dancing of sauce fine herbs today, even after Smith tried to hop it up a little with some rice wine vinegar.

"Culinary fundamentals is what it's all about," he said. "Everything else is fluff. These fundamentals will carry you through your entire culinary career. Searing your meat, cooking your vegetable to the right amount of doneness. It's the fundamentals at every level."

On Route 9G between Hyde Park and Tivoli stood a white house, by all appearances your basic ersatz postwar colonial/ranch-style house with a separate garage in back and, usually, a car or two in the driveway. What caught my eye, every time I drove to the Culinary and every time I returned, was a large teepee pitched on the lawn beside the house. It appeared to be made of some sort of shiny blue synthetic material, was, I would guess, twelve feet high, and would accommodate one person comfortably. A folding metal chair was visible through the entrance. I could not pass this house without thinking about Chef Smith, often wondering if this was where he lived and if, on particularly cold February nights, he would gather his battery-operated light, CD player, water bottles, really good sleeping bag, and make a night of it.

A genuine madman ran Fish Kitchen.
His name was Corky Clark, he'd served in Vietnam, wore a U.S. navy tattoo where most people had watches, and looked ten years older than his forty-nine years. He'd graduated from the Culinary in 1971. "We didn't have to know why something happened," Chef Clark said, recalling the

Culinary Institute of America at its initial location in New Haven, Connecticut. "They'd say cook this and we'd cook it. We did what we were told." He'd been a teacher here thirteen years and he'd been in Fish Kitchen for eight years, near as he could figure. His breath smelled of wintergreen tobacco, and a small wad peaked over the top of his lower lip when he talked. His hair was white and very short and he wore a stretchable chef's hat that hugged his round forehead and included a top, perhaps to keep the heat in. He spent much of his day behind the kitchen in the fish butchering room, which was kept at 45 degrees. Corky Clark had a scratchy voice and when he got excited, which was every day from seven A.M. through service at eleven-thirty, his voice would reach octaves that were virtual squeaks. And he rarely stopped moving, darting about the kitchen, first to broil, then to deep-fry, then to poach, grabbing a handful of toasted almonds and popping them into his mouth, dashing back to the phone, then to the computer. His main function as a chef-instructor was twofold: one, teach students how to identify, purchase, butcher, and cook fish, and two, make this as difficult as the students could possibly bear for seven days.

Whereas Skills lasted twenty-eight days and Intro lasted fourteen, the next three blocks would be halved. Every seven days you'd find yourself in a new kitchen with a new chef who made new demands within the framework of a new cuisine—American Regional and Fish, Oriental and Charcuterie, Breakfast Cookery, and Lunch Cookery—all but Charcuterie were production kitchens meant to produce the majority of the four thousand meals the Culinary Institute served each day. This was by no means a staggering figure. The twelve-hundred-room Trump Taj Mahal Casino Resort in Atlantic City, for instance, might do as many as twenty thousand meals a day. But here, each kitchen was completely restaffed every seven days. And all of the food was high-end, or at least attempted to be. Day One work for Corky Clark's Fish Kitchen included broiled swordfish with anchovy butter, trout almondine, and poached salmon with hollandaise sauce. Most residential colleges contracted a food service company to feed the students. Here food was a by-product of the education.

Clark's kitchen did fewer covers than other kitchens, about forty, because half the class spent the day butchering fish. If you were one of the day's butchers, you might cut, say, twenty whitefish fillets for sauté and fabricate twenty-five pounds of bluefish. You would do well to wear your long underwear. The walk-in beyond the 45-degree butchery was kept at 32 degrees. Forty thousand dollars' worth of fish moved through this kitchen each month; it acted as a sort of in-house purveyor to all the other kitchens at the Culinary.

But as in every kitchen, it was the chef who set the tone for both the mood and the food, and the tone Chef Clark mainly set was one of panic. He seemed to thrive on it. The kitchen would open for students at six-thirty A.M.; the fellow, Clark's assistant, would be there at six. (The four restaurants and Fish Kitchen hired fellows, graduates who wanted to stay on at the school to work for six months.) Clark didn't get there till seven but if you intended to finish your mise en place by service, you got there at six-thirty. This would give you approximately forty-five minutes to begin your work; if any of your products took a long time—if you were on soup and needed to cook out a velouté for the fish chowder, for instance, you'd better have that cooking before Clark began lecture. And you'd better get as much prep done as well because Clark wouldn't let you get back to work till nearly nine, giving you two hours before service.

"If you need an hour and a half to do something, he'll give you an hour," one of Clark's students said. "He puts you in the weeds on purpose, but he's also there with you." Clark loved weeds.

During lecture, you could see the worry creeping up on students' faces. People would nervously eye the clock as Clark rambled, pontificating and questioning. Sometimes the questions were practical, sometimes philosophical.

"Is it ever O.K. to lower your standards?" He repeated the question and waited. "Compromising is like telling a lie. It gets easier and easier. Each compromise you make, *that* becomes your standard."

"Why is lemon traditionally served with fried fish?" he asked a few minutes later.

Someone answered, "To cut the fat?"

Clark smiled and shook his head. He issued a disgusted chuckle. Someone always said that. And he could have told you that that guy in the back row, the one with about as much sense as a *goose*, he was going to be the one. He shook his head some more, chuckling. "Fried fish. This thing is *swimming* in fat!" Tall lanky Clark was squeaking like a mouse. "It's *served* with a fat-based sauce! A little lemon wedge is not going to cut the fat! We *like* the fat!"

In a calmer moment, he said, "Quality is a journey, not a destination. I used to think that was corny, but the more I thought about it, the more it made sense. . . . You're never gonna get good enough, you're never gonna know enough, you're never gonna be fast enough."

He paced the class, crossed his arms, leaned on the steel table. Out of the blue he asked for the definition of escalope. No one answered or even tried. He didn't answer the question for them, just shook his head. "What distinguishes a bisque?" he asked. He received nothing but dead, seven A.M. stares. "Stop torturing me!" he cried.

"You've got to know these things," he said. "You've got to be smarter. How did John Doherty get the position of executive chef at the Waldorf at age twenty-eight?"

Several people sheepishly called out, "He worked harder?"

"Aww!" Clark said, his voice lowering for once. "Everybody *works* hard. You've got to be smarter, you've got to be prepared, you've got to know the answers. You may learn to cook like I did, by repetition, or you may learn to cook like John Doherty."

Such pronouncements, for Chef Clark, were as good a segue into scombrotoxin or Dover sole or Atlantic salmon and aquaculture as any. After lecture, the class would pile into the butchery where Chef Clark would lecture some more, here with visual aids, real fish, and would end with a demo on, say, butchering flat and round fish. People would keep turning around looking at the clock. And then he would send them into their weeds and after class would shake his head. Scorn. Disgust. "The *mayhem* that we called *class* today," he would say. "A hellacious mess."

Clark was not mean. One student in Clark's class told me that in an earlier kitchen, a student had completely botched the chicken pot pies he'd been assigned to cook. Not only did he not have them ready for service; when they *were* ready, after service, he didn't realize the gravity of his error, and asked the chef where he should hold the now-worthless pot pies so that they would stay warm. The chef said, "I don't know, maybe you should stick them up your ass and hold them there." That seemed to me rather harsh, though often the pressures of the kitchen brought this out. Clark was not mean like that. He was simply a madman, a cook by nature. Most of the time you didn't know if he was laughing or screaming.

When I arrived in Clark's kitchen, Day One after a three-day weekend, he didn't know who I was. I always showed up in code, knife bag in hand and ready to work, but he hadn't been told I'd be observing his class for a few days and he ignored me. Eventually he found out what I was doing in his class, but it wasn't till mid-morning, when the class was engaged in the preservice scramble and I was asking Clark questions in the chilly quiet of the butchery that Clark stopped talking, tilted his head, and squinted at me. He ignored the question I'd asked, said nothing, just studied me.

"Who did you have for Skills?" he asked.

"Chef Pardus," I said.

He touched his mouth. He said, "I think I heard about you." He wagged a boney finger at me. "I think I know who you are." He kept squinting at me, as though we'd met long ago, and he didn't like me even then. "I think I remember."

I waited.

Then, in a quiet, almost hushed voice, he said, "It was the end of a block. There was a winter storm."

That was all he said. He nodded slightly.

I said, "That's right." He just kept squinting at me with his head cocked to the side. So I said, "I made it here."

He nodded slightly and said softly, "I know."

Then, in a manner that was not atypical, he paused for what seemed to me an inordinate length of time, then began talking again full steam, telling me I couldn't really understand what he was attempting to do in this class in just a few days; I should spend the entire seven days here. You could spend two years in this kitchen and not learn all there was to know about fish cookery, he said.

Clark, too, had made it the day of the storm. He happened to live in Tivoli, right around the corner from where I lived. And he'd made it when the Blizzard of '96 struck, a storm that had shut down the entire East Coast from D.C. to Boston.

"*Why?*" I asked. I didn't need to, of course; I already knew. But I wanted to see his reaction—surprised disbelief that I would even ask—and hear his response.

"Why?" he said. "I don't know *why*! I just did." The Blizzard of '96 was so severe that the Culinary shut down for the first time ever because of snow. When Clark arrived, along with a dozen or so other faculty, he couldn't believe it. No classes?! He said, "O.K., fuck you. I'm goin' home." And he got back in his car and drove home to Tivoli.

❧

These were the formative kitchens and they were formative in that all one's base skills began here. From Intro through Pantry (lunch and breakfast cookery), students manned production kitchens and cooked the meals for the fellow students, staff, and industry professionals taking part in continuing education programs at the school. For seven days students would hustle through Fish Kitchen, and in the middle of the week, on the eighth day, they would move into American Regional Cuisine in the Continuing Education building, which was attached to Roth Hall by an enclosed walkway. They would cook for seven days there; each day featured a different regional cuisine. One day was devoted to the Gulf States (sautéed fillet of grouper, for example, with a mango and avocado salsa, hoppin' John, and grilled scallions), another to Southwestern states (corn tortilla soup, grilled beef fajitas with salsa cru, lime cream, jicama salad, grilled sweet potatoes), and so on.

After a seven-day tour of the United States, they'd hustle back to Roth Hall, past K-8, past Chef Smith's kitchen, to Oriental. Here, for seven days under Chef Shirley Cheng from the town of Chengdu in Sichuan, they would cruise through Asian cuisines, a day in China, a day in Vietnam, a day in Thailand, and so on.

What students learned in Chef Cheng's kitchen was proper stir-fry technique and Asian ingredients. In a basic braise (chicken with mushrooms), the sachet d'épices contained no thyme, peppercorns, parsley, and bay, as it had in Skills, but rather orange skin, cinnamon, Szechuan peppercorns, and star anise. In Skills and in Intro, one julienned a carrot by squaring the whole thing off, cutting thin rectangular planks, then stacking them and cutting sticks, a time-consuming knife cut that left a lot of trim. Chef Cheng squared nothing off. She thinly sliced the carrot on a severe bias so that she had many long thin ovals of carrot; she then fanned them overlapping across the cutting board and simply rocked her knife lengthwise through the slices and in an instant had a pile of julienned carrot. Carrot julienned this way was uneven in length and therefore unacceptable garnish for Chef Smith's chicken broth, but if you wanted a lot of julienne fast with little waste, this was a new method.

Whoever made the chicken stock for the soup that day would begin by stir-frying garlic, ginger, and scallions—"GGS," the Asian mirepoix that began many dishes in this kitchen—before dumping the water and chicken bones into the wok. There was no lazy bubbling in Chef Cheng's kitchen. She instructed the soup station to boil it like mad and skim it often. She said this resulted in richer, creamier stock, faster.

All the dishes reflected basic cooking techniques and food concepts governing Asian cuisine. Most students would never work in an Asian kitchen, unless they spoke the language in that kitchen, so this was likely to be their only opportunity to learn in a kitchen properly outfitted for Asian techniques.

You had to pay attention here. If you weren't careful, you would miss Chef Cheng's boning demo. She could bone a chicken with a cleaver in fourteen seconds. It was all a matter of knowing where the joints were, she said. But even more impressive, Chef Cheng could take a chicken from living to cooked in less than three minutes. This, as Chef Pardus would say, was really wailing.

Upon leaving Chef Cheng's kitchen students would appear downstairs for seven days of Charcuterie, learning basic grinding and preparation of force-meats for sausages and terrines, as well as brining, curing, and smoking techniques, the results of which were shipped all over the school. After seven days here, they hustled upstairs to Pantry.

These classes were sprints and they took their toll. I bumped into my Skills friends often as they moved through these kitchens and saw, as if through time-lapse photography, that their skin grew increasingly gray and their demeanors haggard. I spotted Dave and Lou, then in American Regional, waiting for the doors of Pantry to open. American Regional with Chef Griffiths was noted for interesting food and high volume. Larry Forgione, who had returned to his alma mater to do a demo in the Danny Kaye Theater and promote a cookbook a few days earlier, stopped by their class to talk with the students. But Dave said he was tired, had stayed up late the night before writing a paper on the cuisine of the American Northwest. "Food, food, food," he said, "that's all you ever think about." He looked dizzy.

Lou, who had dropped the kids at his in-laws at six-thirty this morning as usual, to be at IBM for his seven-to-eleven shift, was nervous. He was on veg today, one of the hardest stations because of the volume. He would be prepping kale, turnip, and other tough greens—like, a *ton*, he said—and he didn't know how he was supposed to prep them or how to cook them for service. And the zucchini—the course guide said grilled but the chef had told him the night before he'd be julienning the squash.

"You'll be sautéing it," said Erica, also waiting for lunch. "We didn't grill any vegetables." Erica, who had already gone through American Regional, was in Fish kitchen. Adam had been elected leader of her group when they'd moved to Intro and I asked about him. She scowled and said, "He's getting kinda militant."

I later bumped into Adam in the quad. He wore a distant, half-there expression, as though he hadn't slept for a few days.

"I'm really burnt out," he confessed. "I can't wait to get out of here."

He still commuted to Brooklyn on weekends; this Saturday he would be trailing at Lutèce, hoping Soltner's former restaurant would make a good externship. Lespinasse, his first choice, had turned down his request. He was angry at the Culinary's curriculum. After American Regional and Fish kitchens, there was no sense of urgency. He was presently in Charcuterie, not even a production kitchen. "It should build," he said. "You should be in the restaurants before extern."

Lola appeared looking exhausted, ill, on the verge of tipping over right there. "I gotta question," she said. "Did you think about duck at all?"

"Yeah, we're gonna dry-cure it," he told her. "A nice piece of duck, the last thing I wanna do is soak it in *brine*." Adam then elaborated on the sauce, hoping he could work currants into it, along with pistachios for some color.

Lola was visibly relieved that Adam had done the homework. She put a hand to her chest and said, "I got in my car and I thought, 'Oh my God.' "

I asked about Erica.

"Erica's doing well," Adam said. "She's got an awesome extern—the Trellis."

Lola and Travis, living together in Kingston now, remained a solid couple. Adam, she, and I talked a few moments longer; I discussed with Adam duck confit and a related question about whether it would be possible to make a puff pastry with clarified duck fat instead of butter. Lola's eyes glazed. People were tired. The overload of incoming data was understandable. A lifetime of study and practice would not result in a comprehensive mastery of gastronomy; the administrators and chef-instructors knew this and it merely increased their determination to get it done in a matter of months. And in all but Adam, food passions seemed to be ebbing.

Lunch Cookery and the Burnt Parsnip

The kitchen that cranks out the food at the Culinary is Pantry. There are two pantry kitchens, downstairs and upstairs, and the upstairs Pantry sits like an anchor in the center of Roth Hall, off the main hallway, just outside the dining chapel. It's a volume kitchen, serving between four and five hundred meals a day at breakfast and lunch. At twelve-forty-five P.M. Pantry doors open and students, identical in their white jackets, checked pants, and black shoes, and extending all the way back to the hospitality office, pour through; the sous chef, or aboyeur, stands at the door with a clipboard marking down orders and simultaneously calling them out: "Pick up one deli! Pick up one hot plate, pick up two, pick up three hot plates! Pick up one veg! Pick up one hot plate, pick up one deli! Pick up one, pick up two pastas! Pick up a pasta! Pick up a pasta!" There are no commands of order or fire. This is lunch cookery: there's a lot of it, *fast*—between 200 and 250 meals before the doors close forty-five minutes later, the bulk of the meals having been served in the first twenty minutes.

I'd stuffed my notebook onto a shelf of a rolling steel cart earlier in the day to julienne two pounds of snow peas and, eventually, to help plate the pasta: lo mein noodles seasoned with sesame oil, cilantro, and black sesame seeds, encircling a bed of sautéed vegetables—julienned peppers, carrots, shiitakes, leeks, water chestnuts, celery, bamboo shoots, seasoned with GGS, tamari, chicken stock, and rice vinegar—which formed the bed for two marinated broiled shrimp skewered in a yin-yang design. James faced the stove, sautéing in batches of ten and broiling shrimp; K.C. and I plated; the orders fell like hail and the chef, Katherine Shepard, jumped in with a wet cloth to wipe our plates and slide them onto the steel counter where they were whisked away by a steady stream of students. Ours were tasty, good-looking plates. The noodles had been cooked the day before, but everything else had been prepped that morning and cooked at service. In a half hour we'd served fifty plates; amid the clatter a "no more pasta" and "eighty-six the pasta" sounded out; the sous chef wiped the item off the menu board and we cleaned the station.

There had been a single pause in the frenzy of service when the chef left us upon seeing a woman dressed in civilian clothes who had returned with a plate and a sour expression. Chef Shepard, short and plump, apologized profusely, turned toward the kitchen, held the plate at face level, and removed a hair from the potato salad. This was not good. Pinky aloft, Chef Shepard lifted the hair to the light and said, "The worst part is it looks like *mine*," she said to us. "I'm the only one with long red hair." Then, pleadingly, "And, I'm in *code*, too."

Fifteen minutes later, the kitchen closed, having served more than two hundred plates. Reuben sandwiches with ill-fated potato salad; oil-brushed pita stuffed with Greek salad; meatloaf with a spicy ketchup gravy, garlic smashed potatoes, peas and carrots; a plate of fruit and cheeses; and the yin-yang shrimp. Pantry students picked up what they'd ordered for family meal, returned by two o'clock, cleaned and prepped for tomorrow's menu— pan bagnat with pasta salad, chef salad with fresh bread sticks, chicken-fried steak with a spicy onion-milk gravy, sautéed greens and garlic cheese grits; a Middle Eastern–tasting plate; and pasta fagioli with bruschetta.

"Some people," Chef Shepard said, "even within the industry, feel that the breakfast line and the lunch line are where you put people who aren't worthy yet of doing dinner.

"It's critical for a chef to think fast for lunch foods," she continued, "to actually be able to manufacture foods at that speed because you don't have the cushion of, 'Well, they're going to have aps, they're going to have soup.' They want to be in and out, they want it on the table ten minutes after they put the order in. So that's why, when somebody says 'That's beneath me' or 'A real chef wouldn't cook like that,' well, I don't know that that's true. I think a chef has to be able to cook like that, in that environment."

We'd taken a small round table in the dining hall, mainly empty since Pantry ate well after everyone else had been served. She removed her toque and let her straight bright hair fall. Behind her wire-rimmed glasses were eyes as blue as her hair was red. She had brought half a sandwich. "I'm on a never-ending diet," she explained.

I was spending a few days in her class, working as much as I could and talking to the students. Half of this group had left Chef Pardus's Skills kitchen as my group had arrived (my group presently hustled through Fish and American Regional), and they were an unusually diverse batch. David had cooked on a kibbutz in Israel, Krista was a twenty-nine-year-old former human rights worker who had received a bachelor's from the University of Washington in anthropology; she'd always been pushed into cerebral areas, she said, and figured it was now or never to follow her passion for cooking; she'd worked in restaurants all through school and had come here because she wanted a broad, solid base fast. Jason had been, at his peak, the nation's eleventh-ranked hammer thrower. And Darren Sample, twenty-four, had spent the past four years as a cook on the USS *Michigan*, a trident nuclear submarine. He worked sixteen hours feeding four meals a day to one hundred fifty people. Noise was such a consideration under water that if he dropped a pot, he'd force the ship to change course and descend to a new thermal level. You could tell by the look in his eyes that this guy was not easily fazed. He was a good cook and a qualified torpedo man. Having been deprived of weather for four years, he now loved all weather, any kind; you name it, he loved it. The night before, there had been a cold rainstorm. Darren used the opportunity to go jogging.

He'd been sent to the Culinary while still in the Navy for a two-week continuing education course. The Navy didn't care much about teaching cooking and Darren learned as he went along; when he left the Culinary after the course, he knew he had to come back: "I came here," he remembered, "and anytime I asked why, everyone had an answer."

Chef Shepard knew this was a solid group, and there were plenty of them to get all the work done. Occasionally a group of ten would arrive, not the usual seventeen or eighteen, to cook the same amount of food. Small groups were interesting, she said: "They either come together or they're a complete abomination." And her students seemed to like her and the kitchen. This was not always the case. For years, some chefs and students looked at Pantry as though it were Siberia.

Timothy Rodgers, a 1981 CIA graduate and now team leader for various kitchens including Pantry, said, "I'm on an individual campaign to change 'Pantry' to 'Lunch Cookery' and 'Breakfast Cookery.'" He, too, lamented the fact that Lunch Cookery was looked down upon. Why should the time of a meal period determine its importance, he wondered, noting that it's one of the biggest selling meal periods? (Fifteen billion dinners are sold annually, according to the National Restaurant Association, considerably fewer than the twenty-six billion lunches sold each year.) The business is huge. "If I were going to do a book right now, it would be soups, sandwiches, and salads," he said. But until a couple years ago, he noted, Pantry was "a lost area" usually staffed by chefs on their way to retirement or by a chef who was more "ethereal" than was desired of a chef at this school. Then James Maraldo, now teaching in the Catarina de Medici kitchen, arrived in Pantry and introduced food that Rodgers described as "atypical." Rodgers jumped to reign Maraldo in, but when he saw what Maraldo was doing, he found the food intriguing and realized that Pantry chefs needed a lot more leeway.

Maraldo's dishes had a decided Italian bent. When Jean-Luc Kieffer was brought in, he added new recipes with French elements. Chef Shepard, a former executive chef at the Beekman Arms in Rhinebeck, kept Lunch Pantry rooted in the Hudson Valley. And soon, Eve Felder, a former Chez Panisse chef, would introduce Californian overtones and stress fresh unusual heirloom ingredients. Suddenly, Pantry was an exciting place to cook.

Part of what made Lunch Cookery distinct from other forms, Rodgers said, was the use of ordinary products; you couldn't sell lunch the way you could dinner. Also, it resembled banquet cooking given the high volume over a short time, requiring thought and organization as far as determining what can be cooked in advance and how far—"There are good ways and there are negligent ways," Rodgers said. Because of these differences, he added, "You learn how to think differently."

Not only did Pantry produce some of the most interesting food in the school, the food seemed almost contrary to all the kitchens that preceded it. No more sautéed veal with sauce champignon and sautéed spinach. This was American bistro food that included a cross-cultural range of ingredients and methods. Students arrived to find on Day One's menu herb focaccia with Tuscan sausage, mixed greens and a balsamic vinaigrette, and vegetable chili with a cheese quesadilla and cilantro-lime rice. The students, Chef Shepard said, arrive thinking, "Finally, here is food I can *sell*."

Classics were not ignored. Salad niçoise remains popular throughout the country despite its age and in this kitchen it fulfilled the Day Seven composed-salad requirement. Every day there must be a composed salad—a main item, greens, dressing, and garnish. Instead of niçoise it might be a buffalo-wing salad with macaroni in a dill dressing. There was always a deli plate—typically a sandwich. On Day Four, it was a cheeseburger with avocado, tomato, red onion with an herbed mayo-mustard, and Yukon golds cut to matchsticks and deep-fried. On Day Seven it was the ever-popular CIA Club. Knowing how to make a decent sandwich was important.

The Reuben, a traditional grilled cheese sandwich, was a good example. "We all used to do it however we ever made Reubens—there was no science to it," Shepard said. "One day we really did get a memo from the president that said, 'In order to produce a Reuben sandwich that is not soggy, this is the correct procedure.' That drawing in the course guide now reflects what has been determined by the president of this school, and all the other master chefs he powwows with, to be the way to make a Reuben that doesn't get soggy. It's all about putting the cheese in the right position so that the meat and the sauerkraut aren't in touch with the bread, so the cheese seals the bread off. How many people in life make Reubens that taste just fine without having this diagram?" She shrugged. "But the reason those diagrams are there is to produce a consistently better-quality product."

The CIA club was another example of the importance of sandwich-making.

"There has to be a club because in the world of sandwich-making," Chef Shepard said, "you have to learn how to make double-decker sandwiches."

I asked her what distinguished the CIA club from your run-of-the-mill club.

She said, "I don't know that there was a decree that came down from upstairs that said, 'And we shall have our own sandwich. Let it be known as . . .' " The CIA club used a combination of turkey and ham, that was all, but Shepard returned the discussion to technique. "Teaching how to make a club is very important, how to weight it so that the top isn't heavier than the bottom, so that when you cut it, it doesn't fall over; that's why you put the light stuff on top, the lettuce, tomato, and bacon."

"The CIA club sounds like a piece of cake," Chef Shepard began her double-decker-sandwich lecture. "It's not. It's a lot of work. Roast the turkey, bone and slice it today. Slice the ham. The recipe says two ounces of turkey and two ounces of ham. It won't work that way. We never get quite enough turkey, so portion out an ounce and a half of turkey and two and a half ounces of ham. It says slice the ham paper thin. That *means* paper *thin*. You want to pile it, you don't want to fold it. Portion your meat ahead of time. You can get your bacon trayed up and get your mayonnaise done." Garnish for the plate would be deep-fried root vegetables. "It's a lot of work. Whoever does it, it will take all morning to get them fried in our little baby fryer. We're going to have a meat tub full of chips. We need that many for sixty portions and for all the grazers. If you haven't tasted these, you will find that it's a pleasant experience. If you hate beets, this may totally change your life."

The chef went to the board and diagrammed the production line for the club: toast, mayo, meat, toast, mayo, lettuce-tomato-bacon, mayo, toast. Sixty slices of toast at each point. Whenever she worked a lunch line, the chef said, the club was what she hated. It took up all your work space. You'd have five other sandwiches to get out and club components cluttered your whole station. The number of parts and volume make it a challenge. When the sandwich was assembled, then came 240 toothpicks.

"This is critical," she warned. "The most important part. They've got to go straight down through all layers. If they don't go straight down, the knife catches them and pulls the sandwich apart and the toothpick gets cut in half and whoever eats that half will not be a happy camper. The science of doing a club sandwich is really, really important."

Pantry began at nine-thirty A.M. in a classroom on the fourth floor of the east wing near Julia Hill's Culinary Math class and Jay Stein's Product Identification and Food Purchasing class. Students in their whites took seats and opened notebooks. Chef Shepard would first address each station—deli, pasta, veg plate, composed salad, and hot plate—to inquire where prep stood and address questions, then move to the following day's menu.

Most days there was no time to spare. Lecture ended at 10:15 and you had two hours to prep before the chef began demo plates. But on Day Seven there was no lecture so we had plenty of time. And the chef looked nervous. She said, "It's an oy vey day. Too much time." Rarely a good thing in a kitchen. The chef would spend most of the morning, she said, "putting out little fires."

Tim, who was making the ciabatta, forgot to put the counterweight on the scale to compensate for the weight of the bowl he had the flour in and consequently the Hobart whipped up bread dough that looked like cake batter.

The chef told him to add more flour, watching as he did, till he reached the right consistency. Then she asked him why the herbs and calamata olives weren't in there. He rolled his eyes—oh, yeah. Tim dumped them in but the moisture from the olives ruined the consistency and he needed more flour.

He was headed home to Minnesota after the next block to extern at a country club and also to help open a friend's restaurant; he couldn't wait to leave, he said, and he wasn't focused.

This was what happened when you had too much time. The creamy, black pepper dressing for the niçoise kept breaking. The mayonnaise for the club, a gallon of it, was soupy. James, who had the job of deep-frying the root vegetables in the little baby fryer, found that they took so long he had to remove them before they were done in order to get them all cooked by service. Here I did something that would become instructive: I said nothing. Vats of chips waited to be deep-fried. I'd cut half of them, on the mandolin, myself. Taro root, sweet potatoes, parsnips, carrots, potatoes, and beets— twenty-six pounds in all. When they were fried properly, they made a beautiful hill of red, orange, and golden brown chips. But James was loading up the tub with soggy masses of starch. I was part of the team working on that plate, but I wasn't really part of the group and didn't want to overstep my bounds.

I continued helping with the construction of the sandwiches. As service approached everyone began to work a little faster. We still had a lot of sandwiches to make. Cutting them in quarters was indeed the tricky part, as the chef had said. James had almost finished all the chips, such as they were. As service approached it grew more and more clear to me that unless somebody did something, we were going to have to put soggy, undercooked chips on the plate. At last, about five minutes before service, right after the chef and the hammer thrower tried to reemulsify the dressing for the niçoise, I asked the chef if we could serve the chips like this. She shook her head, partly to say no but partly in disbelief. She glanced at the clock.

I said, "We can refry them at service. They'll cook fast."

"We don't have any choice," she said.

The doors opened and the chef herself began to refry the soggy chips. Everyone else on the deli plate was occupied, two people constructing, one person on toothpicks, another cutting, and I rushing them from our station to the service counter that ran the length of the kitchen, as the volley of "Pick up one deli! Pick up a deli! Pick up a deli!" descended. A frenzy reminiscent of Chef Clark's kitchen took hold. No time. Get it out. I had donned latex gloves to plate the chips that Chef Shepard was refrying, along with pickle and olives. The fryer, which James had cranked for mass loads, had grown too hot and the blanched chips burned before Chef Shepard could get them out. There was little the chef could do. It would take time and several batches to drop the temperature of the oil. I continued to plate the burnt chips as fast as I could and they disappeared as soon as I put it on the counter. It seemed as if everybody wanted the club today.

The phone rang and the chef was called away. I took over the fryer, just now starting to cool. Tim, whose herb-olive ciabatta had come out nicely in the end, stepped in to help me with the chips.

"*What* is *this*?" a voice across the counter asked.

It was Chef LeBlanc, formerly executive chef at the Ritz and Maxwell's Plum in New York City, now the P.M. instructor in Charcuterie. He had a round head, dark hair, dark eyes, and a mustache. He leaned on the counter to display to Tim and myself a very crisp, dark chip. "What *is* this?" he repeated.

Tim looked carefully at the chip pinched between LeBlanc's thumb and forefinger. "I believe," Tim said, pausing, "it's a parsnip."

"It *was* a parsnip," LeBlanc exclaimed. "Now it's burnt!" With that, LeBlanc took his club, pickle, two olives, burnt root vegetables, and departed.

As this was Day Seven, the class prepped for the incoming class's Day One. It was important to prep well for the new students since they'd be walking into a new kitchen with two and a half hours to prepare lunch for two hundred fifty people. After prep the class moved next door to Burns Demo, one of the original demonstration kitchens in the building. Chef Shepard herself had sat in this kitchen-cum-lecture-hall as a student straight out of high school. The Culinary relocated from its New Haven, Connecticut, location in 1972, and when the young Katherine arrived, wire still hung from the ceilings. Her first classes were putting the kitchens together. It was a time when students would sit for six hours watching Chef Czack or Chef Weissenberg cook (both 1958 graduates still at the school). The next day students would watch another chef cook, asking questions and taking notes, but never tasting (unless it was MSG, which they were required to taste, since it was an oft-used flavor enhancer at the time). The

Culinary then was a learn-as-you-go place; you picked up knife cuts as you needed them.

Chef Shepard would be doing doubles next for the rest of the block, teaching A.M. Pantry to her current group, beginning at three-thirty, and then sticking around to teach a new group in P.M. Pantry.

Eighty percent of A.M. Pantry was egg cookery, which she loved. Adam Shepard, who was no relation and who would not enjoy Chef Shepard's A.M. Pantry, told me, "She sleeps with her omelet pans."

Chef Shepard's goals in both classes were similar: to encourage a respect for these forms of cookery, to teach the ingredients and methods of these forms, which often differed from P.M. Cooking, and to develop in her students speed and agility required of a volume kitchen. "When you're cooking eggs that take one and a half minutes per order," she asked, "how slow do you think you can move? How much time can you take to do that job? It should take a minute and a half to two minutes to make an omelet. Period. If you can't do it that fast, then you're not *good* enough."

On graduation day, two of her students would be chosen to make omelets in the president's dining room for Mr. Metz and his guests, including the graduation speaker, typically a prominent figure in the food industry. "Mr. Metz is right there in front of you," Chef Shepard told me. "Mr. Metz likes to show off his students. It's an exciting feeling to cook for, maybe, Robert Mondavi."

Chef Shepard distributed a test (among the questions: list the components of a composed salad; list the steps for preparing and holding salad greens for service; define three types of vegetarianism). Everyone would arrive tomorrow morning at three-thirty for Breakfast Cookery. Students who lived off campus, the chef warned, should beware of drunks and deer on Route 9 as they headed into class.

I couldn't stop thinking about LeBlanc and the burnt parsnip. I'd told the chef about what had happened when she got off the phone. She felt bad and mad and asked me if I thought we should bring him some properly cooked ones. I said yes. I put a handful in a bowl I'd lined with a paper napkin and strode into the dining room. LeBlanc was eating with Chef Reilly, his back to the dining room.

"Chef LeBlanc?" I said, holding out my offering.

He turned, looked at the chips. He managed to convey surprise, scorn, and irritation with one expression. He said "Thanks" and took the chips. I returned to the kitchen to finish service.

This small gesture made up for nothing in my mind; LeBlanc was simply receiving what he should have had in the first place. I couldn't shake the image of him pinching that burnt chip in our faces. Why the chips burned was easy. A chain of bad decisions: James's hurry to finish the chips; my decision not to say anything when I saw he was undercooking them; the chef's cooking the chips in oil she knew to be too hot; and finally my decision to lift these burnt chips in my own gloved hand and float them into the center of a plate containing four triangles of juicy club sandwich. For me, a series of bad judgments had condensed into one crisp black parsnip chip.

The fact that LeBlanc and the parsnip ran on a loop in my mind was not, I believe, the result of some inner sensitivity of my own; rather, it was in the very nature of the Culinary Institute of America and the changes it wrought in its students. Unlike many educational institutions these days, this place dealt not only in knowledge and skill but also in value judgments. It taught a system of values that was almost religious in scope and beautifully concrete, physical, immediate. And because of this, a great human dilemma bound itself up in me and that parsnip chip.

I'd served numerous people chips I knew very well were burnt, that I myself would leave on the plate had they been served to me. I *decided* to do this. Why had I given them something visibly inedible? Wasn't this a question of morality? It was wrong, I knew it, I did it *anyway*. Wasn't this the very kind of decision that defined a mediocre cook?

I returned to Pantry kitchen the next day. Chef Shepard was in her first day of doubles, had been in the kitchen since three A.M., and was finishing up her P.M. class.

"I can't stop thinking about those chips," I told her.

She nodded immediately and said she was still mad at herself for that. "If this had been a real restaurant," she said, "those chips wouldn't have gone out."

"Why did you send them out then?" I asked.

I wanted to know for myself. I could follow my own moves through service. It was always the same: the day started out slow, and the pace picked up, and then suddenly you're in the weeds without knowing how you got there and all you can think about is get the plates out, get 'em out. You don't have *time* to think—if you stop to think, you're buried, so you simply *act*. You give people burnt food.

I continued to press Chef Shepard. "Why did you send out burnt chips?" Finally, clearly troubled, she said, "I didn't want to *lose*."

 President Metz

I had been at the Culinary for three months and had yet to meet the man who ran the place, Ferdinand Metz. At first this seemed odd. I was a writer who was being given fairly broad access to a large institution with an operating budget of $65 million, an institution that influenced the enormous food service industry, an institution that he cared a lot about. He had chosen not to meet me. And I had chosen not to meet him, at first because my questions would be fruitless before I knew the school, but also because I felt I was getting to know him better by not meeting him.

Details, anecdotes, what people said about the man, how people reacted when they passed him in the hall, how people reacted to the mention of his name, my own glimpses of him—these small bursts of information, as they accrued, began to form a silhouette of the president of the Culinary Institute of America.

That he was thoroughly corporate, for example, solidified in my mind from the beginning. When I first met with Senior Vice President Tim Ryan my first day at the Culinary, Mr. Metz called from, I believe, the West Coast. Leaving to take the call, Ryan guessed aloud and with a friendly chuckle that Metz was calling from his StairMaster.

Metz, always perfectly and beautifully dressed in stylish but not corporate attire, was tall, trim, athletic. His fine gold hair never seemed to move it was so well coiffed. He wore a tidy mustache. His eyes were slivers, his cheekbones angular and high above concave cheeks. His was a presence that never failed to arrest me, fix me, as though he were a celebrity, or maybe dangerous. Though one caught glimpses of the corporeal Metz maybe half a dozen times a year, one couldn't get away from the idea of Metz if one tried. His spirit was omnipresent.

If his name came up in conversation with a chef-instructor, I always probed for thoughts on the man. One of the instructors said simply that Mr. Metz was walking perfection and there was nothing more to say on the matter.

Among the spare details I knew of his history were the facts that he had spent his first twenty years in Munich, Germany, and that he retained a distinct German accent. I knew that he had worked at Manhattan's famed Le Pavillon shortly after he arrived in the United States in 1962, that he was subsequently banquet chef at the Plaza Hotel, and that he had left his job as senior manager of new product development at Heinz U.S.A. in 1980 to become president of the Culinary.

Once a month, on the Thursday before graduation, the school put on what was called the Grand Buffet in the dining chapel, a formal buffet dinner featuring competition-style platters of galantines, pâté en croutes, roulades, terrines, and cured salmons from the Garde Manger classes, and vast perfect mirrored trays of cakes, tortes, candies, and petit fours by Patisserie classes. Intro, Fish, and Oriental also served food at this buffet. The chapel would remain empty until Mr. Metz arrived with the graduation speaker and guests to tour the food. Mr. Metz often stopped to ask questions of the students about the food they'd prepared.

On Day Twelve of Intro, after dinner, Rudy Smith said to the broil station, which was preparing salmon for the Grand Buffet, "I'll bet you Mr. Metz will ask you how he can tell whether it was salted before it was cooked." The salt, Chef Smith explained, drew concentrations of protein to the surface of the meat; protein is what caramelizes; if the salmon had a good deep caramelization on the grill marks without being overcooked, it had been salted before cooking. "Mr. Metz wants you to impress him," Chef Smith said. "He wants you to impress his guests."

Mr. Metz loved blanquette de veau, Chef Smith continued, directing his words to Lola, who would be making it. He always had some. The blanquette was similar to the fricassee, which Ben had done the day before, but there were distinctions. The blanquette was a highly refined white stew:

chunks of veal were blanched to remove impurities; the sauce was strained; it was a bright, elegant dish. Small attention to details would make a huge difference in the outcome. When Mr. Metz ate stew, it was this highly refined version. "It's real important for you to understand the difference, where they came from," he said to Lola.

This was the group's first Grand Buffet and Chef Smith ran down general rules. "Nobody eats before Mr. Metz. Make sure you know the whole menu. Be proud of what you know; share it with him. One thing you should not do is try to bullshit the man. If you even *think* about it he'll know.

"The man plays to win," Chef Smith concluded. "He cooks that way. He's a damn good cook."

Lola, clearly anxious, asked, "What should we *call* him."

"Mr. Metz," Smith answered, unsmiling. "He's a *man*. He's a damn good cook, but he started out just like you."

Chef Shepard remembered the day Mr. Metz, on one of his periodic tours through the school, stopped by her kitchen. She was then teaching introduction to Hot Foods. "We had made quiche," Shepard recalled, "and Mr. Metz was talking to my students about the menu and he wanted to know how we made the quiche." They told him the chef had instructed them to sprinkle cheese into the quiche shell. Mr. Metz said, "Did she? Why did she do that?" The students were unable to answer. "We hadn't had the lecture, so they didn't know why," Shepard said. "And he told them, 'That's how you produce a quiche with a crisp crust on the bottom. By putting the cheese on the bottom, the egg batter doesn't penetrate so quickly.' "

She remembers with equal clarity an "unpleasant" call from the president, "something I did not want to hear."

As a pantry chef, she was in charge of the student, the specials tournant, who prepared a morning snack for the president. "He likes things very plain," Shepard said, "very simple. Carrots, turnips, rutabaga, and celery sticks, that's it." An easy assignment—revealing, even, in its spartan crispness. On one occasion, though, her kitchen was under a heavy production load and had only ten students. The specials tournant was to prepare Mr. Metz's crudité. The vegetables were a couple days old and the chef asked the tournant how they looked. The tournant said O.K., then prepped and plated them, and covered them with plastic wrap. Shepard checked them but not carefully. They looked fine beneath the wrap but were in fact somewhat dry and limp. Crudité would not seem to be the pressing issue in Pantry with only ten students. The crudité then sat for several hours at room temperature before Mr. Metz got to them.

Shortly thereafter, the pantry telephone rang. It was Mr. Metz. He asked Chef Shepard what she had sent. She apologized, made excuses, knowing no excuse was adequate. The crudité were bad and she had sent them to President Metz. Those were the only facts that mattered. He said, she recalled, "If you didn't have time, you should have said so. We could have made other arrangements."

She knew this was true. But it was also true that you did not say no to Mr. Metz. That, too, was losing.

I quickly became fascinated with this man—who loved blanquette de veau for its rich refinement and ate raw turnips for breakfast—because of his effect on people. One almost never saw him, except at graduation time, less so now than ever given the two campuses on separate coasts. But everyone wanted to please him, and everyone wanted to impress him. I was once walking with a young, tough, cocky student. We passed Mr. Metz in the hall; the student's eyes enlarged and he turned to me, did not speak, but mouthed the words *That was President Metz.*

Mr. Metz set the standard. That standard was perfection. Pantry had access to fresh turnip, rutabaga, carrot, celery; there was no reason not to serve them. There was something both gentle and ferocious in his tone and it remained in Chef Shepard's mind. "If you didn't have time, we could have made other arrangements." *Do you understand what I am saying? If you can't do it perfectly, we will find someone who can.*

Nothing short of perfection was acceptable. Would you serve President Metz burned root vegetables? Never. Therefore, you should never serve to *anyone* burned root vegetables. Here was the morality of cooking and service, and at the CIA, it rose to an almost religious dimension. Eventually, I grew to understand that the source of this perfection, this wanting to do it right, the anger at not living up to the task, the deep gratification when you did well—whether in Pardus's Skills kitchen or Shepard's Pantry—was Ferdinand Metz.

Part III

Keepers of the Food

 Garde Manger

"Eve Felder," Chef Pardus had told me during Skills, "is a food *goddess*." Felder currently taught Garde Manger, the last block of the first year of the CIA curriculum, and I had the good fortune to rejoin my old Skills class—Adam, Erica, Lola-and-Travis, the silent Bianca, Ben, Paul, and Greg—and watch this woman in action.

Her class was their final block before they left on their externships, and they all ached to flee Hyde Park. The dizzy fatigue that began in Intro had only increased as they moved into Garde Manger, and all seemed to be counting the days till the end of the block.

A similar mood ran through the entire school; this was the final block before the seventeen-day summer recess when the Institute shut down to clean and repair itself. Students and faculty alike, all of whom began this half-year stretch in a series of blizzards, would end it in lazy, hot July as if leaning into a marathon finish-line tape and a heavenly stretch of rest.

All except for Chef Pardus.

On my way out of Alumni Hall, carrying a lunch tray with the remnants of my calamari salad, I passed Chef Pardus, who stopped to tell me the news.

"Guess what I'm doing over summer break," he said, almost smirking.

"What?" I asked.

"Teaching *Skills*."

"Skills?"

"In *Brazil*," he said.

The Culinary has a certification program at a hotel in São Paulo, with many of the same courses taught exactly the way they were here. The main difference was that the students stayed in one kitchen, and CIA instructors rotated in. When Chef Pardus finished Skills, Rudy Smith would fly down to teach Intro. Pardus, ever the squeaky wheel, had gone to scheduling Chef Bob Briggs and asked when was he going to get one of those nifty overseas assignments? Briggs said, "What are you doing summer break?"

While others fished, lounged, weeded their vegetable gardens, and cooked squash, corn, and new potatoes, Chef Pardus would be simmering beef bones at a lazy bubble, tasting brown sauce after brown sauce, and building consommé rafts.

But almost all the rest were anticipating the restorative weeks of summer. Garde Manger was not a production kitchen serving daily meals, but instead served prepared-in-advance-food, so the work was mainly prep with no last-minute scrambling—a fine way to spend the final three weeks of school.

Classically, Garde Manger handled cold items, hors d'oeuvres, some desserts, and decorations such as ice sculptures. Today, Garde Manger, or Pantry station (the term is French for pantry, and loosely translates as keeper or protector of the food), does much of the same. Garde Manger would be in charge of hot and cold appetizers, salads, sandwiches. Our Garde Manger class would focus on cocktail canapés, plated appetizers, and finally, buffet platters of cold food, attempted at near-competition level and served on the Thursday before graduation to Mr. Metz and guests at the Grand Buffet.

But, Chef Felder explained in her Day One lecture, "Forcemeat is the backbone of this class."

Forcemeat is defined very generally as cooked or raw meat, ground or minced. The word derives from the French *farcir* and *farce* (to stuff and stuffing), but I could never hear or use it without a small shudder. Such a crude word. On either side of this term one found only elegance. At the scientific or molecular level, for example, classical forcemeats are often emulsions of meat, fat, and water—a complex colloidal system. On the other side of this dreary term were the types of emulsions, delicate on the ear, even regal-sounding: galantine, ballottine, pâté de foie gras. Mousselines, mousses, quenelles, and terrines were all . . . forcemeats! Even the hearty-sounding sausage and the American hero, the hot dog, were better than forcemeat. And that's no baloney.

But all the above were forcemeats and forcemeats we would grind and roast and bake and poach.

Chef Felder, of course, had a deep respect for forcemeats. She called forcemeat "a liberator."

Indeed, it provided a method for using leftover meats that would soon be past fresh, and this was the soul of garde manger—to protect what is to be eaten.

Chef Felder said the first garde mangers were cavemen. American Indians were garde mangers when they packed fish in salt to cure and preserve them. Duck confit, legs cooked in, then submerged and stored in, their own fat was a garde manger technique. A garde manger kitchen relied more than any other on seasoning and spices because the food was usually served cold and therefore needed a flavor kick to replace the steamy aromatic effect of hot food. Garde manger techniques flourished in the Middle Ages when spices, a sign of affluence, were the rage. The meat is cold, molded, and is often suspended in aspic; the first thing many people think when they hear these words is Spam, so the food had to be beautiful, visually enticing as well as tasty.

"You have to *see* taste," Chef Felder said. " 'Look at what they're eating. Oh my lord, it looks delicious. Look at that carrot, it is cut to perfection. Look at that terrine, look at that pâté en croûte, look at all the garnish that's in it!' It has to scream out for the customer to want to eat it. It has to invite the customer in. In the garde manger kitchen, we garnish heavier, we season heavier, our knife skills have to be beautiful so that the flavor becomes visible. President Metz will come through on the Grand Buffet and press the meat to see if juices come to the surface.

"One of the most exciting things for me," she continued, "I am going to teach you how to utilize, without a recipe, leftovers. So if last night we had a duck left over, I'm going to teach you how you can turn that duck for two or four servings into sixteen or twenty servings by making a forcemeat."

"Y'all?" she asked. Chef Felder was from Charleston, South Carolina, and used y'all the way a writer uses a tab key to begin a new paragraph. "Y'all, how do you make a forcemeat without a recipe?"

Ratios, of course. Ratios and proper technique freed you, she said. Know the ratio and you were golden. How much meat, to how much fatback, to how much water. A typical emulsion used five parts meat, four parts fat, and three parts ice (everything—including the grinder itself—must be cold as ice; if the mixture became hotter than 40 degrees, the proteins and fat might not bind properly and result in a broken forcemeat). This emulsion was *named* after its ratio; it was called a 5/4/3 forcemeat. Commoners know the 5/4/3 forcemeat as knockwurst, frankfurters, and other fine-textured sausages.

Chef Felder was in her early forties, slender, with short wavy brown hair, almost all of which could be contained within her toque. Her complexion had the familiar heat-baked texture of a chef. Her dark eyes pointed down slightly toward her narrow nose, like two upended teardrops; when she talked about food, her eyes sparkled, and her entire body and mien grew pixilated.

Chef Felder was a self-taught cook. In Omaha, Nebraska, she worked her way up from restaurant manager at Cafe Eggspress to executive chef of V. Mertz Restaurant. She read everything she could, and began following a column in *Cooks* magazine written by Lindsey Shere, Alice Water's partner and pastry chef at Chez Panisse, who spoke eloquently on the necessity of chefs and farmers to work together. Shere's words enchanted Felder, and she grew determined to work at Chez Panisse. With this single hope, she enrolled at the CIA. She kept her sights on the beacon of Chez Panisse, the landmark Berkeley restaurant. She wangled an externship there, and when she graduated in 1988, she returned to Chez Panisse and stayed seven years, until a former teacher invited her to take the chef's practical at the Culinary.

On this Day One, Chef Eve Felder talked about forcemeat almost non-stop for five hours, then flew to Wisconsin for the rest of the week. We would have a different chef the following day, while Felder taught basic cooking techniques to public-school kitchen workers, in a joint effort between the CIA and the USDA to improve school lunches throughout the country.

Our stand-in chef was Mark Ainsworth, the A.M. Garde Manger instructor who would do doubles till Felder's return the following week.

Now, I don't know if it was the strain of doing doubles, if it was the fact that this was a cold kitchen, or maybe that Chef Ainsworth spent too long in the Virgin Islands (executive chef at Passers Landing in Tortolla), but Chef Ainsworth, a tall thirty-seven-year-old with feathery brown hair, was placid. Calm. *Mellow.* He'd worked at La Bernardin. That had to be intense. He'd been the chef on the *Yorktown Clipper,* of Clipper Cruise Lines, a tiny kitchen on a speedy clipper ship with little storage space but all the demands of a production kitchen and gravity going every which way while you're cooking. This, I would imagine, was nerve-racking. But you could not faze this guy. Sometimes he would raise his eyebrows, sometimes he would smile and nod. That was about it.

His near-deadpan tone somehow made him a great storyteller; he passed along a lot of information by story. We would be diligently at work on our cocktail reception canapés and Ainsworth would call out "Demo!"

Time to cure salmon, gravlax cure and smoked cure. Among the information he imparted on the subject of salmon—farm-raised versus Alaskan, his buddy who started an Alaskan salmon business and how he makes money by smoking the fish, how this friend figured a way to smoke salmon fat to make money off what used to be trim, how sea lions can see from a quarter mile what kind of salmon were caught in his friend's net—was that David Burke, the star chef of Park Avenue Cafe, made salmon pastrami. "It's mainly marketing," Chef Ainsworth said. "You guys know how to cure pastrami. What are some of the seasonings?" Students called out answers they learned in Charcuterie and Ainsworth said, "Right, it's simple. David Burke does the same thing with salmon, sells it as a salmon pastrami, and is making a fortune.

"The relationship between the salt and the sugar is important," he continued. "Seasonings, the bay leaf, cloves, allspice, that's not really important. You want a Southwestern cure, add Southwestern seasonings. You want an Oriental cure, add Oriental seasonings." Ratios, again, were all important. Gravlax, cured only one day, would need two pounds of salt to one pound of sugar. For salmon that will be smoked, we used less salt. "Why?" he asked. "Because it's a three-day curing job."

He had a good story for everything. Adam Shepard had recently trailed at Lutèce, now led by Eberhard Muller, and Chef Ainsworth stopped to listen to Adam describe his night in that kitchen. They hadn't let Adam do much, but he watched and tasted. "The food going out of there was *perfect*," Adam recounted. "Perfect. Everything. I tasted everything that went out of that kitchen and I could not think of one thing to improve any of it. His lobster stock was incredible. It was the best lobster stock I've tasted."

Chef Ainsworth nodded. Eberhard had amazing taste capabilities, Ainsworth said. He'd worked with Eberhard at La Bernardin. The cooks there were making lobster stock once, but they couldn't get it right, the taste wasn't quite there. So someone added a smidgen of chicken stock base.

"There was maybe ten gallons of this stuff," Chef Ainsworth recalled, "and we added a tablespoon, and Eberhard tasted it and said, 'WHO PUT BASE IN THIS STOCK?!' "

The world of the Culinary often seemed so hermetic that it was gratifying to hear stories like these from the outside.

We learned food tips in Garde Manger. The fresh marinated mozzarella balls, occasionally called buffalo mozzarella (in Italy, some mozzarella is made from the curd of buffalo milk), now ubiquitous in gourmet delis for ten bucks a pound, were simply cheap cheese curds melted in salt water (five or six ounces of salt per gallon) that had been heated to 160 degrees. You worked the curd in the water, with your hands if you could stand the temperature, or with spoons, till it was gooey as taffy. Then you could do anything you wanted to it before cooling it. Form it into large balls and marinate them in oil and herbs. Roll them into a long tube, wrap the tube in plastic wrap, and tie off little one-inch sections for bocconcini, or, as Chef Felder liked to do, serve the little mozzarella balls with roasted red peppers and a red-wine-balsamic vinaigrette. You could smear the gooey cheese curd into a thin sheet across your cutting board, spread some pesto on it, roll it into a tube, and slice it for mozzarella-pesto swirled discs. Chef Ainsworth had my table (we'd been divided into groups of four) make this for a cocktail reception for prospective students, but half the sheet would be spread with an intriguing vinaigrette: to the red-wine-and-olive-oil base we added four roasted red peppers, a head of roasted garlic, and two chipotle peppers.

No end of canapé innovation could be found in salt water and two-dollar-per-pound cheese curd. Of the gourmet deli counters selling it, Ainsworth nodded sagely and said, "It's quite a racket."

We would bone out a lot of meat for our forcemeats, which we began to make on the second or third day, and Chef Ainsworth—more or less in passing—said sometimes it was fun to bone out a chicken from the inside, leaving the chicken intact, then stuff it and roast it, so that it appeared to have all its bones. Something to do for Mom, he said. "We bone out a quail this way," he continued. "Some of you may have seen the Euro quail we get here. Like that. Then we do it to a hen and put the quail in the hen, and then we put the hen inside a pheasant, and the pheasant inside the duck, and we roast it." Sometimes he stuffed the initial quail with foie gras molded around a truffle. As he said this, Adam smiled and nodded, which he rarely did. Then Ainsworth told an apocryphal tale, from the more decadent years of ancient Rome, about the practice of continuing this idea: the cook wouldn't stop at the duck stuffed with hen stuffed with quail stuffed with a wren stuffed with foie gras around a truffle; Romans would then stuff the stuffed duck into a boned chicken, and the boned chicken into a suckling pig, and so on all the way up to cow. They would roast it for hours and hours and hours and when it was done, the Romans would share the truffle and throw the rest away.

But Ainsworth's main philosophy was to give assignments, hang back, and not instruct too much. "They're about to go out on extern," he told me. "They've got to be able to answer their own questions."

The Second-Term Practical

The second-term practical is among the final tests a CIA student takes before departing for extern. It is a cooking test taken during the first week of Garde Manger. A group of six students arrives in the Practical kitchen off the mail room at seven A.M. (if they are P.M. students). The six menus the students may prepare, printed in the handout everyone receives before the test and also posted on a bulletin board, consist of a soup, an entrée (a meat and sauce), two vegetables, and one starch. Before they cook, students answer questions, such as what mother sauce is used in preparing most cream soups, or, what is the protein in ground beef and egg whites? (Velouté, albumen.)

The menu is basic. Entrées include roast chicken with pan gravy, sautéed chicken with sauce fines herbes, and poached salmon with hollandaise—Skills Two food. Soups were straight out of Skills One. This was after all a test of basic methods (sauté, shallow- and deep-poach, braise, roast, broil) employed in a timely fashion. The soup was to be presented after two hours and fifteen minutes, entrées fifteen minutes later. Everything you needed was either on a tray or in the reach-in, and you had exactly the right time to prepare a full meal for two from scratch provided you made no mistakes.

But the practical made most people nervous. If you were late with your food, you failed. If your food could not be eaten—say you misjudged done-ness of the roast chicken and the thigh meat was bloody—you failed and would have to pay to retake the test. You cooked in an unfamiliar kitchen for a chef you didn't know. This was a test and test anxiety went along with it.

I arrived for the practical at seven A.M with Len Mormondo, who had moved through his standard daily mise en place like a sullen workhorse across from me in Skills, and beside Eun-Jung, who was also scheduled to take the practical today, as was big, sweet-as-a-Teddy-bear Lou. When Eun-Jung arrived and saw me, she said, "I am so happy. It is just like Skills." And it was. We were asked to do nothing that we hadn't already done in Skills long ago. The only difficulty was that no one knew what menu they would be preparing and therefore had to know all the menus, and the uncertainty weighed heavily. Eun-Jung, like many students, had written all the menu recipes on three-by-five cards and carried them in her breast pocket. I had not done this; I carried a few of my Skills cards to ensure I had the right amounts for items such as the court bouillon in which the salmon was to be poached, but I would rely on the techniques and hoped, somewhat nervously, that the rest would follow.

Chef Felder's advice seemed best of all: "It's only dinner," she had told us on Day One. "You're only doing what you love to do."

The chef-instructor, Adam Balough, was a weathered man with a large nose, strawberry-blond hair, and a Hungarian accent as thick as his glasses. As a youth he had served his four-year apprenticeship at Karpatia Restaurant in Budapest. He had been at the Culinary for twenty-three years. "People call me a lot of things," he told us, chuckling gruffly, "but not a bad cook."

He didn't much look at any of us. We gathered in the kitchen around a small rectangular table scattered with the chef's papers, a silverware container, and a silver bowl containing six small wads of yellow paper. He extended the bowl to Lou. Lou took one and unfolded it. "Shallow poach," Lou said, and then took a breath. He had spoken with emotion, but I could not say whether it was worry, happiness, or simply relief that at last he knew what he was responsible for: cream of broccoli soup, rice pilaf, broccoli and carrots, and poached fillet of sole. We then toured the kitchen with the chef, who more or less pointed and mumbled. "Keep the ovens at three-fifty." "Wash your own pots as you use them." "Don't be late for your entrée."

"Chef, are there tasting spoons?" asked Lou.

"Yah," said Chef Balough, and set them with a clank on the table.

The stations were numbered one through six. There were two stoves and a small alcove with barely enough room for the table and a few chairs. Chef Balough asked us to fill out a form with pertinent data, including the name of our Skills instructor—"So I know where to send you back," he grunted. He then tried to put us at ease. "Cook like you cook for your mother. If your mother would eat it, so would I." He paused, reconsidering this wisdom. "Maybe your mother would eat it anyway, so you don't feel bad." He chuckled and continued. "We sit down and I tell you what I think and maybe we disagree. But when people see the grade, they don't usually disagree."

And then it began. Five of us departed, leaving Lou to the shallow poach and fate, with the small advantages of more time to study and the knowledge that we no longer needed to be concerned with the menu Lou was beginning.

I returned at ten to a bustling kitchen and a single yellow wad in the bowl that read "Braise, Steak/Lamb Shank, Cauliflower, Snow Peas, Mashed Potatoes, Onion." Lou had started late and was just presenting his soup as I sat down to take my verbal test. After a perfect score there I was up and cooking. I'd drawn one of the easier menus. The deep poach, for instance, requiring hollandaise, court bouillon, and a consommé, was a headache.

The key to the braise was to get the meat seared and the mirepoix caramelized first since the braise would take about an hour and a half to cook. So while my meat seared at one end of the kitchen, I was back at the other end chopping mirepoix and fine-slicing onions for the soup, which would also take a long time, since a good caramelization was the critical element in onion soup. The veg and starch were no-brainers. I'd cook and shock the veg once the soup was simmering—I wanted a nice long slow simmer to really develop the flavor—and the lamb shank was braising. The mashed potatoes could be done just before the soup was ready and held above the stove. The chef had made it easier still for me. Don't pipe the mashed potatoes, he said. Keep the veg plain. And garnish for the soup can be a simple slice of bread toasted with melted Parmesan and Gruyère.

Meanwhile Lou was making a critical error. The shallow poach method was simple: sweat shallots in a sauté pan, add fish stock and a little white wine, bring it to a simmer, lay the sole into the liquid, called a cuisson, on the bed of shallots, cover it with parchment, and pop it in the oven for several minutes. The cuisson, reduced and thickened, would become the sauce.

And there Lou made his error. He held his fish on a rack while he reduced his cuisson to sauce consistency. The problem was that, though reduced, it remained thin as water. Lou panicked and turned up the heat. It was nearly time to plate his entrée. In moments, Lou's sauce was gone. He had failed to add velouté or beurre manié (butter with flour worked into it) that would have thickened his cuisson.

The chef evaluated everything, tabulated Lou's score, and gave him an 83. "He boiled away his sauce," Balough told me when I asked. "He had no sauce and he served his fish dry. I could have failed him. But everything else was perfect." Balough shrugged. "Other chefs might have said, 'You fail.' They don't care." It was difficult to fail with Chef Balough. He noted that some students get so flustered they give up entirely, or serve their entrée a half hour late, both of which result in failure. One student would fail the practical this block; his consommé raft broke and he simply fell apart after that.

In the meantime I had everything under control and worked efficiently at the stove beside Len and Eun-Jung, who frantically simmered her gravy for the roast chicken. Suddenly a burst of flame engulfed her, then disappeared, and her expression never changed. Often she was in my way, or Len's, or she'd take the burner that I'd been using and still needed, apparently oblivious to the awkwardnesses. Waves of nostalgia would sweep over me.

My soup was ready at twelve-fifteen as planned, had been ready for some time. I had forgotten my crouton in the broiler and it had turned to cinder, but I had saved enough cheese to quickly make another. I presented the soup and went about reheating the veg with butter and some salt, holding the perfectly cooked fork-tender shank above the stove while I strained the sauce and kept it hot on the stove. I plated the veg and mashed potatoes first. As I reached for the shank with my tongs, I noticed that a thin film of grease had separated out of the sauce and hung on top. I placed the shank on the plate, grabbed the sauce, and spread a spoonful of sauce over the shank. Chef Balough, having finished with all the rest, hovered over my shoulder at that moment.

"Let me see," he said, pulling my sauce pot to him. "You need to degrease it."

He had spoken as if I were a blockhead. I got flustered and stirred the sauce quickly.

"Now you're stirring the fat back into the sauce," he exclaimed.

I halted and looked at him. I did not know what to do.

"Leave it," he said, giving up. "Go on."

I looked down at the shank. Already bright orange grease was bleeding out of the sauce I'd already spooned. I finished plating and sat to taste and evaluate with the chef.

My soup was overdone, simmered too long with too many onions that had been overcaramelized, and a few that had been scorched gave the soup a faint bitterness (I had not cut them uniformly). But mainly it was too rich. I argued that I was after rich.

"You wouldn't want to eat the whole thing," the chef said.

"Not in this hot kitchen in the middle of July you wouldn't," I argued. "Imagine a blustery winter evening and you're famished." The chef was not buying. He liked a lighter flavor. And by the way, I shouldn't have cut the crust off my toasted bread; the French way is to leave the crust on.

My vegetables were cooked well. As was the shank, but it was a little dry; I should have covered it when I held it instead of simply setting it on the rack. Besides being greasy, the sauce was too thick. I had used brown sauce for my braising liquid. I should have used half veal stock. The potatoes were nicely done. "That's *something*," he said, then tabulated my score.

I got a 91.7, and while I'd fared better than the chef's comments would lead one to expect, I was nonetheless disheartened by my many errors. My food was completely edible, pretty good in fact. But it was far from excellent. I had forsaken many details.

Most of my Skills class had done better than I. Greg Lynch drew the braise and scored a perfect 100. Balough had told him one would not find a better braised shank anywhere in the world. Ben scored a 99 on the braise. "My sauce was soooo good," he bragged. "The chef grunted when he tasted my braise." He begrudged Greg his 100, said Greg was still a "shoemaker," which had become the popular sleight of the block.

I returned on the last day to ask Balough how the group had done relative to others. "The group did unusually well," he said. "Two high passes today, three high passes yesterday." He shook his head. "They knew all the questions, their knife skills were good."

Half of my Skills class returned to thank the person they felt responsible for their high score, Chef Pardus. Pardus told me pretty soon he was going to need a bigger hat.

Adam had scored a 99 on the sautéed chicken with sauce fine herbs, zucchini, carrots, pasta, and split pea soup. When I asked him to tell me about his practical, he sounded like he was reliving a legendary sports moment.

"If I'd given him the other piece of chicken, I'd have gotten a hundred," Adam said, noting that one tip of one chicken breast was a tad overdone. "Everything else was perfect. I couldn't believe it. It wasn't supposed to go that good. I don't know why it did. I knew that he didn't want bacon in the split pea soup because he doesn't like color, heavy flavor; he wants things to be what they are. He wants split pea soup to be split pea soup. So I rendered the bacon and cooked the shallot and the garlic and the celery in the bacon fat, but I took the lardons out and held them on the side, and I took part of the bacon fat and made the croutons with the bacon fat. And I put the lardons in a sachet into the soup for the last minutes of cooking. I never would have thought of that. I don't know why I thought of that. It was the perfect amount of flavor. And I cooked the potatoes in chicken stock instead of cooking them with the peas and the hock, right? And I saved the chicken stock to thin out my soup. That worked out pretty well. I glazed the carrots with chicken sauce, butter, and zucchini I just blanched, shocked, reheated, and tossed in whole butter."

I asked him what he thought of Balough.

"I think he knows what he's doing," Adam said. "People are like 'He shouldn't be grading the practical, he grades so easy, he's got no sense of flavor.' Bullshit. He's lenient, but he's right. I tasted Melissa's soup, and she said, 'He said it has too much flavor.' And she looked at me like 'I don't understand what he's talking about.' But it's true. You know what broccoli tastes like when you cook it till it turns gray, you know how it's got that weird sort of mushy gray underneath flavor? Well, that was the way the food finished. I knew exactly what he was talking about."

Vic scorched his consommé, just as he had done in Skills. And Erica scored a 91. She too had drawn the sauté. "I'm pleased, yeah," she told me, smiling, shrugging modestly and looking away. Then she looked at me with those incredibly blue eyes and said, "I got the pea soup. And you *know* how I feel about pea soup."

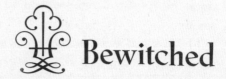 Bewitched

The following Monday, Chef Felder was back. I didn't know who I liked better. Ainsworth was like a cool older brother in town for the weekend hanging out. "Duck fat is one of the best kinds of fat to use because it's so tasty," I heard him say as he strolled through the long narrow kitchen. "The only better kind of fat is fat that comes off foie gras." When someone asked how much mirepoix to use for stock that would be used for aspic, he said, "If you go to measure for your stock on extern, they may laugh at you. You should know by now how much mirepoix to use."

Felder, on the other hand, had arrived from another realm to bewitch us. "Cooking is *magic*, cooking is *alchemy*," she said, eyes asparkle. She could even make aspic, a flavored liquid made solid with gelatin, exciting.

"Lobster consommé with quenelles of wild mushrooms was served last night," she announced to the class during lecture, snatching an example out of the air the way a magician produces a flapping, fluttering dove. "We have left over a quart of consommé, and we have one lobster. Our choices with that are to give it to the staff or throw it out or come up with something to do with it. A quick method is to change that consommé into an aspic.

"We have one lobster and we have now made lobster aspic. What we do is we cook off that lobster, large-dice it, take a little bit of scallion, a little bit of watercress, small-dice some chervil, blanch it, small-dice some chives, and blanch it. We combine the lobster aspic—we have probably seasoned it up high because it's going to be served cold—together with our lobster meat and our chervil, chives, put that into a terrine mold, triangular shape. And what was going to be thrown out has now turned into a lobster terrine that we can slice and make sixteen to twenty orders out of. Two small slices, serve it with a little bit of baby greens, a little bit of lobster-stock-reduction mayonnaise, and make back our money. A quick method if you already have a consommé. Total utilization."

I felt like clapping.

Our plated appetizers were due on Day Eight, and our table, Bianca and two others from a different Skills class, had been assigned the following menu:

> Chicken galantine with cranberry-orange coulis, wild rice and wild pecan rice salad with toasted-pecan vinaigrette, and pears poached in a port wine syrup.
>
> Lobster salad with mache, haricot verts, artichoke hearts, tomatoes, and truffles with truffle-oil vinaigrette.
>
> Shaved vegetable salad with olive oil, lemon juice, Parmesan, and black pepper.

These would be beautiful plates, the kinds you see in the pages of *Gourmet* magazine. Each of the six groups had its own menu. One, if not several, of these plates would float into a Day Eight Skills-kitchen gale of pots scorched with béchamel, bowls of chicken velouté, and clam chowder the consistency of oatmeal, as if out of a mirage.

The galantine was intriguing and worth mentioning, if only as an example of a forcemeat other than the de riguer pâté en croûte (Chef Ainsworth had defended this dowager of the buffet table by saying that if you could make this classical forcemeat preparation, you knew how to work with dough, forcemeat, and aspic, and you could put this basic knowledge to use in many ways). A galantine is typically a poultry forcemeat poached in gelatinous stock.

"Y'all?" We had gathered round for a demo. "Write this down: preparing a skin for a galantine." Chef Felder, who had spread before her on a cutting board the entire skin of a chicken in one continuous sheet, bumpy side down, with two little pant legs where the drumsticks had been, explained the preparation technique. She scraped the fat off the skin and squared it off, noting how very, very delicious chicken skin could be if you cooked it in a moderate oven until it became crispy enough to sprinkle over salad greens and sautéed chicken livers. She trimmed the pant legs, laid the skin on a sheet of plastic wrap to help with the rolling, and continued through the entire preparation of the galantine.

Our forcemeat, made from the marinated dark meat of the chicken, pork butt, and fatback, was spread in a long strip down the skin; we would lay two chicken breasts on top, then cover the breasts with the remaining forcemeat, into which we had mixed dried cherries and pistachios. We would wrap it all tightly in the chicken skin so that it formed a cylinder about nine inches long and about three inches in diameter. We would then secure the cylinder with cheesecloth and butcher's string. Chef Felder tied the string at both ends, then supported the cylinder in three places with more string, saying, "Little cummerbunds. Gentleman, you know what a cummerbund is—holds the tummy in."

"Not necessary, Chef," said Ben, serious as a marine.

We would poach our galantine in 170-degree chicken stock to an internal temperature of 160 degrees. We would cool it in the stock overnight, then remove it from the cheesecloth, paint it with glace, roll it in finely chopped pistachios, and then it was ready to slice. Each piece, rimmed in green, would contain a chunk of moist white chicken breast surrounded by forcemeat that was brightly dotted with red and green of cherry and pistachio, the secondary internal garnish. We would serve the slices with a bright cranberry-orange coulis, rice, and poached pears.

Not a recipe for the working, single parent of three, perhaps, but an intriguing classical preparation. "This is a basic galantine," Chef Felder said. "I want you to learn the technique first. Once you've got the technique, you've got the world by the toes."

After the chicken galantine—a two-day preparation—the lobster salad would be a no-brainer, or so I thought until the mache didn't show up in the order. Mache, a small light-green leaf at the end of a pale twisting stem, had a fresh delicate flavor perfectly paired with lobster, both in looks and taste. Without mache, we had no lobster salad.

I found Adam, food steward for this block. He said he'd ordered mache but hadn't seen it come in; we checked the order sheet, which showed the storeroom had filled this order. I went to the storeroom. They didn't know anything but promised to send the mache as soon as it came in. I explained the problem to Chef Felder upon my return and she went to the storeroom. She tangled with these folks all the time—this was how she got heirloom tomatoes, how she got both fresh sardines and very expensive anchovies packed in salt and imported from Italy.

She returned, subduing indignation, and said to me, "Mr. Metz has taken our box of mache."

The mache the Culinary bought was hydroponically grown by a nearby farmer and shipped in plastic bags inside sturdy brown boxes; it grows in dense bunches and these are intact when shipped. It's a beautiful product that's usually plentiful here, but with the summer break approaching, the storeroom had cut back on ordering perishables. Felder made another call, then gave me instructions. "I want you to go up to the functions office, across from Fish kitchen," she said quietly. I want you to pick out eight perfect, *beautiful* bunches of mache without disturbing it. Talk to Dora." Chef Felder told me to bring a half hotel pan with damp paper towels and reiterated that I was to gather the mache bunches as delicately as possible, so that one would scarcely notice their absence.

I assumed she'd worked all this out with Dora, who was in charge of filling Mr. Metz's order, but I'd failed to notice the subversive hush in her voice. When I arrived at the functions office I was met by a woman with dark hair wearing business attire. I had often seen this woman in the halls; I didn't know where she actually hailed from, perhaps Latin America, but she always reminded me of the spooky Malaysian matron who blackmails Betty Davis in *The Letter*. In real life she was probably as generous and kind as Mother Teresa—she always seemed friendly when she appeared in Pantry for Mr. Metz's utabaga, or popped into Coppedge's bakeshop to pick up Mr. Metz's sourdough. I told her I was looking for Dora.

"You're looking for Dora?" she said. "Well, that's me."

I said my name, explained I was from Chef Felder's kitchen, and that Chef Felder had told me she, Dora, would be able to help me out. I fully thought she would say, "Yes, I was expecting you," but instead she shook her head. "This is all we have." She pointed to a box on a rolling cart loaded with food. "We ordered from the storeroom two pounds and they sent us this." The box read two pounds. Dora removed its contents, two plastic bags filled with mache, and put them on the scale, which acted as a paperweight for Mr. Metz's order. Each bag weighed ten ounces, twelve ounces short of two pounds. She shook her head saying, "Mr. Metz doesn't mess around with boxes."

I asked if I might be able to remove—very delicately, one would scarcely notice—eight perfect, very very beautiful bunches.

She said no. But she told me to wait while she made a phone call.

An assistant appeared and began to go over the order being placed on the cart.

"Wouldn't it be possible for me to take just a little?" I asked the assistant. "Do you really need *all* this?"

The assistant said yes.

"Could we call Mr. Metz and find out if he needs all of this?"

The assistant smiled and said, "Sure, go ahead. Call him." This was clearly a dare.

"Would he be at home?" I said.

"He's probably still in his office."

Something told me then that it would not be cute if I called Mr. Metz's office asking how much mache he planned to use. But I kept trying anyway, for the heck of it, the paper toweling in my hotel pan growing dry.

"Is he using it now, tonight?" I asked.

"He's taking it with him."

"Where is he going?"

"I believe he's going to his home in Pennsylvania." This would make sense. We were one day away from a four-day Fourth of July weekend. I remained focused on the task at hand.

"It's summer," I said. "Mache is in season. Surely there's a farmer's market near his home in Pennsylvania where he can pick up some fresh-picked mache."

The assistant shook her head.

"Surely he can buy it somewhere."

She smiled at me, still shaking her head, and said, "I don't think he's been to a grocery store in his life!" Then she turned her head completely away from me, chuckling in disbelief at what she had just said. (Heaven forbid she would slander President Metz!) This was undoubtedly one great perquisite of being president of the Culinary Institute of America—having the Culinary storeroom at your disposal. I wouldn't spend much time in the Shoprite either.

"I only need eight tiny bunches. I'll settle for less."

More grave shaking of the head. I sensed she was growing weary of me, but I pressed on blindly. "Perhaps we could FedEx Mr. Metz some mache tomorrow."

This suggestion was not taken seriously. Dora returned, saying the storeroom was completely out of mache.

"I need just a little bit, and I need it by six o'clock."

"We need this by four o'clock, which is right now," and onto the cart went the box of mache, and off I was sent with my little empty hotel pan.

I began to beg at other kitchens. Chef Kief, in Pantry, had a box of mache, winced at its contents, and said, "I need all of this. This has to garnish fifty plates tomorrow." Then he sighed, pulled one bunch, pulled a second and a third, put his fingers on a fourth, then thought better of it and said, "That's really all I can spare." I wanted to say "Bless you," but I only thanked him.

When I returned and explained to Chef Felder what had happened, she rolled her eyes thinking, "If Mr. Metz knew that we needed it, he'd surely give up the few sprigs we needed," but she only sighed. She decided that we would do four lobster salads instead of eight.

I saw why she liked to use mache for this dish: she directed us to plate the appetizer with the lobster tail, in thick slices but apparently intact, as if the lobster were alive in a tangle of seaweedlike mache. The presentation was a good one, especially with the black truffle slices sprinkled on top in vivid contrast to the orange lobster. I had never peeled a truffle and asked Chef Felder how I should do it; as I watched her peel one—she had wrinkled her nose that we had to use canned—she said, "When you get fresh truffles, which are about eight hundred dollars a pound, store the truffles in rice. The rice pulls flavor out of the truffles. Then put two eggs into the rice and store it in a cooler. The eggs will absorb the flavor of the truffles. They breathe. And then here's what you do. You gently scramble those eggs. Gently, gently scramble those eggs and put them in the middle of the plate and serve them with pain de mie toast and champagne. It is a very romantic New Year's Eve supper for two." Having finished her story and her truffle, she departed.

Garde Manger students, outgoing students, ate on stage, as did incoming A Blockers, and students in the wines and menus block of the curriculum. Stage—the raised platform of the former chapel's alter—was served by the Classical Banquet Cuisine class, which prepared classical European cuisine; student waiters, in their first table-service class, used silverware to nestle fresh rolls onto your bread plate as you sat down, and they refilled your coffee after dinner. In our whites, we could at six-thirty have dinner on stage and be served, for instance, a mikado salad (rice with oysters), followed by game consommé, followed by osso buco with freshly made noodles.

Many students skipped stage altogether because it took too long (and left no time for a smoke afterward) or because they had had enough rich food. Adam never missed stage, nor did I, so I typically ate with him. Usually we talked about food, but this was also the only time outside class I had to hear how my old Skills class was doing and where they were headed.

Over a plate of poached sea bass Adam and Susanne talked about their externships. Adam had the night before called John Schenk at the Monkey Bar and found out that he got the job. Susanne had trailed at Gramercy Tavern and had gotten the externship there that she'd hoped for.

"I trailed at four places," Adam told her. "Lutèce—they didn't want me—Match, Oceana, and Monkey Bar. They didn't want me at Lutèce."

"Why?" I asked.

"I dunno. I called Eberhard and he said"—Adam intoned a deep German accent—" 'We have no positions available right now.' "

"What did you think of Oceana?" Susanne asked.

"I liked it a lot. I liked Rick, I liked Rad; he's the night sous chef."

Susanne said she'd heard the kitchen at Oceana was too macho. Adam said maybe, but Lutèce was more so. "At Lutèce," Adam said, "the poissonier burned himself while he was trying to plate about twenty plates at the same time. Everybody came all at once. He burned himself, and the sous chef said, 'If you're going to burn yourself, do it quietly. If you don't want to burn yourself, you shouldn't have become a cook.' " Adam chuckled and shook his head. "He wasn't anybody. He was the sous chef, he wasn't even the chef. He was just standing there expediting. He wasn't doing a thing."

One night I sat beside Eun-Jung, who picked mussels and scallops out of her coquilles St.-Jacques to drain off the sauce. "I miss Korean food," she said sadly. Too much butter and cream here. Of Garde Manger she said, "Reception food is not our culture. This is very new to me." Eun-Jung was not allowed to work in the United States, and thus not allowed to extern, so she would move straight into Introduction to Bread Baking after Garde Manger. When she returned to Korea the following spring, she hoped to work in fine hotels while she earned a master's degree; then she hoped to teach.

"Yeah, me too," Erica joined in. "That's what I want to do."

Erica would be heading south to Marcel Desaulniers's Trellis Restaurant and Cafe in Williamsburg, Virginia.

The subject of Adam's photography came up as we finished the sea bass, and waiters arrived to whisk the plates away. He often brought his camera to class and photographed finished plates. He said he hoped to photograph food not for magazines or cookbooks, but rather as fine art. "I think photography and food have a lot in common," he said.

"Such as?" I asked.

"Contrast," he said without hesitating. "Textures. Light and dark. Emotion."

"What emotion is in food?" I asked.

"Every emotion there is," he said.

"What emotion was in our sea bass?"

Adam smiled and shook his head. The fish had been overcooked, the sauce pale and weak.

A stranger at the table, listening to our conversation, said, "Hatred."

Adam said, "I have a thing for shooting people while they're eating." Adam explained that whenever he went to dinner parties, he carried a little disposable camera with him and photographed people as they were putting food into their mouth. "People don't really like it," he admitted. At home he had an entire envelope stuffed with negatives of such photos. He had not made a print of a single image. Apparently, it was the subversive act of the picture-taking that was important.

When Chef Felder introduced herself on Day One, she had done so in an uncommonly elegant way. She had begun by saying her name and origin and then, invoking the name of her mentor, Alice Waters and Waters's command that cooks must support the farmers near them, Felder told us about what she'd done the day before. She had gone to an organic strawberry farm and picked strawberries. She had then gone to a farm that grew peas, and she picked peas. From there she went to a farm that raised chickens and bought chickens that had been butchered that morning. She returned home, snagged some grape leaves, lettuce, and herbs from her garden, and, surprised by all this Hudson Valley bounty, asked six people to dinner. "That is what food is all about," she said. "Food is about community. It's about the earth and really taking care of the earth."

Erica sat spellbound—she had never heard such things before. She had never before considered that food had an emotional and philosophical element to it, and while Chef Pardus and Chef Smith and no doubt several other chefs had at least implied such ideas, something in Chef Felder made this knowledge accessible to Erica.

"Garde manger takes time," Chef Felder said to us. "Cooking . . . *takes time*. I don't care how much you like burning and turning on the line. If you don't take time to pay attention to details, you'll never be great cooks."

Sometimes I imagined that Chef Felder more or less materialized out of ether but when we met for an interview at her cubicle, she was huffing from the hike up four flights of stairs, clearly mortal and carrying a wrinkled brown paper sack filled with fresh new potatoes from a farm near her house, the dirt on them scarcely dry. I had asked to meet with her outside class to know her better and because I thought she might have unusual thoughts on what made a good cook, how one became a good cook. Ratios, of course. Ratios had to be grafted into your bones. Technique, the physical skill, skills of the craft, combined with the knowledge of how food behaves, that too. And experience. But there was something more, and I hoped Chef Felder might lead me there.

Eve Felder grew up in the "low country" of Charleston, South Carolina, within a family that loved food and cooking. She knew all along that she wanted to cook, but her parents insisted she get a college degree. After she received her bachelor's in psychology from the College of Charleston, she found that her desire to cook remained. "I always wanted to cook," she explained, "but, you see, I was a Southern *lady*, and cooking was *domestic* work." She would therefore receive no encouragement from her parents here; she learned to cook by herself and eventually, through sheer determination, found her place at Chez Panisse.

"I learned so much," she said, referring to the seminal chef-farmer restaurant. "Mostly that you need to develop relationships with farmers. At Chez Panisse, we bought our fish from Paul Johnson. Paul worked at the restaurant when he was younger and they've been buying fish from him for twenty years. Alice helped set him up. Steven Sullivan, with Acme Bakery, used to bake in the restaurant. Now he makes a lot of money in a bakery and provides bread for the restaurant twice a day. Most of all I learned that what is most important is to maintain those relationships so that you are building community within your restaurant as well as outside your restaurant. And that the bottom line is: what does the food *want*?

"What does the food *want*? What does it taste like in its unadulterated form? As young chefs, you'll notice, certainly in my class, I have a group that wants to continue to add more and more ingredients to something—they want to smoke this, they want to do that—well, in fact, these potatoes are going to be delicious with just a little bit of sherry-shallot vinaigrette and roasted garlic. They are going to be *delicious*. And I think what they need as young chefs is to taste the food for what it is, and not to impose their ego upon it, but be with it. What does it need, and do I have the technique and taste buds yet to *know* what it needs? Taste it. I try to say, 'Taste it, taste it.' I will not use recipes because it needs to be tasted.

"To taste," she continued. "Most important is to teach students to taste, and expand their taste buds, to get them to know that when you buy olive oil it's not about buying a brand of olive oil, it's about tasting ten different olive oils and *choosing* the one that you're going to use. Comparative tasting. Just because your child hates foie gras or your child hates caviar, I mean the child inside of you that has never had it—it's an *acquired taste*—as a chef, you need to learn to distinguish what's good. You may not like beets because you haven't had the best beets, but for pete's sake, don't turn yourself off."

It was a beautiful July noon and we'd taken a seat at a table on the St. Andrew's terrace. Craig Edwards, the St. Andrew's fellow, appeared to ask if he could get us something to drink. Craig told me he was infatuated with Chef Felder. She had "this incredible aura," he said. When he brought us some sparkling water, Chef Felder, in her best Southern-lady accent, said, "Well, I'm honored," and Craig beamed.

I narrowed the focus to Garde Manger. What in this class was fundamental to a cook's education?

"One is to teach the students formulas," she said, "so that they are working from basic ratios rather than recipes, and from that basic formula, how to taste whether or not it's good. I truly believe in using ratios. And then once you have a foundation you can start going crazy. But until you know that one cup of flour and one egg will make pasta, and until you know that one cup of oil and one egg yolk will make a cup of mayonnaise, until it's ingrained in your head, then you are tied to a recipe book that's going to have various formulas that may or may not be true because they are not necessarily written by someone who has the technique. . . . A simple syrup. If you can take a cup of fruit, and you add a half a cup of sugar to that and let it sit overnight, it's going to release all its juices, and you bring that up to a simmer, and when the fruit is tender, remove the fruit; reduce the juice down to the consistency you want by checking it on a plate. I mean you can then make preserves and jam, you have freedom. . . . Professionally you need to know those techniques so that you are liberated to do whatever you want to do."

Clearly, part of food passion is a relentless curiosity. Chef Felder was the sort of person who did not simply read about foie gras, for instance. She would travel to the Dordogne region in France and spend several days on a farm that raised ducks and geese for foie gras, observing the entire process, from the forced feeding to slaughter.

"As a chef," she explained, "I need to know how to cure a leg of pro-sciutto—it's an inquisitive mind—how to cure a belly of pork to make pancetta or to make bacon, so that I understand the basics of cooking. What is it that this person in the south of France does? How do they make a jambon bayonne? I want to know how to do that. No one can tell me this. I know what it's like to force-feed a duck now. I know what it's like to kill a quail. I know what it's like to kill and clean a squab. I know what it's like to take down a full pig, to take down a full lamb. I'm not queasy about that, I can't be. Because that's the connection of working with food."

I asked Felder if she thought great cooking was innate or could be learned.

"This is the million-dollar question," she said, "and I get in so much trouble with this one. I believe that cooking is a craft. And it's a craft that can be taught, it's a skill that can be taught. I do not believe it's an art. I think that if you have a good positive attitude and drive and focus and have your eyes set on a goal, then you can be trained to cook. If the passion is there. You have to have that passion, because it's hard work, it's hard on your body. It's hard. It's very physical."

The difficulty of work, I sensed, partly contributed to a macho ethic in the kitchen. And it tended to produce, as far as I could see, a fair share of lunatics. I used lunatics, I explained, in the best way—lunacy, moonstruck.

"I do not like working in an all-female kitchen," she said, "and I *do* not like working in an all-male kitchen. We feel like different species, we per-ceive the world totally, totally differently, and the beauty of that is to work in harmony, because the males are going to contribute something that only they can contribute, and the females are going to contribute something that only they can contribute. Wow! It's outstanding! And if you have a whole male environment, it becomes a bunch of goats trying to get to the top of the mountain and kicking everybody off!"

She laughed loudly.

"I'm going through in my head and thinking about chefs I admire, and would I say it's lunacy? I would say it is. It verges on a bit of an obsession. . . . If you have a passion for food then it's not only your life and your avocation but it's also your vocation and maybe that's the lunacy." She smiled thoughtfully. "Yeah, it can be a little whacky."

W e would break for the Fourth of July weekend (after an ice-carving class, picks, chisels, and chain saws ripping away in the ice-carving shed out back by the Dumpsters), and return to prepare immediately for Grand Buffet, a three-day operation. Felder's Grand Buffet philosophy combined a highly stylized main platter with casual, eccentric side platters. One team, for instance, prepared pork tenderloin pâté en croûte, turkey mousseline with smoked pork tenderloin, and a foie-gras-and-sweetbread terrine for their main platter, while grilled vegetables with a grape-leaf salsa and herbed flat bread with romescu sauce—an outstanding Spanish base sauce made from roasted tomatoes and ancho chilis—spread across their side platters. Contrived and casual, classical and modern.

My table's assignments were salmon mousseline pâté en croûte (each table was required to do a pâté en croûte), saffron mousseline and scallop terrine, and a salmon-and-lemon terrine. Our side platters would be ricotta-and-Parmesan-filled ravioli with a cherry tomato vinaigrette and salmon pastrami. Each table was required to write down and compile all the recipes that went into their platter; these would be graded. In all, about seventy-five recipes would be executed for Grand Buffet.

Chef Felder, the day before, commanded all to work clean, look good, be professional. "You're representing the CIA. Pres Metz will bring the graduation speaker through," she said, then reminded us that for tomorrow we needed "impeccably clean jackets" (Erica would have to buy a new one), "no apron, no gloves, no side towel." She led us through the journey from our downstairs kitchen to Alumni Hall, pointing out danger spots where trays can be upended by unforeseen door openings and corners.

"I want you to taste everything," she continued. "If you've never had fresh sardines before, taste the damn things." A friend and cook in New

York City had told her where she could get her hands on fresh sardines; Felder got the storeroom to work on obtaining the order, and she concocted an intriguing side platter of grilled sardines wrapped in grape leaves. Adam, who did the grilling, said this was a nuisance because the heads kept wanting to fall off. "President Metz will come by and ask you questions," Chef Felder continued. " 'How do you make a mousseline?' 'What's the difference between a mousseline and a mousse?' 'What temperature did you cook your mousseline to?' If he stops in front of you, regain your composure and answer him. Don't panic. You will panic, but regain your composure and answer. He's a very, very nice man and he's very proud of this stuff." Felder was perched high on several stacked stools, and with her toque extending her height, knees up high, she seemed like an odd Cheshire cat expounding in her ecstatic way on food. "We have a big day tomorrow. We have the Grand Buffet. We have the president's reception. We have *Gourmet* in here watching us. We're also having a foie gras tasting. Taste the relish with it. It's very good, but just a little bit to balance the richness of the foie gras."

A photographer and art director from *Gourmet* magazine, which was preparing an article on the CIA's fiftieth anniversary, did appear to photograph some of the more ornate and visually dazzling pâtés and terrines, lending our exercises an increased air of importance. At six P.M., we carried our platters, all checked by Chef Felder, to Alumni Hall, where two long rows of tables waited. Beyond us, giant mirrors served as platters for Patisserie classes. In the wings, Intro, Fish, and Oriental kitchens set their serving stations. A line formed at the doors; no one was allowed in until Mr. Metz—who in a few months would be judging the culinary olympics in Frankfurt—arrived to survey each platter, ask questions, point out errors, praise, and more or less sanctify the occasion as he did every third week without fail.

"Very nice, very nice," he said in all but a whisper as he viewed our platter. His eye moved to each item, locked on it for a moment, then moved to the next. He asked Ben Grossman, "Where are you doing your extern?" Ben said, "La Grenouille." He caught an error in one group's platter, a pâté overlapping in the wrong direction. Only after he had surveyed every platter in both Garde Manger classes, both Patisserie classes, and the items from Intro to Oriental, did the doors open and a stream of students and faculty pour in carrying plates and asking questions about what we'd prepared.

In an hour, after all had eaten, we returned with our beautiful platters—

many of them full, to be dumped in the recyclable bin—and we cleaned the kitchen. The following day, we took inventory of kitchen supplies, cleaned it thoroughly, cleared out the coolers and walk-in, took a final exam, and departed one by one as we completed the test. Erica finished the test before I did. I watched her, recalling the flaming roux and scrambled eggs. She was becoming a good cook. The door closed behind her, but she peeked through the window for one last glance, just her head visible through the small frame, and waved good-bye to me.

The class would spread out through the entire country for externship and would not be back till the blizzards of January struck again.

It was for me a peculiar sensation, watching the school that never stopped empty and shut down. Now, it felt very much like a school, with school's seasonal rhythm, the acute sense of transition and growth. As I walked to my car in the vast parking lot in the bright warm evening, I found myself missing my Skills class, remembering Chef Pardus (safely landed by then in São Paulo), his voice still clear in my head—*This is your Skills kitchen for the next six weeks, keep it clean; notice my fingers are curled, I'm not gonna cut myself, I'm not goin' to the nurse, I'm not goin' to the hospital, I got other things to do!*—and wanting some sort of closure for it all. But there was rarely closure in this business, and there was no closure here at the Culinary. Service was over, the kitchens were clean. Everyone, almost all solitary, packed and left the campus.

And I thought about Felder's final message to the class—or plea, rather—to be responsible for the earth as much as we could possibly be; examine whether or not herbicides affected our water supply, find out if our agriculture will sustain us, care about what we dump in the ocean. We were on the banks of the once bountiful Hudson River, a literal example of her warning. General Electric had all but killed it with chemical sludge, and while it was once again showing signs of life, huge concentrations of toxic PCBs still contaminated the river bottom. "Care about the earth," she said, "it's what our livelihoods are *based* on." She was right. If we completely screw up the earth, we'll have rotten food.

Externship

Adam Shepard got a long weekend off after Garde Manger and began work as a lunch-line cook in mid-July at the Monkey Bar on East Fifty-fourth Street in Manhattan. Adam worried that lunch would be less interesting than dinner—again, lunch, the poor stepchild of real food. About a week later, Adam said to his wife Jessica, "I think I love my job." This was an eyebrow-raising statement, according to Jessica. "I haven't heard Adam use the word love for anything," she said.

"It's nutso," Adam told me. "Absolutely fuckin' nuts. Today, from quarter to one till two, we probably did a hundred thirty lunches. We-got-*slammed. Hammered.* Absolutely unbelievable." Adam had shown up for work on a Tuesday and was alone on his station by Friday. He loved it, admired the chef, John Schenk, but people were still taking his tongs when he needed them. I wondered if it were the ghost of Eun-Jung. "Fuckin' Tony does it," Adam said. "Tony the grill cook takes my tongs all the time. If there were six tongs on our one oven door, he'd wind up with all of them. He just puts them down wherever he goes. He'll take a bunch of fries out of the fryer, put his tongs down, grab some salt, walk over to his station, leave his tongs behind him, then grab another pair, and then I don't have any."

Adam, dressed in jeans and a T-shirt, carrying coffee mug and a knapsack, arrived at the Monkey Bar at seven-forty-five, having taken the

F train from his home in Brooklyn. He descended the stairway to the cavernous basement below the restaurant. I followed. He grabbed a pair of pants and a jacket from the laundry room, handed me the same, and we changed in a dark ancient locker room, long and narrow. The lockers were marked with graffiti. He removed a chef's knife, a small Chinese cleaver, and a serving spoon from his black briefcase, closed his locker, and headed to his station. The first thing he did was turn on all the ovens. He set out a bain-marie for tools. He got me slicing celery root first while he looked for the key to the walk-in and the only twelve-ounce ladle in the kitchen ("It's exactly one order of soup," he explained).

I'd asked Chef Schenk if I might trail Adam for a couple days. Schenk chuckled and said, "Sure, I don't mind." Adam didn't mind either since I could help with his mise en place.

"A lot of mise en place," Adam told me. "Like crazy amounts of mise en place. Cutting and cooking and setting up and just all kinds of stuff. I have to dice peppers, mince shallots, and then I have to take the corn off five ears of corn; I have to small-dice a large handful of haricots verts; I have to fry a ton of julienned leeks, I have to make probably fifteen pounds of mashed potatoes. I have to make eighteen potato cakes; I have to prep asparagus for soup, sauté half a case of oyster mushrooms; I have to fill all the oil bottles, refill the stock bottles, set up my bain-marie with all my sauces, bring the soup up to temperature, cut potatoes for the soup set, prepare the meat for the soup set, pick thyme for the chef; and I have to cut shallots for the chef as well, along with a bunch of miscellaneous other things, like I have to clean and slice and fry four celery roots for celery-root chips for the cod plate."

Adam got to work on the potato pancakes, using last night's mashed potatoes and two old baked potatoes, a big handful of chopped sage, butter, and cream, all of it bound with flour. He molded them to the size of a baseball, flattened each to about an inch thick, and cooked them on an electric flattop. These would serve as the base for his pan-roasted chicken, huge chicken breasts that he'd sear off in butter and olive oil at around eleven.

Vinnie Flauto, the thirty-one-year-old A.M. sous chef from Atlantic City, had arrived an hour after Adam and did not seem to be in a good mood. "I'm sick of this fucking shit," he said. "I've got to make this sauce and I have no wine. This is a fucking restaurant and I have no wine." A woman from the front of the house eventually got him two bottles and he dumped them into a giant kettle.

Generally though, there wasn't much talking, just cutting. As Adam had said, a lot of mise en place to get through. I'm not sure why, but I was surprised by how much like a CIA kitchen this was. It was 90 percent mise en place. It would take all morning and by service Adam's station would be set with frisé, grilled white potatoes, oven-dried cherry tomatoes, haricots verts, a ratatouille of diced haricots, corn, red pepper, and roasted carrots, and plastic containers filled with roasted carrot strips, cooked Swiss chard, julienned leeks, and containers of small towels, rolled and soaking in water to wipe plates, and still more containers of dill, chives, rosemary, asparagus, and diced carrots. A bowl of mashed potatoes covered with waxed butter wrappers. Steak sauce, chicken sauce, barbecue sauce for the salmon, and lamb jus, all of which he kept in a hotel-pan water bath.

"I saw Susanne yesterday," I told Adam as I brunoised red pepper for his ratatouille, which went with the lamb chops. I'd stopped by to say hello to Susanne and see how she was liking Gramercy Tavern.

"Spellacy?" Adam asked, excited.

"Yeah."

"Did you work there?"

"No."

"Did you eat?"

"No."

"Aw, man," Adam said.

Susanne was on desserts and the first thing *she* did after changing was make caramel for the peach Tatin. She made a blackberry and blueberry compote, mascerated raspberries with sugar and thyme. She made peanut brittle and a cornmeal pound cake. Claudia, the pastry chef, wanted everything very fresh, Susanne said, so each day she began anew. Susanne gave me a tour of the kitchens, the walk-ins, then her station. She ducked into a lowboy to show me a little white espresso mug filled with a gelled mixture of buttermilk, cream, and sugar, an old Italian country-style dessert she called panna cotta. "James Carville had one of these today, and *I* made it," she told me with aggressive pleasure.

She showed me the dessert menus. Reviewing it, I said, "So this is your day."

"That is my life," she said. And she liked it. "I'm all alone," she said. "It's kinda like Pardus. You're all alone, it's a lot of production, plenty of room." She was relying heavily on McGee to figure out how and why her sugar was behaving as it did.

Ben Grossman was on the *amuse bouche* station at La Grenouille. First couple days he was there he was making terrines and mousses. "Just like we did in Garde Manger class," he said with surprise. "Same ratios and everything. They do a caper-and-foie-gras terrine. They did a cauliflower mousse and we made them into quenelles and served them with cumin oil and basil oil. They were all right; there was a little too much cumin flavor. But I was like, 'Hey, I know how to do that. No, really, I know how to do that. I can do that, no problem.' Same way we did it in class."

Monkey Bar chef John Schenk arrived shortly before twelve. Schenk, named one of the ten best new chefs of 1995 by *Food & Wine* magazine, had *staged* in Paris, worked four years under Alfred Portale at Gotham Bar and Grill, been executive chef at two restaurants before the Monkey Bar, and would soon move downtown to head the kitchen of Clementine. Forty-one years old, he had been a cook for twenty years and busyness swirled around him, even when the kitchen wasn't busy. He was tall, had dark short hair, wore a bandanna during service (as Adam had taken to doing). I asked him about Adam. "I wasn't going to hire him," Schenk told me. "I don't know why I did. His schedule just happened to work out perfectly." Schenk shook his head. "But he's really come into his own. He had plenty of training and he thinks. That's good."

"He thinks," I repeated.

Schenk said, "Let's just say this business isn't filled with Einsteins."

I asked him why he hired externs (he himself had no formal culinary education). He said they were a good deal. Cheap labor, available when you want them, they show up, they can fill in anywhere, and they speak English. (Externs typically earn seven dollars an hour or so, but can earn as much as twelve or as little as nothing.)

When I asked Vinnie how Adam was doing, he reiterated Schenk's concerns, then grew protective of Adam and told me how wonderful he was.

John Schenk was a hands-on executive chef and this impressed Adam. "He's there *all* the fuckin' time," Adam told me. "He comes in at twelve o'clock, gets behind the line at twelve-thirty, does lunch. At two-thirty, three o'clock, he splits for maybe an hour; then he comes back and does all the inventory and puts together the order sheet and he gets behind the line at five-thirty, cooks dinner, and after dinner he does the prep sheets for the next day and goes home."

And so it was today. Adam began the soup sets at twelve-twenty-five, placing diced potato, asparagus tips, and leeks into bowls ready for the asparagus soup, and soon Schenk, moving onto the line between Vinnie and Adam, started calling out orders and cooking. Lunch is fast, "a free fall," as Schenk put it. By twelve-forty, orders were coming out as fast as ticker tape, and in an instant Schenk had two long white rows of tickets dangling from the service shelves above his station.

"Ordering two monk," Schenk called, turning back and forth to the oven behind him, cooking as he expedited. "Ordering a soup, fire crab, pick up the tuna. Cook cook cook. Ordering chicken. Fire ravioli, fire two paillards medium, firing a monk, fire squid." And the runners circled down into the kitchen and back up the stairs with giant trays above their shoulders.

At one point, mid-service, a tad weeded and trying to keep straight in his head what he'd ordered and what he'd fired, he looked up from a sea of tickets with a breezy smile and said, "Why don't we just fire every fucking table, solve all our problems." Then he cooked some more, Adam beside him a blur of motion.

"Ordering a double," Schenk said. "Pop three chickens." Adam had them ready above the oven on sizzle platters and spun to put them in the oven. "Let's pick up a chicken, four bass, and a tuna," Schenk said.

When it was over, Adam seemed disappointed. "By the time you get in the groove, it's over." Adam hadn't gotten out of there until six-thirty, the night before, prepping P.M.'s new menu—chopping and searing oyster, cremini, chanterelle, morel, and shiitake mushrooms, and chorizo—nearly eleven hours after he'd arrived. He would be here late again this night, searing more mushrooms. He liked the hours, the hot-and-heavy service, but he was looking forward to returning to the Culinary the following January. There was still a lot to learn.

Meanwhile Travis worked the P.M. line at the Duck Club in Kansas City, where he'd cooked for, among others, Marcus Allen and Steve Bono of the Kansas City Chiefs. Lola had gotten a job at the Rainbow Room and the job would pass in a blink. When they returned five months later it would seem as if they'd never left. School went on. Every three weeks, seventy-two students would graduate and seventy-two students would begin Introduction to Gastronomy, as the same number left for and returned from externship. Erica would be back from her externship at the Trellis, older and more skilled; by the time she was back in a hot kitchen she was not only a competent student, she was a desirable partner to have because of her speed and proficiency.

And her old friend Dave had one of the most interesting externs of all—a job at Michel Richard's Citronelle in Georgetown, working under head chef Larbi Darouche, who had worked under Jean-Louis Palladin at Jean-Louis at the Watergate Hotel. This was the big time. Dave was doing prep work his first day when Darouche asked him if he wanted to help out with a banquet for eighty people. Dave would never dream of saying no, of course, though it would take him out of the kitchen. As it turned out, Dave found himself at a swank Washington club. Larbi's buddy, Jean-Louis Palladin, stopped by to help out. As did Richard. So, on his first day of externship, David Scott, veteran of Michael Pardus's Skills class, worked a banquet with Michel Richard on his right and Jean-Louis Palladin on his left. He spilled mashed potatoes on Richard's shoe.

Part IV

Second Year

⚜ Thermal Death Point

I arrived shortly before six A.M. on Day One and hung back in the hallway outside Bakeshop Two as sleepy students materialized in the hall, their first day back from externship. A couple were lively enough to offer happy exclamations upon being reunited with friends, but the hall was mainly quiet. Chef Richard Coppedge strode into his bakeshop and locked the door behind him. A few people muttered questions about which chef that was and which class they were in—we were evenly divided among pastry and bread—and at six on the nose, Chef Coppedge's head emerged from the doorway and he said, "O.K."

Chef Coppedge, a bone-thin giant black man, baked bread. According to Chef Shepard, he had galvanized the entire bread-baking program, which had apparently been stuck for years in hard-roll hell. I often used Chef Pardus as a sounding board before I moved into a new kitchen. "I happen to like him," Pardus said when I asked about Coppedge. "Some people don't like him. *Everyone* respects the hell out of him." Pardus concluded simply: "He's the bread guru." And Marcus Färbinger, former pastry chef of Le Cirque and now a team leader for curriculum and instruction, told me that when Coppedge showed faculty and students what you could do with bread, overt passion for bread became possible. Coppedge had made bread cool.

We filed in. Chef Coppedge stood at the door examining each of us as we entered. "You need black shoes," he said to a student who wore black canvas sneakers with white trim. Come back when you have them."

"I don't have any," the student said.

Coppedge shook his head. "Get some by tomorrow." He notified all those with long sideburns to get rid of them. Anyone with fingernails, cut them. "Your hands are in the dough all the time," he said.

When all were in the bakeshop he said, "You've got till tomorrow to be in code. These are not my rules, they're the school's rules, so don't gripe at me. If I've got to do it, you've got to do it. If it were up to me, I'd have a beard, I'd be wearing shorts, and baking bread. But there has to be some continuity."

"Welcome back from externship," Chef Coppedge said, then paused. "We'll be making all the bread for the entire school for lunch. As you know, this place goes on no matter what. It has to. So turn to page thirty-three and let's get mixing."

And that was all the welcome there was time for. Some of the students had returned to Hyde Park as recently as last night. Some had been gone the requisite eighteen weeks, others longer, until they'd saved enough money for the second half of the program. Josh had been gone eighteen months. A guy named Jerry had worked in the test kitchen of *Cooking Light* magazine in Birmingham, Alabama. He hoped to go into journalism after graduation seven months from now. Another student named Ross had been on the line at Gramercy Tavern while Ruth Reichl, restaurant critic for *The New York Times*, was reviewing the restaurant. He made three dishes that went to Reichl's table, everyone at her table having ordered tasting menus. This was exciting, Ross said. The cooks found out what she looked like—if they didn't already know—after Patrick Clark, chef at Tavern on the Green who had recently been skewered and roasted by Reichl, had sent a copy of her picture with a description of what the woman could do to your restaurant to every restaurant in New York. An exaggeration perhaps, but Gramercy Tavern had Clark's letter pinned to the board "like a wanted poster," Ross said. He had seen the same letter in the kitchen of the Union Square Cafe. Serving Reichl wasn't different from serving anyone else, Ross said, except that for Reichl, you tasted everything twice before sending it out. After Reichl gave the restaurant and chef Tom Colicchio three stars, little changed because they'd been booked to capacity every night anyway.

Anthony had externed at the Hudson River Club under Chef Waldy Malouf and now answered "Oui, Chef!" to every instructor out of habit; he was threatened with termination if he didn't respond this way in Malouf's kitchen. Steve had externed at a restaurant outside Cleveland that I had once written about; Steve called returning to the Culinary "a necessary evil."

And Jason Dante had been at a hotel in Dallas, cooking starch for five months, and was glad to be back in school. Dante was from West Monroe, Louisiana. He pronounced it MON-roe. He said "own" for "on" and "earl" for "oil." Chef Coppedge had hardly begun before Dante spoke: "Question of the day, Chef. Do we get to eat what we cook?"

"We're not cooking, we're *baking*," Coppedge said, and that was all the answer Dante got.

Our first stop was the oblique mixer, which could handle two hundred pounds of dough. We would get lean dough number one mixing first. A different team would be responsible for lean dough number one each day. At six A.M. that team would put thirty-six pounds of water into the giant Hobart mixer and dissolve eighteen ounces of fresh yeast in it, then dump in forty-five pounds of high-gluten flour, nine pounds of organic wheat flour, and more than a pound of salt. This would give us a little more than ninety-two pounds of dough. Coppedge wanted his bread doughs kept at 70–75 degrees, something one could regulate by water temperature; Coppedge knew what the temperature of the water should be each day from the feel of the room.

Once the first lean dough was mixing, Coppedge said, "I know you're used to cooking. Cooking is a mad dash. Baking is different. Baking is regimented. It is disciplined."

One noticed the differences between a kitchen and a bakeshop immediately. This bakeshop, located in the Continuing Education building across from Roth Hall, was large, quiet, and cool, with five rows of wood workstations, or benches. There were no stoves, only ovens. The majority of the ingredients were kept in large rolling bins labeled "white rye," "dark rye," "coarse rye," "King Arthur all-purpose," "90% organic," "bleached all-purpose," "stone ground whole wheat," "bran," "1st clear," "cake," "milk powder," "durham," "pumpernickle."

One felt an ease in this bakeshop that did not exist in a kitchen. In a bakeshop, you only put things together; you did not break, tear, or cut things apart first. In a kitchen, everything was about speed, and you could regulate that speed by moving faster, cutting faster. Here, everything was determined by flour and yeast, and you had to accept that. In America, a land of durable wheat, ingredients are measured in relation to flour (in France they are measured in relation to water). No matter how much lean dough we'd make, the starting formula was the same: 100 percent flour, 60 percent water, 3 percent fresh yeast, and 2 percent salt. This was called the Baker's Percentage.

The names of major appliances in a bakeshop were named for their effect on yeast. The refrigerator was neither a cooler nor a reach-in, but instead a retarder; cool temperatures slow yeast. You let dough rise in a proof box. The very term "proof"—letting the dough rise—was in fact a term that originated when bakers needed to prove their yeast was alive, gobbling dough and releasing the gases that leaven the bread.

Here was the crux of the matter: yeast was alive. We would always be working with something that was actively responding to its environment. "A dough waits for no one," Coppedge would say. "Dough is alive until we bake it. Steak has no opinions. This has an opinion until we bake it."

Each team of three or four people would be responsible for a different dough. While we would follow recipes, and there were general proofing times and baking times, Coppedge explained, "I'd rather you look at it, listen to it, watch it, see what happens." Coppedge could tell a dough was properly mixed by the sound it made in the mixer. He cut a chunk of lean dough and began to spread it with his long fingers into a square. When we could stretch the dough so that it would become almost translucent and not tear, he taught us, we had developed a good dough.

"The dough is in your hands," he said. "It's not like you're sautéing. You're not using a knife. It's in your hands. It's alive. You work with it, it works with you."

"It's very romantic stuff," Dante said.

Chef Coppedge said, "That's why my wife married me."

Because yeast is alive, it's possible to overlook the substance without which yeast would be irrelevant: gluten. Here one needed only to turn to the pages of the redoubtable McGee for imaginative explanation. Flour contains many substances—starch, enzymes, sugars, lipids—all rather prosaic constructions. "The one exception," McGee writes, "is the proteins which, when mixed with water, form that remarkable substance we call gluten." He defines gluten, which is not water-soluble, as "the gumlike residue that remains after you have chewed on a piece of raw dough for a few minutes." Without it there would be no such thing as raised bread. Gluten is a network of proteins strong and flexible enough to expand without breaking and therefore contain gas as it is released by our helpful fungi. The more flexible the dough, the more gas it can retain; the more gas, the bigger the volume and finer the texture.

When you read about bread, whether in McGee or any other book that examined the science of the stuff, it sounded terrifically complicated, what with the gluten forming, yeast consuming carbohydrates and releasing carbon dioxide and ethanol, starch gelatinizing at 140 degrees, protein coagulating at 160 degrees. This was not the simple staff of life we had always considered it to be.

For Chef Coppedge bread was an enormously complex physical system and simple at the same time. The man lived bread. When Coppedge took a vacation, he relaxed by traveling to Boise, Idaho, and baking bread with his friend and former student, Gary Ebert, who opened the Zeppole Bakery. When they were not baking bread, they talked about baking bread. The kind of bread they discussed was called artisan bread, which Coppedge said accounted for about 5 percent of all bread consumed in the United States. Most of the bread sold in the United States is white, presliced, and stacked on grocery store shelves in colorful plastic bags. Artisan bread had become enormously popular recently, but, as Coppedge said, "You've got to sell a lot of bread to make a little money."

Chef Coppedge, forty years old, received his culinary education at Johnson & Wales immediately after high school and returned to that school to teach after working throughout the East Coast as a baker and pastry chef; he had been at the Culinary for four years and had been baking for fifteen years. Every now and then he felt an urge to move to Idaho permanently to bake bread with Ebert, but he knew that he was a teacher as well as a baker. Also, Coppedge said, "I like that oven there." The Culinary had installed in his bakeshop a magnificent hearthstone deck oven—three tiers of refractory cement, two meters deep; two tiers were gas-heated, one electrically heated, and all included steam injection and were computer-controlled. The steam was crucial for great crust. He had never had access to such a good hearth. "You can just leave me here forever," he said.

As a bread-baking skills instructor, Coppedge taught two things, mixing dough ("I can hear it from across the room") and fermentation.

Mixing, even with the aid of the massive Hobarts (in olden times, Coppedge said, bakers didn't need to use salt; the dough became salty from the sweat of the people kneading huge quantities of dough), was not a simple combining of ingredients. Yeast, crumbled into the water, must be dispersed evenly. Flour was added and immediately the water began to bind with it; gluten began to form, and yeast began to feed on the carbohydrates in the flour. The salt, added next, tended to slow the yeast down. If the day were cool and dry and you began with cool water, you could mix the dough long and slow and develop the glutens nicely. But the very act of mixing the dough heated it, as did the gobbling yeast. If the day were hot and humid, you'd want to watch the dough carefully. Coppedge taught us to mix dough not by direction, but rather by "looking at it, feeling it, hearing it." The behavior of dough varied because it was alive. And it would stay alive until it had nothing left to eat or you brought it to 138 degrees. This was called the Thermal Death Point for *Saccharomyces cerevisiea*.

Fermentation was what made bread baking a science and an art, Coppedge said. Raised dough began with the "chance contamination by airborne yeasts," according to McGee, probably in Egypt around 4000 B.C. Today this is the method chosen by artisans, and it's called sourdough; sourdough is not a flavor (throughout most of history, sour bread was as desirable as sour wine). One allows a mixture of equal parts flour, which likely has yeast on it already, and water to become contaminated by yeast in the air; at room temperature, these yeasts feed on the flour and reproduce; if you keep adding more flour and water to this slack dough, the yeast culture will grow, feasting on carbs and releasing gas, leaving lactic and acetic acids in its wake. McGee says American sourdough began in California when gold miners had no access to yeast and had to use leftover dough to start a new fermentation. The air in San Francisco, the city now associated with sourdough, will, it is said, create a different-tasting starter than the air in Hyde Park. Some practitioners of the form believe that the sourdough starters have nuances as rich as wines, depending on where they are from and how old they are. Good sourdoughs will have a deeper, more complex flavor than loaves made from commercial yeast.

When I talked to Chef Coppedge about bread, hoping to get a sense of the spirit of his work, the spirit of baking, and what distinguished it, he spoke of "putting the microflora to work . . ." but trailed off there, reverentially. Sourdough was, he said, "the pinnacle"—I assumed of bread making, but he trailed off again. Whenever I asked him to locate the source of his passion, he could scarcely finish a sentence, so ineffable was the notion of leavened bread. Chef Coppedge stopped naming his sourdough starters after friends' dogs, he said, but his oldest starter dated to February 8, 1985. There was a bit of a scare last block when one of his students used the entire starter by mistake in one of the doughs. Coppedge called his wife. They rent a house on twenty-eight acres in neighboring Staatsburg and he'd put a spare sample of that starter in the barn a while back. He hadn't touched it in years. His wife retrieved the sample, drove it down to the Culinary, and met her husband in front of the school. Liquid had risen to the top, but Coppedge poured that off and the starter was still good; the yeast was dormant, still alive. We would continue to build it daily with equal parts rye and wheat flour.

Losing the starter would not be the same as losing a great old cabernet vine—Coppedge said the main thing was to have starter available when you needed it—but he did believe that the acids in the starter became more refined over time, as with wines and cheeses, and he was glad his eleven-year-old starter would continue to live on.

"If I could make bread every day like that, I would," he told the class. "I wouldn't use any baker's yeast whatsoever, but for the time we have, the number of days, it's very difficult to work in. In fact, this is the way most artisan bakers are going. Most people agree that the bread has a different flavor. So what are we doing? We're going back to the way breads were made before yeast was fabricated. We're going full circle, toward less refined foods, whole foods."

Once the dough was mixed, it was fermented, usually in white plastic tubs or as a giant expanding blob covered with plastic wrap on one of the benches. We would then fold the dough over to release gas and redistribute the yeast to fresh food supplies, and scale the dough, dividing it into the weight Chef Coppedge wanted. It would then rest before we shaped it.

Shaping, whether we were making baguettes for the Escoffier Room or hoagies for the Walk-In, an on-campus deli, was a skill that took practice. The main idea was to fold the dough over on itself and seal it with the heel of your hand, folding again, banging with the heel of your palm to pinch the fold shut, until you had a long thin tube. This shaping created the internal structure of the loaf. Chef Coppedge would demo various shapes. On Day One he demoed ciabatta, Italian for slipper. One simply pulled on a pound of dough till it was a long flat oval. When it had proofed one last time, it would be stippled with one's fingers, brushed with olive oil, and sprinkled with kosher salt, then shot into the oven.

This bakeshop had a machine that rolled baguettes, but we usually rolled the baguettes by hand. Chef Coppedge rolled beautiful baguettes. Once he had constructed the tube of dough and had a perfectly straight seam along the bottom, he rolled it out to lengthen it and tighten its internal structure. He rolled it gracefully back and forth, spreading his lanky hands farther apart as he rolled. His touch appeared to be strong and delicate at the same time. He demoed three for us the first time we made them, and all three were virtually identical. When you tried to do it yourself, you understood how remarkable this was. I asked Coppedge if he liked rolling baguettes. He stared at me, his eyes enlarged behind round spectacles, then nodded gravely. "I am always trying to perfect them," he said.

I felt no urgency here. Coppedge more or less loped through the bakeshop from one dough to the next, or to the oven to check its temperature. Often he would simply sit—like dough, resting. But dough, as we learned, was deceptive—within that placid pale ball of flour and water was a hive of activity. Also deceptive was bread-baking class—while much of the time one simply scraped down one's bench or engaged in idle conversation while the dough proofed, this kitchen was, as Coppedge said, producing bread for nearly the entire school, between two hundred and three hundred loaves a day. Every day, waiters from the four public restaurants appeared for the restaurants' bread. Students in green aprons arrived from the Escoffier Room for baguettes. Students working in the Walk-In deli would arrive for hoagie rolls. Students from Pantry would take whatever was available that day.

And because yeast doughs acted independently of you, the urgency took a different form. Urgency was determined largely by yeast. You felt the urgency underground and spread out. In a kitchen you could avoid weeds by efficiency of movement and thought. In a bakeshop, efficiency didn't matter; you could be as efficient as you wanted but you still had to wait for the yeast and watch it, do what it told you to do. In a production kitchen one normally found oneself in the weeds just before service or during service. In the bakeshop, weeds could happen at any moment.

On Day Three Dante and I had been assigned the hoagie dough. We used a basic hard-roll dough, which was seasoned with salt and sugar and softened with egg whites and vegetable oil. Focaccia and Italian bread could also be made—depending on how you shaped the dough.

Somehow, we'd scaled the flour wrong. Dante and I dumbly stared into the eighty-quart mixing bowl. From across the room, Coppedge told us we needed more water. We argued that we had measured everything correctly, then slowly began to add water. The dough mixed and mixed and mixed and by the time Coppedge came over to ask us where we screwed up, we had added an extra four pounds of water. We mixed till it was well developed, and hefted the dough to the bench to bulk ferment. The air was warm and humid. After fifteen minutes, Coppedge strolled by and, noting our dough's size, put his hand on the dough.

"This is running," he said. "It's about eighty-seven degrees. This is running really fast." He inserted a large digital thermometer into the dough. It read 86 degrees. "And that's not even at its core." He called it "a fever" and said it had gotten hot from overmixing. We'd have to reevaluate the times of all the fermenting, scaling, and what time the dough would eventually go into the oven—there was a lot of bread to bake and finite oven space.

If somebody screwed up their dough, Coppedge would have to tell a waiter from American Bounty or St. Andrew's Cafe that the bread wasn't ready yet. Sometimes a restaurant would begin seating customers before a panting waiter came jogging in with a large plastic crate filled with bread still hot.

Dante had pulled a small chunk of our feverish dough and was kneading it in both hands. The chef regarded him skeptically. "I'm just overworking it to see what it feels like," Dante said. "And I'm fidgeting."

"Bakers don't fidget," Coppedge said. "Cooks fidget."

Hoagies and hard rolls were the chore breads. The best breads were the flavored doughs, and here Coppedge was not unlike a painter choosing from a palette flavors that would transform his lean dough canvas into something brilliant. Sometimes it would simply be a matter of adding roasted garlic to the lean dough, brushing it with olive oil, and sprinkling it with coarse salt. Sometimes he liked to add calamata olives and walnuts, resulting in a purple dough that was salty and nutty and moist.

After lunch and final kitchen cleaning, we met in a classroom down the hall, where Chef Coppedge would call out bread assignments. Team Three, for example, would do his frito diablo to the lean dough number two. "We're gonna add pine nuts," he said, "raisins, and crushed red pepper. It's gonna be kind of crusty, kind of hot, kind of chewy, kind of sweet. I think you'll like it." The sourdough would be the coveted chocolate cherry sourdough, big round loaves of golden bread riddled with sun-dried cherries and pockets of melted chocolate. "If anyone lets the word out that we're doing chocolate cherry bread," Coppedge warned, "you don't get one."

This was a decided perk of Baking Skill Development. The bread was good. Really good. Best-bread-I've-ever-tasted good. And you could take a loaf home. When we made a new bread, we'd stand around chewing away, nodding, and someone, stunned by surprised, would always say, "*Damn* good bread." Good bread like this, when you knew how complicated it was, seemed out of our reach, and yet we had made this bread.

We made rye bread, which we proofed in a canvas-lined basket called a banneton because rye flour lacked the supportive protein of wheat flour and needed the structure, as well as pumpernickle with cracked rye and pumpernickle flours, soaked overnight; the sharp grains would shred the gluten network if they were not soaked. According to Chef Coppedge, the net of gluten was like an intricate web of muscle tendons.

We made a wheat bread that was about seven parts flour and one part cooked potatoes, flecked inside with fresh chopped dill. The superb sunflower-seed bread was flavored with milk powder, sugar, sunflower oil, honey, and whole eggs, with sunflower seeds baked into the hard golden crust. We would also make classical doughs: soft rolls, brioche, and puff pastry. And we would mix, roll, proof, then boil bagels in malt-seasoned water, and then bake them to chewy perfection.

We mixed a sourdough multigrain, a San Francisco–style sourdough that used a starter of water, flour, and buttermilk, a standard wheat sourdough that was amenable to the chef's artistic whims—"Team four, you're gonna be making an apple sourdough; we're gonna take the sourdough and we're gonna substitute in the final dough some apple cider and we're gonna incorporate some apple, and we're not going to add any yeast, any commercial yeast."

"It's getting humid," the chef said as class rolled into gear. "And we're gonna have to deal with that. When it gets humid, the dough is going to kick our behinds." The chef was always saying something along lines that I didn't fully understand. He could explain it to me—the effects of heat and moisture on the dough, and how this would make the dough race, but somehow an explanation was never enough.

At least for me it wasn't enough. The differences between cooking and baking were so deep, so acute—and I was so unprepared for them—that the work of this kitchen confounded me. I didn't get it, *couldn't* get it. It was not in my nature. This was a fact I could do nothing about, a fact embodied by my physical state: I began bread baking with abounding eagerness, and with each day I grew more weary, teary, and decrepit. It was as though I were coming down with a powerful illness. Each day, my brain grew cloudy, my shoulders sagged, I moved more slowly, I struggled through a growing fog to ask questions I thought needed answers. On Day Four, Chef Coppedge looked at me. I was sneezing, my eyes were oceans, and I believe I shook my head to see him clearly. He said blandly, "You're allergic to flour."

"Allergic to *flour*?" I asked.

"I see it every now and then," he said.

Sure enough, an allergy to flour hit me like winter had hit the Hudson Valley that year. And I'm not talking about flour for a pound of pasta dough or a pie crust. I would heft a fifty-pound sack of flour to the oblique mixer and dump it in. My head and shoulders would all but vanish in a white cloud.

I'd be sneezing my head off, even when Coppedge wasn't shaking a big plastic container of dried red pepper flakes into the lean dough number one mixing in the Hobart oblique. I would go to the nurse's office for antihistamines. "I'm from Chef Coppedge's bakeshop," I'd say.

"Chef *Coppedge*," they would swoon.

They actually *swooned*. Such was the power of bread. I knew then, with sadness, such power over women was beyond my reach because I was not a baker.

As in all matters of food, there was an intellectual and spiritual correlative. I'd already discovered that I was cook. I could know what cooking was, fully, in my bones. Cooks, I had learned, came to cooking not to fulfill a desire, but rather, by chance, to fulfill something already in their nature. The same, I believe, was true of bakers. They were different. I have no doubt that there are people in this world, toiling away, in offices and backhoes alike, who are fundamentally unhappy because they never tried working in kitchens. And many are likewise unhappy because they are, by nature, bakers.

Because I was a cook or, rather, had "the cook" in my nature (I did not presume to call myself a cook), I could not fully comprehend baking. Baking was a sphere of knowledge and experience—as cooking was such a sphere—that I could not enter, could only observe from without, even though I was, like everyone, baking the bread, stretching the dough in my hands to gauge if it had been mixed enough, had developed the necessary gluten network; I had scraped down my bench, had put boiling hot water into the giant Hobart oblique mixer, and covered it with plastic wrap to steam off the dough, and then cleaned it; I'd pounded the baguettes into tight rolls with the heel of my hand, and lengthened them with strong, gentle palms in hopeful imitation of Chef Coppedge. I'd scored and stippled the loaves with knives and my fingers and brushed them with oil and sprinkled them with salt and shot the loaves into the oven and watched the loaves *puff*, suddenly—an effect called oven spring, the yeast becoming hyperactive from the heat just before death; and I'd cooled the loaves and eaten the bread and swept the hearthstone with a long mop heavy with vinegar and water. But I was not a baker and I would not then, not ever, understand the true nature of bread or the nature of bakers.

Instead, I had to learn from Coppedge by intuiting his urgency, an urgency in his tone rather than expression or movement, an urgency that made me pay attention. Chef Coppedge would be loping, no hurry, toward his desk; he would stagger that lope for an instant as his eyes looked at the air. Then, resuming the long slow stride, he would call out, "You're going to be using ice water today. Twenty-five percent of your water you will weigh as ice." Later that hot day, he had a student throw a bowlful of ice directly into a tub of dough to try to keep it cool.

Coppedge brought books for the students to peruse—one had time to read in a bakeshop. He seemed to like a new one just out, Nancy Silverton's *Breads of La Brea Bakery*; it was the best on theory, he said. But he was also vaguely dismissive of books.

He sat and, as we perused, he said, "You've got to experience bread. You can't say, 'I tried her recipe and it didn't work.' To understand bread, you've really got to hang out with a baker for three to six months."

I recalled Pardus's remark that the difference between baking and cooking was purely semantic. But here I realized that cooking and baking were two different processes entirely, as distinct as Eastern and Western philosophies. In baking, there were so many things you had to be able to see that weren't visible—moisture in the air, yeast, the components of flour. You never heard a cook complaining about how humid it was in the kitchen. If a consommé wasn't clear, you could *fix* it by making a new clarification, this time with more acid and protein. Baked stuff was harder to fix. The pressure in baking was all beneath the surface, underground, within the crust, and would remain there until you hit the thermal death point. If the pressure ever became visible, it was too late. If you scaled your dough right, you were fine, but if something was out of balance, what you had on your hands was a disaster because there was not time to mix, ferment, scale, rest, shape, proof, and bake more. The pressure here came from within and, in a bakeshop as in bread, the secret was to create and maintain that pressure.

M y friend Jason Dante from West MON-roc, Loosiana, had been a lively partner in bread baking, as I sneezed away and gouged my knuckles into my liquid eyes. As we rebuilt the rye starter, he'd look at me and say, "Man, I dig this fermentin' shit." He liked all things fermented. As a teenager he and a buddy made moonshine (they never drank it, fearing they'd made something lethal). In his room at the Culinary, Dante had fermented cabbage into sauerkraut. Bread baking was his favorite class, he said. All week he'd been bugging the chef to let us do a chipotle pepper bread. On Day Six, the chef, perhaps from fatigue, relented and ordered four cans of chipotles packed in adobe sauce, twelve poblanos, and several heads of garlic, and told us to go to it.

As we roasted the poblanos and garlic in the deck ovens, we discussed what kind of bread we were in fact trying to make. Jason, unsure of himself, suggested sourdough. I reminded him that the frito diablo—with the pine nuts, red pepper flakes, and raisins—had been done with a lean dough and suggested we stick with that. Chef Coppedge, ambling by, stopped to listen to our uninformed conversation. "Poblanos and chipotles," he said. "Southwestern, isn't it?"

"I was thinking about adding corn," Dante offered vaguely.

Chef Coppedge nodded and said, "I'd add some cornmeal, soaked. Make like a porridge."

"You mean . . . ," Dante said, narrowing his eyes.

"I'm stepping in here now," the chef said.

"Oh, no, Chef!" Dante exclaimed, as if being taken out of the game.

"I'm stepping in here," he continued. "Use twenty-five percent cornmeal, cooked in equal parts water. You're gonna make a porridge. Add it to the basic lean dough." He leaned over our course guide opened to the lean dough grid and pointed to the smallest quantity resulting in ten pounds of dough. "One and a half times this," he said and ambled off.

We cooked the cornmeal, peeled, seeded, and chopped the poblanos, and Dante took to fine-chopping the chipotles. He lifted one from the can and said, "These look like little dried turds. They *do*." He saved the adobe sauce to add to the dough as it was mixing. He licked the top of the can before throwing it away.

Once you had the basic lean dough, and understood the texture of the dough you needed—if you could stretch it till it was nearly translucent, you could actually see the gluten pattern, the web in the dough—then you could flavor it with just about anything. The chef, while a purist as far as method was concerned, did not think ill of flavored breads, so long as the flavors didn't overpower the fermented flavor of the bread itself. Coppedge noted that New York City, for instance, was killer competitive, and artisan bakers had to have some way of distinguishing their bread from another baker's bread. In America, you could not distinguish yourself with a plain baguette, even if your baguettes happened to be ethereal.

Our chipotle-poblano bread was indeed distinctive. We had added the right amount of chipotles and adobe sauce for good smoky heat, the roasted poblanos speckled the dough with their flavor, the cornmeal came through robustly; we had dusted it with cornmeal to impart some rustic grittiness.

I stayed with Coppedge to bake the last loaves of it while Dante went to lunch. The chef examined the finished loaves, which we'd shaped into ciabatta and foccacia. He noted it was a little flat and had overproofed just a little; also, he said it smelled just a tad heavy on the salt, which Dante had already told me he'd gone heavy on. But Chef Coppedge admired it nonetheless. "I like what you got here," he said. "I may send some of this down to the Bounty as a test. If they like it . . ." He shrugged.

When I told Dante Chef Coppedge would be sending our bread to the Culinary's best restaurant, Dante whooped and gave me a high five.

Chef Coppedge would release various teams to lunch depending on when their bread was finished. This meant a staggered departure and return, but Coppedge always arranged it so that he would have fifteen or twenty minutes alone in his bakeshop. Sometimes, he would have a bite to eat at his desk. Sometimes he would lean against his desk, arms folded, and stare at the bread baking perfectly in his hearthstone deck oven.

A bakeshop was a different kind of place. A white patina seemed to cover everything, softening the room, making it almost dreamlike. It was gentle here. Cool. Calm. *Poof,* flour into a mixer. *Puff,* the croissants rise.

Shhh, the dough is resting. And Coppedge was a baker. You could see it in his stride, in the way he thought, in the stories he told.

He always had a loaf or two of sourdough into which he had incorporated sauerkraut and chunks of red onion. This was a regularly featured bread at the Culinary because of President Metz. About three years ago, Coppedge told me, Metz had gotten crazy for bread. One day, the president's secretary summoned Chef Coppedge to Mr. Metz's office on the second floor of Roth Hall. When Coppedge arrived, the secretary handed him a piece of sourdough bread from a restaurant in San Francisco. Mr. Metz wanted to know, the secretary said, if Chef Coppedge could re-create it. Coppedge said the president now eats about a half a loaf of sauerkraut-and-onion bread each day: "He likes his dough really sour." Then, in a manner reflecting a dichotomy perhaps common among bakers that balanced extreme humility with extreme hubris, Coppedge added, "It's a matter of educating him."

This sort of talk about the president could only have come from a baker. Coppedge could say this because he was a baker and Mr. Metz was a cook. Bakers and cooks were two different creatures entirely.

Upon leaving Baking one would enter the more refined Patisserie, an even colder kitchen. Much of the work was done on chilly granite. Here students learned how to make vanilla sauce and ganache, how to temper chocolate, bloom sheets of gelatin, make linzertortes, marzipan roses, and pastry cream. They learned how to cut and roll parchment into a tight cone for fine-line decoration on their petit fours, designs they practiced nightly on cardboard cutouts. After these six weeks of Baking and Patisserie, they hung up their whites for six weeks of lecture and book work for the wines-and-menus chunk of the curriculum.

For these students, it felt odd to be out of the kitchen for so long, but those who intended to earn their bachelor's degree would spend two years out of the kitchen.

I'd had a chance to sit in on several bachelor's classes and to enjoy the polished hardwood floors and muted carpeted bachelor's classrooms on the third floor of Roth Hall's west wing. Bachelor's students dressed in street clothes, though they were older and neater than your average college students. Bachelor's candidates, who had gone through the associate degree here, paid about twenty-five thousand dollars for seventeen months of study and a six-week food-and-wine tour of California. The program, which began in August of 1994, had a capacity of 250 students and had yet to live up to the Culinary's expectations regarding enrollment. By the end of fiscal 1996 it had admitted a total of 225 students and graduated 106 students. The numbers were increasing, though, as many incoming students now arrived intending from the outset to spend four years here.

The emphasis in the bachelor's program was on food service, unlike other schools geared more generally toward hospitality and management. In addition to classes such as "Accounting and Budget Management" and "Marketing and Promoting Food," there were also foreign-language requirements, English composition, and other general liberal arts courses. It was almost disorienting to find oneself in a classroom in the Culinary Institute of America, listening to an intricate lecture on Japan's rise as an economic power. Krishnendu Ray, the instructor of the class called Asian Culture, was a deft lecturer; he could, in the middle of a class on his native India, posit the notion that all religion was an attempt to control women's fertility and man's jealousy of that fertility, be convincing about it, then return the focus to Western stereotypes of Indian society. One felt far from the madness of Fish kitchen and burnt root vegetables here.

After students in the associate's program had passed Menus and Facilities Planning, Management of Wines and Spirits, and Restaurant Law, they once more donned whites for International Cookery, Advanced Culinary Principles, and Classical Banquet Cuisine before moving into the final four blocks of the CIA curriculum, restaurant row. Here, students were playing for real; these were public restaurants, and if you called for a reservation at any one of them, you were likely to be told that there was nothing available for at least two weeks.

These restaurants were the true measure of what the Culinary Institute of America could accomplish in as little as a year and a half. They were reviewed in newspapers and magazines, were well regarded, and often displayed awards and citations they'd won. The most remarkable thing about these restaurants, though, was not that they were good restaurants but that they changed staff every seven days. Every seven days, the entire staff of the restaurant would depart, and eighteen or so new waiters and eighteen or so new cooks would arrive to begin work for the first day.

♣ St. Andrew's Cafe

The bright warm day permitted the pre–Day One meeting to be held on the terrace of St. Andrew's Cafe around glass tables shaded by white-and-green-striped sun umbrellas. Craig Edwards, a tall, natty man with an immaculate smile and a mischievous lift of his black eyebrows, was in the final stage of his front-of-the-house fellowship under table service instructor Philip Papineau. The new class, arriving piecemeal in green aprons, had finished Introduction to Table Service, waiting on their fellow students for the past seven days in Alumni Hall, the dining chapel. Craig welcomed everyone and ran through dress requirements, homework assignments, and general timing. I was the only one in whites—finishing up Patisserie—but a stranger in the group was commonplace; students regularly made up classes or dropped behind into a new group because of illness or failure.

"You're actually going to be waiting on humans, live people," Craig began. This, he said, would be different from anything we had done so far at the Culinary. "Shoes," he continued. "You can wear your skid busters, but make sure there's no food on them. Wear your chef's jackets to class; they'll keep your apron clean. Please wear T-shirts; it's starting to get hot and they absorb moisture, O.K.?" He asked that the maître d' of the day dress conservatively; bar people were to dress for regular service. Black pants, of course either CIA-issued polyester or black trousers of your own, but please, no cotton Dockers, which tend to fade, unless you planned to dry-clean them. A sign-in sheet would be in the foyer and served as the attendance sheet. Day One began at six-thirty, Day Two through Day Seven began at seven-forty-five. Setup till eight-thirty, lecture ended when family meal came up at ten-thirty, final inspection at eleven-twenty, and the restaurant, St. Andrew's Cafe, opened for business at eleven-thirty. We must learn the buzzwords he'd handed out—shorthand terms for all menu items—before we arrived for Day One.

"You're free to smoke," he said, "but please do it on your own time, and do it in the back entrance. We have customers going through here." He pointed to the entrance doors. This was important information; nonsmoking students at the Culinary were the exception, or so it would seem given a glance at the quad. "If you do smoke, please wash your hands and use a breath mint afterward. Mr. Papineau is very serious about this. If he smells it, he will instruct you to do something about it."

Craig, his toothpaste-advertisement smile shining brightly, had repeated this information exactly once every seven days since his graduation nearly half a year ago.

I n preparation for St. Andrew's Cafe, I had taken my wife and daughter to the restaurant for lunch to sample the fare and get a feel for the place as an anonymous customer. St. Andrew's Cafe, the only restaurant with a building of its own (the General Foods Nutrition Center was its proper name), formed one side of the quad where, in clement weather, hoards of uniformed students hung out before class or inhaled after-meal cigarettes. One entered into a vestibule that contained a large maître d's desk where menus and the reservations list were kept; beside this homey item was a large glass window looking into the kitchen where students sautéed and grilled and the chef or his fellow called orders into a microphone.

We were greeted by Philip Papineau, a tall dapper man with a smooth dark Mediterranean complexion. His manner was formal but at ease. No, he said, reiterating what he'd told me when I'd made the reservation, an eleven-month-old was not a problem at all, and he showed us to our table, the student maître d' being engaged in a similar activity across the room.

St. Andrew's dining room reminded me of a large sunroom where much bridge playing might be done from the comfort of its bentwood-and-stretched-leather chairs. In warm weather, French doors opened onto the terrace, separated from the quad by a low brick wall. The facing wall, mostly window, allowed plenty of natural light to play upon the rich blue carpet and daily-polished silverware. The bar was tucked back against the observation kitchen and faced a large fireplace and oak mantle on the far side of the room.

After the smoothness of Mr. Papineau, our waiter seemed Cro-Magnon. He welcomed us to St. Andrew's Cafe, nodding slowly, as if trying to sell us on the restaurant we'd already chosen. He asked if we'd like anything to drink. I said we'd be having a bottle of wine with lunch and would order that in a moment. Our waiter nodded, holding a steady pen to his waiter's pad. I had ample time to notice his lips, which curled out to expose his broad teeth. He kept nodding and staring at me, pen still perched on the pad. At about the time I considered saying, "I'll need a *moment, thanks,*" he raised his eyebrows, gave me a slight smile, and continued his slow nodding. Then, in the manner of a hulky wrestler leaving the mat, he walked away and stood in the corner beside another waiter, with his hands behind his back.

When you dine with an eleven-month-old, you must, upon sitting, reset everything except the tablecloth on the far end while the eleven-month-old throws her body across the now-barren landscape, grasping, inevitably, for the knife as passionately as she would the tree root that would keep her from plummeting off a cliff. No sooner had we accomplished this than another waiter arrived bearing a small plate of Chef Coppedge's delicious bread. He asked if our daughter could have some (our bread would be delivered in a basket along with flavored olive oil and a white-bean spread soon). Favorably impressed, Donna said, "You must have children." The waiter said, no, he didn't, but another member of the class did and had suggested that we might want bread immediately. We were grateful, indeed.

Here, I would eventually realize, was table service at CIA restaurants in microcosm. It ranged from dull and awkward to gracefully attentive. One received far more attention than one was used to, by more waiters than one typically saw in a room twice the size, and their service was unfailingly solicitous. Some of the students had waited tables before and felt at ease, but most had not and this was a new experience. All of them were paying money to wait tables and were being graded on their conduct. Even at its awkward, Cro-Magnon worst, waiters here projected the attitude that they would do anything within their power, limited though it may be, to answer every question and fulfill every request with alacrity. I have never felt more at ease in a restaurant than at any of the CIA restaurants—even the very formal Escoffier Room, and even with our prehistoric friend, who, after a clumsy and labored service, gave us the wrong bill at the end of the meal.

It was the delivery of the bread to our daughter, however, that created and fixed the tone of the afternoon. (Of three breads served, I feel obliged to note, our daughter opted for the sauerkraut-red-onion sourdough, a very sour bread indeed; as this was a matter of education, we did not worry overly.) We had been at St. Andrew's less than two minutes and had already had the attention of four servers; this had both overt and unconscious effects, as I would soon learn from the impressive Mr. Papineau.

I arrived at 6:30, having fastened my bow tie and draped a green apron over my neck. I had grown accustomed to arriving in kitchens but here one arrived into a cool carpeted room with innocuous jazz music piped quietly into the background. Mr. Papineau noted that my apron was tied wrong. I'd tied it like a kitchen apron; one must tie a waiter's apron underneath itself so that the tie does not show. Then Craig told me to put my briefcase in a locker downstairs. No book bags or briefcases of any kind were allowed here: too much valuable silverware lying about.

I knew none of my fellow students, but what struck me from the beginning was how much older they seemed than the students I'd known in the earlier kitchens. They were not literally older, but there was a maturity to them, even to nineteen-year-old Manning Shaffer, a confidence that must be another by-product of the education and of a five-month externship in the field.

It's possible, too, that fast aging is caused by the work. I was continually surprised to discover that the age of this or that chef was not fifty-six but rather thirty-nine. None looked haggard—simply older, weathered, properly seasoned.

The oldest in our group was a guy named John Marshall, age thirty-seven. He had spent most of his career in front-of-the-house work. His wife worked and before he came to the Culinary, they had a combined income of about ninety thousand dollars. They'd given that income up (John had to sell his sailboat to pay for tuition), and John now had to work full-time in addition to going to school. He lived in Pine Plains, forty-five minutes northeast of the Culinary. In the evenings he was the chef of Mashomack Shooting Preserve where, as John put it, the very rich come to shoot live, prebought birds, and drink Bloody Marys. He would not make it for Day One's six-thirty starting time.

Tables had been pushed aside and chairs lined in two rows in front of the fireplace where Mr. Papineau began Day One.

"My name is Mr. Papineau. You know Craig. Chef Hanyzeski will be in the kitchen this week. Chef De Santis will be back next week when you rotate into the kitchen. Martin is the fellow and Dan is the fellow-in-training." These were the customary formalities of every class. He took attendance. As every instructor had, he asked that anyone with learning disabilities see him. He ran down the daily routine and times.

"Everybody needs to have: pen, dupe pad, crumber, and wine key," he said. "I'm being incredibly dumb and repetitive about this because I don't want anyone to misinterpret me. *Everyone . . . must* have *. . .* these *four* items *every day*." If he reprimanded anyone, he said, "Don't take it personally. I don't know you well enough for you to take anything personally."

A word about dress would seem to be unnecessary, but Mr. Papineau brought his own table-side sentiments to the matter: "We all need to be in uniform. I think the school is right on the money with that. It says a lot about you. Customers only have to look skin deep. They don't *need* to look for the *real* you."

Shortly thereafter, Mr. Papineau gave us our assignments and we were off to do our side work, all of us wearing a chef's jacket over our apron but for Todd Sargent, who dressed in coat and tie and had wrapped his hair into a rope of a ponytail.

I set tables with a knife and fork, bread and butter plate, butter knife and napkin. I wiped down every salt and pepper shaker in the sixty-five seat house; twenty-one matching vases filled with stems of estamaria, a vase for each table, waited in the cooler. Others inventoried the bar, set the coffee station, filled small dishes with bean spread and olive oil, set the side stations, while five or six sat at one large round table polishing silverware. Mr. Papineau showed me how to unfold the tablecloth, touching it as little as possible, so that the crease was facing the right direction, always pointing to seat number one; soon, but not today, we would learn the unusual and clever mechanics of changing a tablecloth in the middle of service without showing the vinyl covering of the table itself.

I asked how this group seemed to him.

"Very even," he said. He had sent me a confident, no-problem expression, and he had swept a broad hand across the air. "I get to see this every seven days. You're off to a very auspicious start."

Only when the side work had been completed and we took our seats again for a quiz on buzzwords for every item on the menu—"orzo" for the pasta with morels, Parma ham and Parmesan, for instance; "open-face" for

Mediterranean roast beef sandwich on focaccia with aïoli—did it occur to me that we were actually going to be serving *people* today.

"Order-taking is the single biggest issue in the class," Mr. Papineau said. Into order-taking was condensed everything that table service was about—timing, finesse, self-control, graceful movement, clarity of mind and voice—and required some understanding of human nature, salesmanship, and hospitality. During the next seven days, we would scrutinize the "competencies"—an oft-used word at the Culinary—that went into professional table service. But, as this was Day One and guests were due in a couple hours, Mr. Papineau's first concerns were that we understand the menu. He began with the wines, describing each simply. "The kitchen really tries to moderate fat; the food has a different mouth-feel to it, so the wine list can be tricky." He ran through the various aperitifs offered as well as the beer.

"Beer is getting to be like wine," he said. "For those of you who will open your own place, make your beer list as complex, or almost as complex, as your wine list. It's only gonna get bigger and there's a lot of money to be made there. A big area of growth."

He moved into the food. Spice level was moderate. Soups required a bouillon spoon, which would be kept in the drawers of the side stations; the required silver must find its way to the table before the food. The open-face is served medium rare, the salmon medium unless the customer requests otherwise. The chicken and shrimp entrée was served over linguine with a spicy saffron broth and therefore required a broth spoon. Grilled beef tenderloin—a temperature was requested on that. And so on through the entire menu, on into coffee service. He went through the kitchen's procedure, when it fired which course and when it picked up. He rumbled systematically through ordering procedure. The instructions ran from broad—there would be front waiters who would do all the order-taking and there would be back waiters who would deliver the food and clear plates—to specifics. Crumb and remove salt and pepper, *then* set for dessert. Coffee cup handles should be set at four o'clock—let's watch the details, folks. Reset only the twenties and thirties (tables were all numbered), and never strip a table bare. A sloppy table will take the food down a notch, he warned. The customer's eye goes to the mistake first—a crumb on the chair, fleck of tarnish on the tip of a knife in an otherwise sparkling silver setup. "When it's right," Mr. Papineau said, eyes narrowing at the challenge, *"they don't notice a thing."*

Mr. Papineau knew that he was speaking to cooks and he wanted us to give to table service the same passion and precision that we brought to plating the food itself. Use your common sense, he instructed, have confidence, and leave your old waiter techniques, if you had any, behind.

"The greeting includes the beverage list," he said. "Ask if they would like something to drink. Don't say, '*Hi.*' Don't say, '*Howyadoin'?*' Don't introduce yourself by name." And when we saw that the table had finished and needed a check, "Don't mention the C word. Why? *Cuz.*"

If there were questions, ask, and he or Craig would instruct, even if the room were full of guests in the middle of lunch. This was a classroom first, he reminded us.

"The customers are not here to challenge you," Mr. Papineau concluded. "They're here to dig the scene."

Mr. Papineau covered a lot of ground in an hour and a half. Some of my fellow students took notes; others simply listened. How could they be absorbing everything? I was trying to write everything down and could scarcely keep up, so relentless was the volley of information. It seemed only twenty minutes before Mr. Papineau said, "O.K., family meal's up," reminded us that at eleven-twenty there would be final inspection, and headed us into the kitchen to pick up plates of soupy lasagna prepared by the last class.

I was assigned back-waiter duty the first day and therefore did not interact with the customers. Bradley Anderson, a twenty-two-year-old from Wisconsin who asked to be called Shaggy, was the front waiter. He waited tables at American Bounty (which often hired extra waiters in addition to those in the class), and he liked front-of-the-house work so there was little new about this to him. The day proceeded calmly because of Shaggy, because Papineau limited the number of reservations accepted on Day Ones, and because there were two people serving every table. Most of my time was spent standing in the corner with my hands behind my back, rocking from heel to toe, waiting for my tables to finish eating so I could clear and reset. This was going to be easy.

When I asked Craig why he had chosen to do his fellowship in St. Andrew's, he replied, "Mr. Papineau. He's the *man.*"

Philip Papineau, in my mind, was set somewhere in the 1950s in New York City, a bachelor in a small, dimly lit apartment. At night, he would read the newspaper in his T-shirt and slacks, a small plate with half a sandwich to his right and, perhaps, a full glass of tepid water; later that evening he would be seen by a neighbor closing his apartment door, turning the key, and, immaculately dressed, he would stride into the New York City night.

It was not my inclination to create unlikely fantasies about people I watched, but there was something about Mr. Papineau's dark eyes, dark complexion, and broad shoulders that gave him a studio-era leading-man look; his face was long, his dark hair cut short. His beard was heavy but he was always so cleanly shaven that his jaw and upper lip seemed almost to shine. He moved as elegantly as a dancer. He was likely none of the things I saw in him; perhaps he was simply so polished that one could see any number of reflections in him. In truth, one might call him a career waiter; he took his first order at the age of eighteen. The man loved table service, he was expert, and like every great teacher he was able to convey his personal love of the subject directly to his students.

In his lecture on table-clearing he noted that we should, between courses, clear all silverware. You understood this man shuddered at the thought of a customer taking a food-smeared knife or fork off a plate to rest it on the tablecloth. "How many of you have put dirty silver back on the table?" Mr. Papineau asked, raising his own hand. "Come *oooon*," he said in a deep, smooth voice. "Get your hands up. Everyone has done it." He waited for everyone to raise their hand, then asked, "Why?"

Todd Sargent said, "We don't think we're gonna get it *back*."

"Right!" Mr. Papineau exclaimed. "We have been trained by bad service. It's a survival technique: 'Hang on to your knife, *buddy*. You're gonna *need* it.'" We would replace silverware frequently; no food was to be brought to a table until the table had been properly reset by the back waiter.

A question on coffee would raise several dimensions of coffee service. I had already poured coffee for a customer and the coffee had splashed over the rim of the cup and into the saucer, enough to create a puddle in the saucer. I had asked if I might replace the cup and saucer—was this correct?

Mr. Papineau instructed me to take it one step further: "Offer to take it away—*while* you're reaching for it." This gets Mr. Papineau thinking: "A word on coffeepots," he said. "Coffeepots with short stems are drippy. Long spouts, like the ones we have, drip less. Don't overfill a coffeepot; if you overfill it, it can *jump* out of the pot." Once he started thinking about coffee, it seemed he couldn't stop. "Never serve warm coffee," he continued. "There is nothing worse than warm coffee. People will buy it iced, and they will buy it hot, but nothing else in between. Some people like coffee"—he stopped, rose slightly on his toes, and extended his chin—"*melting* hot. Normally older people—I *don't* know why. It must be the dentures. If this is the case, make sure the *cup* is hot. If they can feel it on their lip"—he lifted a mug from the demo table he worked during lecture, pressed it to his lower lip—"they will *perceive* that the *coffee* is hot." In such cases we wanted the mug hot as a soup bowl. And coffee, of course, would get him thinking about tea. "Who's a tea drinker?"

Mimi Anchev, twenty-three, from Westchester County south of Hyde Park, confessed with a tentative hand.

Mr. Papineau glared at her, leaned in, and said, "Oh, you are a *fussy* lot." To the class he said, "Tea service can be *very* complicated," and into tea service he sailed.

"Kids and the elderly," he explained, "are very needy, very selfish." Always, he said, attend to the children first. "If you make the kids happy, then *who's happy*?" He paused. "It's not a difficult concept. Who has made a lot of money on just that?" He paused again. *"McDonald's."*

I grew to understand that Mr. Papineau—"I am a nut for communicating through gesture," he often said—was less a table-service instructor than a professor of sociology and behavior.

One had to be such a creature if one were to be excellent because one had to know what the customer wanted—whether it was water, to place an order, a warmer temperature in the room—then fulfill the need. "And to do this," Mr. Papineau said with a reverential hush, but without losing volume, "*before* the customer *knows* they *need* it. *That's* where it's at. People will spend more if the service is good."

Why? They tend to order the extra course because they trust that it will arrive promptly, and they tend to up their tip by 1 to 2 percent, which is all that you can reasonably hope for. "You've got the big tipper, and you've got the tipper who's incredibly stingy," Mr. Papineau offered sagely. "Everyone else falls somewhere in between. You're not going to change that. You're just looking to move it up one or two percent."

Mr. Papineau stressed promptness. "If you're late," he said, "your service will always be on the defensive."

He could not emphasize this enough. You had no idea how long the time can seem, he said, especially if you were a deuce. He asked who had a second hand on their watch. He said, "Time *one* minute." And Mr. Papineau began. He waited. He appeared to be listening for a small noise, hearing only silence. It seemed a long time before he spoke. With his volume a notch lower than normal, he said, "Can't we get a *drink*?" Disgruntled but patient. He then waited. He looked right, looked left, looked right. A minute passed, and he said, a little more loudly, "All we want is a drink." And then, after what *had* to be yet another minute's wait, he whispered to his imaginary date, "Should we go somewhere else?" When the two people timing both raised their hands to indicate one minute had elapsed, he said in a loud, angry-customer voice, "We have been here for *ten* minutes and can't even get something to drink!"

He shed the angry customer persona, lifted his eyebrows, and tilted his head: *Am I right? See how long a minute can last?* Those who had waited tables were already nodding. Mr. Papineau said, "You can't say, 'Excuse me, sir, but it's only been *one* minute." Timing, promptness were crucial. "These are big issues," he said.

Service today is just terrible, Mr. Papineau would say often. He didn't necessarily want formal, he wanted professional. He wanted polish. "I can tolerate technical errors, I suppose," he said. "I will not tolerate rude, flip behavior." I wondered what it would be like to go out to a restaurant with Mr. Papineau, hear a play-by-play analysis of the service. "For a hundred bucks," Mr. Papineau said, "I don't want *rude*. I want smooth. For a hundred bucks, *I want smooooth*."

He lifted a napkin from the demo table and snapped it free of its folds with a muffled pop. "I like show," he said, "but I'm not big on woofing napkins. If you *do* have waiters woofing napkins, make sure *everyone* woofs napkins. Don't just have one guy woofing napkins." Mr. Papineau was a fine actor and could caricature customers' behavior. "When someone goes to the bathroom?" he said. He lofted the napkin into the air and turned his chin up away from the table. The napkin landed a third on the plate, a third on the table, and the rest draping over the table's edge. Mr. Papineau looked at his audience, raised his eyebrows, and nodded. He said, "Just," and he lifted the napkin by its edges, folded it twice, said, "I'm not big on touching other people's napkins, just fold it," and he set it beside the plate, then over the arm of the chair, either one was fine. "So." He turned to the class. "*Don't* try to refold it into a pheasant."

There were, of course, many *don'ts* in table service. Mr. Papineau jammed his hands into both pockets, rocked from heel to toe, and looked exaggeratedly around the room. "This means," he said, *"not . . . ready."*

"Don't eat, smoke, or drink during service," he continued. "Don't do it. Don't *run* through a restaurant. People think there's a fire. When they see a waiter running, it makes them nervous." Finally and importantly, he said, "You can't laugh. If you're laughing, *who* are you laughing *at*?" The whole class chuckled. "And you *know* there's a *lot* to laugh at," Mr. Papineau said.

Table service was a gorgeous craft to Mr. Papineau. You had not perfected it, he said, "until you can fade into the woodwork and still be in the middle of the room."

Papineau's lectures were not all sociology. They were also formal lessons. He had a large easel with a drawing board onto which he'd drawn a diagram identical to the one on our dupe pad—four course columns running across the top, and seven seat numbers descending the left edge. He turned it away from us, had four students take seats at the demo table, and performed proper order taking. "Grilled beef tenderloin," he said, writing this down, but the point he stressed by caricaturing his own perfect execution was to repeat aloud what had been ordered to ensure the waiter and guest were in sync. "And how would you like that cooked?" He repeated while writing: "Medium rare." And when he had finished the table, having collected all menus, he turned the board around to show us exactly how what had been communicated at the table should appear on our pad.

As always there was something big about Mr. Papineau's movements. He was on stage before us and his actions were loud as stage whispers. When he arrived at the table he didn't simply walk up to it; he more or less *zooped*, his feet arriving first, followed by his waist, shoulders, then head—a figurative indication of speed and promptness. And once he was in place he was Jeeves incarnate, saying in his confident baritone, "Good afternoon. Welcome to St. Andrew's Cafe."

Refinement hid itself within its own virtue. One could not easily recognize genuine refinement because true refinement directed attention away from itself. What made Papineau such a fascinating table-service instructor was that he could reveal his refinement without losing it. He showed us how table service worked. He was the magician revealing to his apprentices the prestidigitations and illusions of his trade.

᭞᭞᭞

Day Two was my first day as front waiter. Shaggy, whose short hair was so blond it was nearly white, would be my back waiter at tables forty-one, a six-top, and forty-two, a four-top. Mr. Papineau had inspired me. I could hardly wait for service. I was eagerness personified.

During setup, I popped out to the foyer to check the reservation list and found that across from table forty-two the name Czack. This would be Richard Czack, a 1958 graduate of the school, executive assistant to Senior Vice President Tim Ryan. We had never met, but I liked him because I knew he had spent part of his professional career in my hometown as a country-club chef and executive chef for Hough Caterers, a division of the venerable Hough Bakeries, once a flour and confectionery landmark of Cleveland. Czack did not look like a chef—balding, glasses, slight of frame; I didn't know his age but he seemed elderly. His voice was nasal, fussy. He looked and sounded more like an accountant's clerk. But Chef Czack was in fact a certified master chef and I was excited to be serving him and his guests, Mr. and Mrs. Forgione, parents of celebrity chef Larry, and an unnamed fourth. This would be fun.

Chef Czack and the Forgiones arrived as scheduled and were shown to table forty-two, at the back of the room, immediately in front of the dormant fireplace. There was no fourth member, but Chef Czack told Gene Huey, group leader and maître d' of the day, to keep the place setting. Then, like a horse out of a starting gate, I broke for the table, greeted the three guests, and, standing at Mrs. Forgione's right, asked if anyone cared for something to drink.

The Forgiones quickly perused the drink menu. Mrs. Forgione wanted something nonalcoholic and ordered a Sea Breeze. Mr. Forgione said that he had no idea what a Sea Breeze was. Chef Czack looked to me and said, "Tell us, what is in a Sea Breeze?"

Certainly, Czack had asked for the benefit of Mr. Forgione. He had not asked because he himself was curious, I don't think, or to test me in front of the guests, to show off the students, yet something in his tone led me to squint a little, as if to show I was working diligently at a tricky problem. I'd long known what a Sea Breeze was and we'd been tested on it as well, but I still made it look difficult. Then, with pride and confidence of having accomplished this difficult task, I said, "A Sea Breeze is three-quarters orange juice and one-quarter cranberry juice."

Chef Czack, if my recollection is correct, said something in response. He could just as well have been speaking Chinese for all I understood. Something had gone wrong with my ears. I nodded and smiled. Chef Czack may have said, "Traditionally, what you described is a Madras. A Sea Breeze is made with cranberry juice and grapefruit juice." I do know that he had not said, "Sorry, pal," and he had not made a Jeopardy wrong-answer noise. Either of those would have penetrated the fog that had rolled into my head. I had become so oblivious that I did not even realize the mistake until later, as I tried to reconstruct the events of the day—much as one might glue together a broken vase.

Mrs. Forgione, perhaps expecting orange juice, perhaps expecting grapefruit juice, said it sounded good and through sheer force of will, I was able to record this on my dupe pad in the proper square. Chef Czack and Mr. Forgione would share a large bottle of Solé sparkling water. I departed for the bar, where Craig poured a proper Sea Breeze.

Mr. Papineau slid up beside me as I waited and, surveying the room, he said, "Take and serve their orders. If Mr. Metz joins them, we'll take care of his order separately."

"Mr. Metz?" I said.

Mr. Papineau nodded, then glided away.

It is a measure, I think, of how thoroughly I had adopted the role of a student that I was all but stricken by this information.

"Mr. *Metz*," I repeated.

My six-top arrived shortly after noon, four of them anyway, and one older gentleman announced upon being seated that they had a tour and would be leaving at one-fifteen, no matter where they stood in their meal. I assured them I'd be prompt and asked if they would like something to drink.

Sometime after this, Craig said to me, "Mr. Metz is here."

I have no clear recollection when this was because from the Sea Breeze on, I had lost utterly my sense of time and other critical faculties of consciousness; the perception of faces, the sound of customers talking to me, depth perception and laws of gravity melted into an amorphous blob of table-service experience. Craig had spoken with a tone that indicated he shouldn't have needed to tell me in the first place. By this point I had lost my composure completely and I said, "*Metz?!* What should I do?"

Craig looked at me, pausing for a moment to observe the thickness of my head, and said, "Ask him if he'd like something to drink."

I knew the moment Craig said it, he was right, and off I scurried.

Mr. Metz, dressed sharply in a blazer and dark slacks, leaned forward on the table, apparently happily engaged in conversation with Mr. Forgione. I approached, pen perched on dupe pad, and waited. I don't know if I spoke, but Mr. Metz, eventually sensing my presence, turned to me, smiled, his eyes their customary slivers, and said, "I'm O.K., thanks," then returned to the conversation. If I recall correctly, I left the table the way a football player enters the game to kick the winning field goal in the final seconds.

Consciousness was impaired, clearly, but it had not abandoned me completely. Later, I glanced at my dupe pad and saw that I had written the words "I'm O.K., thanks" across the page. A small memento of the day, his first words to me.

The rest of the day did not grow smoother, though it was saved several times from disaster by the competence of Shaggy, my back waiter. We used what was called the Squirrel, a computer ordering system that sent, at the touch of its screen, one's order to the kitchen. For some reason, the Czack order for starters did not arrive and was therefore late. Czack scowled at me every time I approached the table. I'd managed to record accurately their main course; everything would have been fine if I'd entered these into the computer. I neglected to do this because I got waylaid at table forty-one—"I just want to remind you that we are *walking* out of this restaurant at one-fifteen." Two people at this table still had not arrived, the four who had arrived placed orders immediately, and one of the women requested herbal iced tea.

This was what stalled me. We had herbal tea that we served hot and we had big pitchers of iced tea at the bar. I explained that our iced tea was not herbal. The woman—no slouch; a tea drinker, after all—explained to me that if we served hot herbal tea, certainly we could put it over ice, no? I said I didn't see why that could not be arranged. Anything for the customer. When I approached the bar and explained this to Craig, normally a happy and delightful soul, he looked at me as if I were being a pain in the ass. Just then, with horror, I remembered that I had not placed the Czack order. After this delay, Shaggy knew to keep a careful eye on the situation. He would eventually take their dessert order and bring their coffee because the problematic six-top, now in its entirety—four people eating their entrées, two people just beginning appetizers—demanded my exclusive attention.

The tea drinker was enormously impressed when I arrived with a teapot, in which an herbal tea bag steeped, along with a glass filled to the brim with ice.

"Now *that* is the way to do it," she said.

I was deeply gratified, but there was a problem. I had noticed it at the bar. The tea bag didn't seem to be steeping so much as soaking; the water was clear. Craig said it would be fine, take it away. I touched the teapot. It was cold. Craig had put cold water in the teapot. That was why the tea bag released none of its fragrant goodness. This was not right, I told Craig. He told me it was fine, go. I did as I was told, knowing it was wrong. I had already spent too much time on this tea, anyway, and Czack was giving me the hairy eyeball from across the room. When I saw the tea drinker pour into her glass what was clear tap water, squint at it, and taste it, my toes curled and my stomach clenched. The burnt root vegetables had come back to haunt me in the form of herbal iced tea.

Desserts, like everything at Czack's table, were late, but coffee cups were low, so I was forced to make another pass with the coffeepot. Czack, who had declined a refill earlier, scowled at this, my second approach, but because everything was taking longer than expected, he said, "I'll have a splash."

I honestly thought this was another test, and I stood there, staring at him, he staring back. Perhaps, unbeknownst to myself, I was nodding, my lips curling out to reveal broad teeth. Eventually, it dawned on me that Chef Czack wanted more coffee and I broke from my Cro-Magnon stupor.

At one-fifteen on the nose, my elderly friend at the six-top and his spouse were making rapidly for the door, having foregone dessert because of their tour. At one-fifteen and a half, I was racing after the man, waving the leather check folder that contained his unsigned Visa slip.

Once the troublesome six-top had been dispatched with their three separate bills, I could attend without distraction to Chef Czack, but "Will there be anything else?" was all there remained to say. I slid the check folder onto the table; Czack did not owe anything but he needed to sign the check. I had taken a spot in the corner, hands behind my back. Czack took out his wallet; I could feel him glaring at me. I looked at him and when I did, he flicked a bill onto the table with a disdain I would do well to be grateful for, or so his expression seemed to suggest. I nodded once. As the Forgiones and Chef Czack stood to leave, Shaggy passed me and said, "Did you see that twenty spot on Czack's table?" A 12 percent service charge was added to each bill to benefit CIA scholarships, all menus explained; "additional tipping is not expected or required." Tips here were generally small, therefore, and often nonexistent; front and back waiters shared tips, thus Shaggy's happy surprise to see a twenty-dollar bill on one of our tables.

Clearly, there was more to waiting tables than I had at first surmised. Weeds, I learned, grew in the front of the house, too. I was humbled and relieved to know that I, in my earnest bumbling way, had done better than some. Mark Zanowski, twenty-seven, a former English teacher from Milwaukee, said he couldn't stop banging people in the head with his elbows. I saw Paul Angelis deliver a chocolate Bavarian to a couple that had yet to order their entrée. And Chen-Hwa Kang, an international student from Taiwan, spilled a glass of water into a woman's lap. All part of a culinary education.

In the field, cooks and waitstaff form a quarrelsome marriage, neither party understanding, or willing to understand, the peculiar stresses of the other's job. Future cooks being trained at the CIA benefited from the rigors of table-waiting—among other things, it enhanced their capacity for sympathy when, later, as they cranked out plates on the sauté station and a waiter failed to appear to whisk the plate away, they might now understand why.

Table-service class was a practical matter as well. If the Culinary were going to have restaurants, it had to staff them. And with all these able available cooks on campus, there was certainly no reason to pay outsiders to wait tables, an option that had been considered; the intent, though, was to ensure that cooks get to know front-of-the-house work and get used to interacting with customers.

And it became a privilege under Papineau's instruction—indeed, it was here that one realized how vital good service was to a restaurant, and this was the most important lesson of all. As Mr. Papineau was quick to point out, many, many restaurants flourish serving bad food well, while few survive whose service is slipshod, rude, or incompetent. Service was selling power. "Learn to keep service happy so service can make money," he told us. Students thus spent thirty-five days, seven weeks, the equivalent of two-and-a-half full blocks, waiting tables.

I engaged Mr. Papineau in conversation after service, when he could relax somewhat, though his sense of decorum and smoothness was such that in this room he always appeared to be on, perfectly smooth, never a wrinkle in his attire, never a skip in his effortless glide through the room. I noted that he appeared to like this work. He told me how lucky and honored he felt to be here; then, looking in both directions first, he grinned and whispered, "I'm like a pig in shit."

I believe I actually jumped when he said this, so jarring was it to hear the polished gentleman use that phrase. But it made me appreciate what a powerful salesman he was. He was not polish to the core, he only appeared to be—which was all that mattered.

Sometimes, when he acted out a scenario during lecture, he was so good I felt that he was dangerous. He was so in control, the other party didn't realize that *he*, not they, controlled the situation; it was merely that Philip Papineau allowed them to feel in control without their knowing it. This was part of the game, and I could not help but sense, for all my admiration of his formidable skills, there was also wound up in the job a thread of wicked insincerity. There had to be, if only to balance the humility necessary to nod and beg a foul guest's pardon.

After service one day, Mr. Papineau and I left the dining room for a small office he shared with the other table-service instructor and their fellows, beneath the restaurant near the lockers and two classrooms where Nutrition was taught (each day after service, kitchen crew and waitstaff would meet for an hour-and-a-half lecture and lab work on protein, carbohydrates, and fat).

"I teach the material, and try to change their perspective on table service," Mr. Papineau said, leaning casually back in his chair, his jacket removed. It struck me then that all his movements were somehow bigger than life.

In truth, while he claimed only to teach, Papineau did much more than that. There were several facets to his work and they blended with each other, mixed, overlapped, and mimicked one another, so that you never knew which he was doing or when—it was all one thing. He was the maî tre d' of a public restaurant. He was a lecturing instructor on the faculty of the Culinary Institute. He was a teacher by example; the posture he held and the values he practiced during service were observed and absorbed by the students around him. And he was a kind of private tutor for Craig. Excellence in one of these areas fed all the others and they fed it; the better maître d' he was, the better teacher he became, and the students learned more. The boundaries between school and business, education and work were in fact nonexistent. Each was an expression of and fed the whole.

He said the dining room was a classroom, but this was not practice; real people came to eat here and pay well for their meal. The students were four blocks away from graduation at this point and it was time for them to know the people who would be eating the food they were learning to cook, but also to know themselves. This was among Mr. Papineau's fundamental maxims.

"In a few short days," he said, swiveling lazily in his chair, hands behind his head, "they learn who they are, they learn confidence. And when they have that they can learn more, faster."

But the biggest thing one gained in table service, he said, was "wisdom about yourself."

"They learn to be sympathetic and sincere, and strong, to lead people," he said. "They'll need to be role models." How could you be all these things if you weren't reflective, he asked, reflective about yourself and about how others responded to your own actions. "Know thyself" would be a waiter's most important rule. Here, at the Culinary Institute of America, one learned Platonic cooking and Socratic table-waiting.

P hilip Papineau was born in Worcester, Massachusetts, in 1954 to parents who believed restaurants were entertainment. "I always loved the show," he said. "I grew up going to restaurants. We weren't rich—there were six of us, four of us and my parents—but every Saturday night, we went out to a restaurant." Throughout school, he had always been the sort of student whose knees rattled during public presentations, pages quivering in his hands. The first table he waited on was at a restaurant owned by his brother and sister-in-law. His sister-in-law had listened in on his maiden voyage, told him he'd spoken so fast no one had understood a word—get back there and do it again. It was his first lesson in table service and he remained grateful for it.

Papineau graduated from Worcester State College in 1977 and continued to wait on tables. He had some friends in Poughkeepsie, moved there, and got a job as a waiter at a place called the Treasure Chest, a high-end formal French restaurant.

"My parents kept waiting for me to get a real job," he recalled. "But to me, that *was* a real job."

His seriousness paid off. When the Captain at the Treasure Chest left, Papineau was offered the job. The restaurant was a favorite of IBM vice presidents during an era of enormous expense accounts. "The money was just incredible," Papineau recalled, with genuine nostalgia.

In 1984 he left the Treasure Chest for another restaurant and eventually applied for a job at the Culinary. He did not feel as though he was good enough—the other maître d's had worked all over Europe; who was he, this American maître d'? "But I *wanted* to be here," he said, his teeth gritted.

He had learned French service. If you only knew American, he said, that's all you could do. If you knew French service, you could do anything. And he lamented the demise of such service.

I told him how much fun I'd had eating at the Culinary's French restaurant, the Escoffier Restaurant, how the waiter, a young woman, had prepared for me the best Caesar salad I had had anywhere ever (it was her first, she told me), how they sautéed tableside in beautiful copper pans. Such service had long been out of fashion, and yet because it was so rare these days, I found it not stuffy, but instead thrilling.

"I - love - that," Papineau said, lustily. "I - *love* - that." To perform something by nature flamboyant and difficult and to do it low-key, he said, to do it with humility and subtlety and grace and perfection—the man's eyes shined brightly. He did not want me to get him wrong though. "I like show," he conceded. And he loved it when, as he said, "somebody's really puttin' on the dog." But "low-key" was where it was at. He adored, he said, "the theater of it."

Like Pardus, Papineau noted the downside: "You can't celebrate Christmas. You can't celebrate Mother's Day. 'I'll have to see you the day after Mother's Day, Mom.'" Christmas, though, that was the rough one. He could manage the rest, but Christmas was when you really felt the rift between restaurant people and the rest of the world.

While he regretted that formal service had fallen out of fashion, he also noted that, as the cup and saucer were slowly reentering the scene, so too might formal service. "And these kids," he said, rising forward in his chair, "will be the ones to do it. These kids will change the service industry."

By Day Four, everything seemed to click. We would huddle at eleventwenty. Mr. Papineau would check that everybody possessed crumber, pad, wine key, and pen, run down any specials of the day, what desserts were being offered. He would look at his watch and say, "It's eleven-thirty. We're officially open, let's have a gooooood Friday."

Service, after a few days, became as natural as conversation with friends. It was fun to serve people, to answer their questions—visitors wanted to know why we were here, what we were doing, where we were going—they were here "to dig the scene," as Papineau had said.

Papineau's lectures remained fascinating through to the end. Even the simplest queries offered him an opportunity to reflect on human nature, the behavior of humans in groups. One of the last things I asked him was how to prioritize various duties, and he said without hesitation words that would serve one just as well in the kitchen as in the dining room: "Do the job that can be done fastest, first. Take the deuce before the four-top, even if the four-top came in first, because the four-top will take longer, and a six-top will take even longer than that. That's just the way it is."

⚜ St. Andrew's Kitchen

I arrived shortly after six A.M., stored my briefcase in a locker, and headed up to the kitchen. The day before, our group had circled around group leader Gene Huey, a native of Omaha, Nebraska, of Chinese descent, as he briefed us. "You have to be here at six-fifteen," he said. "This is not to scare you or anything, but if you're here at six-sixteen, you're late. The chef is very particular. If you're in the bathroom, you're late; if you're downstairs, you're late. Six-fifteen in the kitchen. Standard uniform. Two side-towels, I believe. Keep a locker. Your knife kits up there are fine. So are tool boxes. Remember, this guy talks in grams. It's about thirty grams per ounce. Read the handout, read the handout, read the handout."

I was already familiar with the layout of the kitchen, having been a waiter, but any time I had crossed the line into the kitchen I'd felt like an intruder; my posture and haste whispered "excuse me" and "sorry," whether washing my hands or drinking from the water fountain. Now I was back in my whites and, with my fellow students, could take possession of the place. Part of my possessiveness arose from being added to the class roster. The chef, Ron De Santis, had put me on family meal. This would be the lowest rank in the kitchen; you cooked for your fellow students, often forced to put leftovers and on-their-way-out vegetables to use somehow; if you screwed up, people bitched but it didn't really matter. You were the clerk of the kitchen, the gopher.

Nevertheless I was pumped up and ready because I had a job to do—

John Marshall, Paul Angelis, and I were to make fifty plates of food for waiters, instructors, fellows, and the two St. Andrew's dishwashers.

A voice over loudspeakers said, "Will everyone come up front?" I stowed my knife kit on a standing rack in back of the long kitchen and strode to the front with my comrades. The clock above the display-kitchen window read six-thirteen. We gathered before Chef De Santis. The chef was not tall—five-ten, five-eleven maybe—but he was trim and compact, his chef attire crisp and smooth, a good-looking man with sharp features. He read roll call—all here but for Manning and Mimi; no one knew where they were—and when the chef called the final name, the clock read six-fifteen exactly.

As always, the first order of duties was a tour of the kitchen, beginning with service stations. With our backs to the window looking past the bar and into the cool quiet dining room (Craig and Mr. Papineau were there, preparing for the arrival of a dozen-and-a-half new waiters), and facing the kitchen, pastry station was to our right, followed by garde manger, the cold station that prepared sandwiches and salads, then soup, veg, sauté, pasta, and grill in a counterclockwise semicircle. The kitchen had been built in 1989 and had been designed for cooking and service; that is, it had never been anything else, as was the case with many kitchens, and did not have to confine itself to an already existing space. A Y-shaped service counter, upside down from our vantage point, split the cooking area. The chef would stand in the crux of the Y, calling orders, expediting as it was called, and plates from any station came right down the same runway—an efficient design for getting a lot of different plates with many components from various stoves to the waiters.

"Your stations are set," Chef De Santis said. "You have everything you need there. Day Two, you set your own station."

"At nine A.M.," he continued, "put your plates in the warmer or the cooler. This counter is hot." He rubbed a palm across the bright stainless steel service counter. "Do not keep raw vegetables here." This was the kind of important, small detail you had to learn coming into a new kitchen; every kitchen had its own quirks. And so did every chef. You had to learn these, too, and get a sense of the chef just as fast. Often, the chef and the kitchen were the same thing. De Santis was an easy read because he didn't talk, lecture, or explain; rather he declared things—sometimes directly, sometimes indirectly, but always clearly.

"There is the ice machine," he said as we circled through the kitchen. "Before you take ice, you *must* check with me. We must be sure it's available for service. You'd be surprised how little ice you really need. . . . The most important station here is the hand sink. You should be standing *in line* to use the hand sink. This, for lack of a better term, is the garbage station. We have a problem already." The blue recyclable bin was missing, and someone hustled to roll it back into place beside the gray trash and yellow recyclable bins. "They do not move. That way you *always* know where they are." We passed dry storage to the walk-in. "Only use the left side of the walk-in," he said. "Not the right side. The right side is for P.M. mise en place only. If I catch you there, you will repeat this course. I wanna be *real* clear about that. If I catch you there—you will repeat this course. . . . Plastic wrap. See it?" He pointed to the huge roll beside the sink. "That's where it *always* is. It's a matter of efficiency. . . . While you are with me, you weigh, measure, and scale things. It is not an option. Two reasons. One, it affects quality and consistency. Two, we have nutritional parameters. Otherwise, it's a joke what we're doing." On a board on the wall behind the grill station were kept various sheets (reservations for the week, parties, and so on), as well as a list of our names. "We sweep every half hour," Chef De Santis said. "When you sweep, put an initial by your name. It works well. It's always *nice* and *clean* here."

He had told us a lot about his style already. Promptness. Efficiency. Everything in its place. Cleanliness. And something more. There was clearly something of Jack Nicholson in this man, the way he said *"nice* and *clean"* in almost a whisper, something theatrical and something ever so slightly demented. At first I thought he smiled a lot. But I saw him smiling when I knew he was very angry, and I realized this was just the shape of his mouth. Often his teeth were clenched while his lips were parted in a wide smile. This enhanced your caution when you were near him.

"It's now six-twenty-four," he said. "At six-fifty-five, that's the last time we're going to be able to order supplemental. Check your mise en place. Never assume everything is correct, fresh, servable. You are in charge now. Family meal. We begin plating at ten-fifteen. At ten-thirty, we're gone."

Chef De Santis told us that he considered family meal to be the most important station in the kitchen because it determined the tone and morale of its workers. He told us he'd once worked for a chef who instructed the family meal cook to make a bolognese sauce with the consommé raft and the restaurant suffered for it.

Still, I didn't buy it. I figured he said this because over the years he'd realized that people on family meal have a self-esteem problem. Family meal had to be done, and that was about all there was to be said for it. Today's family meal had been partly prepped by people who were now seated in chairs listening to Mr. Papineau's Day One lecture, so we had plenty of time to put it together and had only one decision to make—the chef wanted us to use several pounds of carrots, to be served with the roast beef and mashed potatoes. John immediately suggested julienning them, then sautéeing them in butter with diced apple and caraway seeds; the chef nodded and left. Everyone had a few minutes to check their mise en place and familiarize themselves with their station before lecture, which began at seven. The restaurant, its new staff formally inducted, opened for business in less than five hours.

D ay One lecture was simply a matter of going through the course guide on policies, dress code expectations, the things everyone had heard in every previous class. But Chef De Santis was going make us interested in this even if we didn't want to be.

"Skills, you'll see three bullets there," Chef De Santis said, looking at his own course guide at the head of the classroom. We'd convened downstairs in a long narrow classroom with rows of white tables on either side, an aisle down the middle, and in front, a desk, a podium, a board, and an overhead projector. "Mise en place, fundamentals, service. When we talk about fundamentals, it means everything you have to do till it's seasoned and on the plate—that is fundamentals. If it says minced garlic, it doesn't mean big chunks of garlic. It means very, very, VERY fine!"

The man knew how to raise his voice. And when he lowered his voice, it moved way down to a delighted, wicked whisper.

"I really believe in the dress code," he said, continuing a description of how we were graded. "I think they've got it just right. I think symbols are important—it's really a symbol. We *can* wear other clothes. We don't. One violation is a seventy percent grade violation; it is possible to fail for the day because of a single violation. The second one, it's a zero for the day. That means you repeat the class. I am serious about this. Work with me on this. I wear this." He tugged at his neckerchief, neatly tucked in. "I button up. You can do the same.

"For the next seven days, you must speak like a professional. . . . I have zero tolerance for discrimination or intolerance. I will dismiss you on the spot if I see it. And I will do everything I can to have you thrown off this campus, *permanently*! Too much garbage goes on out there." He paused.

"Professionalism. You can't buy it. You can't order it from a catalog." He rubbed his thumb and fingers together. "It's not a *thing*. It can't *cut* you. You can't *have* it! It is something you work toward.

"At ten-thirty, you must leave the kitchen. Our industry, there's too much workaholism. You don't have to eat family meal, but you must leave the kitchen. That's the point of being organized. You can't work through family meal.

"By eleven-fifteen, we have to *look* like we're ready to go. Even if we're not. We are a display kitchen. You've seen people looking in. They're ready to come in and *siddown*." His eyes narrowed and he got that evil look in his eye. He said, "We have to *glisten*.

"If no one has said it to you already, welcome to restaurant row. It is the best time here at the Institute. It's *real* fast. You will not believe how fast graduation comes. The work is much more independent. A lot of responsibility is given to you. *You're* in charge. If you need a demo, *ask* me. If you need info, ask me. If you need an opinion, ask me. If you need feedback, ask me." He gave out his office and home phone numbers, should a student need to call at any time. "Real strange hours I'd appreciate if it were an emergency."

"There will not be a meeting at the end of the day. If the day didn't go well we *know* which stations had a bad day.

"If you think you've made a mistake, do *not* throw it away. Maybe we can cook it longer, maybe we can season it. Do not throw it away. That's the wrong message. Any amateur can throw something away and start again. Everybody, when you leave here you are going into business. Do you all understand? Food cost is a part of that." But, he noted, "Don't come to me with burnt. I can't help you with burnt. Black. Crisp. *Burnt?* That's way *past* mistake."

He addressed service commands. "Order" was more or less advance notice. "Fire," he said. "That means *cook* the *food*. Or assemble the item. The last thing the expediter will say is pick up. When is the best time to plate the food?"

A couple of people call out, "As close to pick-up as possible." Chef De Santis asked "Why?" then answered it himself: "The food looks like—*freshly plated FOOD!* It's glistening, *steeeeeeeaming*"—in that whisper of his—"*juicy*. What does food look like when it's been plated too early? It looks like hot plate food. It looks like it's been *sittin' around for a while!*"

I knew a talented actor when I saw one; seven-o'clock lecture would be fine with me.

⤛⧉⤜

By eight-thirty, Mimi and Manning remained AWOL. They had been slated for grill station, and with the restaurant planning to open in three hours, John and I were discussing carrots for family meal when the chef walked up and said, "John, you and Paul are on grill today." To me he said, "Chen and Brian are going to help you with family meal."

Chen-Hwa I think was glad to be in the kitchen. The previous week after table service, I asked him how he was doing and he said, "No broken plate, no water on customer. Good day." Chen's food English was proficient but he had more difficulty in conversation. His classmate, Geoffrey Rassmussen, from Staten Island, was helping him with that. When Brian, looking into a job position in Shanghai, asked Chen if the Chinese were friendly to Americans, Chen said, "Yes, all slant-eyes like honkies." This was Geoff's doing. Geoff was twenty-two, had been on his way to playing college football until an injury ended his career, he said. He had permed strawberry-blond hair, and during table service when the day was slow, he would goof around in the corner striking Calvin Klein–like poses. He said his modeling name was "Tyler" and we often called him Tyler after that.

The morning proceeded with calm industriousness. After family meal, I would prep the next day's family meal (tomorrow: roast pork loin with a honey mustard glaze, rosemary-garlic potatoes, broccoli and carrots tossed with vegetable lié and fresh herbs) and help out where needed. Most other stations were so busy all the way through clean-up you scarcely had time to blink, let alone think about the food you were preparing. My family meal duties allowed me to wander the kitchen.

I was curious about the food. The Culinary billed St. Andrew's, which opened in 1984, as one of the first restaurants in the country attempting to address nutritional and health issues within the context of a standard restaurant menu. It was not a health-food restaurant, but aimed to serve delicious meals—salmon, steak, pork, pasta, hearty soups like gumbo, and rich desserts—while altering technique to make these meals less bad for you. The concepts were simple, and most of America knew them by now: reduce calories, cholesterol, salt, sugar, and protein; increase carbohydrate-rich foods and fresh foods in great variety. This can often lead to serious compromise in pleasure, but some of the solutions CIA chefs came up with were clever and successful. A rich vegetable stock, liéd with cornstarch, replaced two-thirds the oil in vinaigrettes and mayonnaise. Yogurt and ricotta cheese, puréed till it was very, very, VERY smooth, replaced cream and milk for an "ice cream" that was surprisingly creamy and rich. The sausage that topped the sausage pizza used cooked Carolina white rice instead of pork fat. The point was not to eliminate all the stuff that made food taste good (fat), just reduce it when possible by increasing the use of stocks and vegetable purées (the grilled salmon, for example, was served with a grilled tomato coulis and a roasted poblano coulis).

After family meal, all were back in the kitchen quickly. On Day One, Chef De Santis cooked and plated everything on the menu—four pizzas, nine starters, and eight entrées—in about forty minutes, explaining each item in detail as he moved from station to station. This amounted to less than two minutes per plate, so the chef had to hustle.

The pork scallopini with caponata, polenta, and spinach was a popular item—I'd delivered many plates of it the week before—as was the pan-seared chicken and shrimp in a saffron broth. These items were to be handled by Mark Zanowski, the former English teacher, and Scott Stearns at the sauté station. Scott was a very large fellow, twenty-two, from Hanover, New Hampshire; he called me Raymond by mistake the first day and continued to call me Raymond from then on. I squeezed into the veg-sauté-pasta line to watch. The chef first put two pieces of lean pork loin, which had been pounded to about a quarter inch thick, into a very hot, perfectly dry sauté pan, and asked Mark why he did so.

"Because there's fat in the meat?" Mark replied.

"Right. If the pan is properly heated, you shouldn't have a problem."

The pork did in fact stick, but the chef scraped and tugged and lifted the pork off the pan's steel surface to flip it. It had browned nicely. As the pork cooked he got to work on the chicken and shrimp, searing the chicken in another sauté pan. When the chicken had color, he said, "Give me four ounces of broth"—and with a four-ounce ladle, he dropped it bubblingly into the pan—"cover the chicken and poach it." Then back to the pork: "When you see moisture pushing up through the pork and some blood, that's medium rare. That's a good sight way of checking doneness." He let it go a moment longer to medium.

Veg station—Chen-Hwa and Brian Geiger—had already been demoed. They sautéed the spinach, seasoned with shallots and drops of Pernod, and cooked the polenta that accompanied sauté station's pork and caponata. The chef plated this simply, left it on the service table, and turned to the chicken. "This has been poachin' away now for three to four minutes—nice and slow and gentle." In a separate pan over a hot flame he dropped some linguine and a little veg broth to bring them up to heat quickly. "No dry food, O.K., guys? Gotta *see* liquid." During the final couple of minutes, he added two shrimp to the poaching chicken and re-covered the pan. He delivered the linguine, now hot and coated with reduced vegetable broth, to a bowl (servers in the dining room, at about this stage in the item's cooking, would typically be setting a broth spoon at the place setting of the person who would receive this item), placed the chicken breast on the pasta, and the two shrimp, pink and tightly curled, atop the chicken, poured the saffron broth over it all, and garnished the dish with flat leaves of parsley. Good to go.

On to pasta: group leader Gene and Geoff (a.k.a. Tyler) would prepare one appetizer—orzo with morels, Parma ham, and Parmesan cheese—and two entrées—linguine with tomatoes, caperberries, and calamata olives, and potato gnocchi with shitakes, oven-dried tomatoes, and a basil pesto. This station was all mise en place and these were done in a flash.

Next the chef hit the grill station, John and Paul. The clock read eleven-forty, and the chef began to move even faster than he had been. He began by sautéing oyster mushrooms for the grilled bruschetta, and Martin, the outgoing fellow, said into the microphone, "Ordering one salmon, medium well." The microphone, necessary for the folks on pizza in the back, made any speaker's voice sound deep and formidable; the first order of the day— coming as if from the God of the Old Testament—always surprised me. John looked at Martin, surprised, looked back at the chef, then turned back to Martin and said, "Ordering one salmon, medium well."

"Get the pan hot with a little oil, they sear up well," the chef was saying. "It gives them some taste." He reached for the hotel pan containing the white mushrooms he was talking about, looked at them carefully, and said, "Someone didn't wash these mushrooms." Some chefs instructed students not to wash mushrooms, only to brush them off, because they absorb water, which dilutes their taste. Chef De Santis looked at John and Paul and said, "Wash mushrooms. They grow in *sterilized* horse manure, but I don't want to eat it. *Wash* mushrooms." These would go with the steak as would some freshly shucked peas that he popped into boiling water. He spooned tomato relish—scallions, tomato concassé, brunoise green pepper and cucumber, minced garlic, seasoned with cider vinegar, salt, and pepper, and cooked just enough to heat through—into the center of the plate, placed the beef tenderloin John had grilled onto that. "You've also got roasted potatoes that

go with that," he said. "You've got a lot of things on this plate." He returned
to the bruschetta, the oyster mushrooms having sautéed nicely by now. The
chef was moving like a speeded-up movie. "Load it up with mushrooms,"
he said, heaping them on top of the grilled bruschetta, which had been
rubbed with garlic. "Don't be stingy with the mushrooms." He popped this
into the oven to heat it all through and pulled out a sizzle platter with four
long wedges of roasted potato. "These got a little too roasted; don't roast 'em
so much." The chef piped four dabs of mashed potatoes around the beef.

"Fire four beef, two medium, two medium rare," Martin intoned into the
microphone.

John, startled again—priority was unclear; was this classroom or restaurant?—looked at Martin, looked back at the chef, appeared to consider not
saying anything, then thought again, said, "Firing four beef, two medium,
two medium rare." He turned to put them on the grill and the chef, with an
adrenaline glare, said, "Hey! I need you *here*."

"I was just going to put them on the grill."

"Just put them in the dry rub for now."

John did and turned back just as the chef placed the point of a wedge of
potato into the dollop of mashed potato saying, "This is your anchor," and
leaned it onto the beef. He sauced the plate with fond de veau, and moved
on to the grilled salmon, served with roasted beets and smokey black-eyed
peas along with the two vegetable coulis.

After the grill demo, I strolled back to bone out two pork loins for
tomorrow's family meal. A whole loin is about two-and-a-half feet long with
an oddly shaped bone concealed within the lean meat; I had never boned an
entire loin before and set about with curiosity, sliding my very sharp boning
knife along the ribs to separate them from the meat.

Craig Walker, an amiable fellow who worked for a nearby wine maker,
and David Sellers, who hoped to return to his home in Cullowhee, North
Carolina, to open a restaurant at a defunct boys' camp owned by his father,
had been assigned to the St. Andrew's wood-burning pizza station. This was
a prized station to be on—David and Craig were excited to learn to make
St. Andrew's pizza. I happened to be boning the loins at the veg-prep table
right next to the pizza station when the chef hustled back for his demo.
Martin's ordering and firing were now pretty constant. I could tell from the
sound of Chef De Santis's voice that he was getting a little excited after all
this demoing.

He squatted at the racks below the station, pulling out trays of mise en place, while Craig stood over him.

"That's not how I set this up today!" He looked up at Craig for an answer. Craig mumbled words to the effect that whatever the chef said, it wasn't his fault. "I had two sheets here!" He was pulling out all the sheet trays and rummaging through them. Craig raised his hands in the air and mumbled something incoherent. "I had two sheets here! One had aps! *I* did that this morning! Are you running this station?! Who's running this station?!"

It was a reflexive reaction of course to deflect the heat of chef-anger off oneself and onto your partner whenever possible, and this Craig did by mentioning David Sellers, who was nowhere to be seen.

"Where is *he*?!"

Scott McGowan, on pastry beside pizza, had initially planned on watching the pizza demo, too, but decided instead, with eyes comically enlarged, to help me out with the pork loins to avoid any spillover wrath.

David Sellers wore a crew cut beneath his toque, had earnest brown eyes behind glasses and a ready, friendly smile. He wore this smile—*Oh good,* he thought happily, *we're going to get our demo!*—as he bounced up to the station.

"*Where were you?!*" the chef cried.

David halted abruptly, unprepared for the chef's anger. "I-I-I was in the bathroom," he offered

"*NOW?!*" said the chef. "*Did you have to go NOW?! During service?!*" David stammered and shrugged meekly. The chef shook his head in disgust and disbelief and quickly began rolling out a ball of dough on the floured wood surface of the pizza station.

Meanwhile, grill station was getting clobbered. Orders came at them twice as fast and at twice the rate they'd prepped for. I was wrapping up the pork loin as Paul—a swarthy Italian with dark eyes and a heavy shadow of whiskers—approached out of breath and, I believe, with little bits of weed in his curly black hair. "Can you cut some mushrooms for me?" he asked and was just as quickly gone.

I found mushrooms, gave them a good blast of water to remove the sterilized manure, and got chopping. That was when I learned how to chop fast; the knife virtually rattled on the cutting board, leaving a wake of sliced button mushrooms. But no matter how fast I cut, I could not keep up. As soon as I'd finished half, Paul was rushing back for more. It seemed that everyone in the restaurant was ordering grilled salmon and beef tenderloin on this warm sunny day.

I caught up on the mushrooms eventually, and Dan LeStrud, the incoming fellow who had graduated less than three weeks ago, appeared and asked, "Can you run over to fish kitchen for a side of salmon?"

Off I ran. It was, of course, Day One in Corky Clark's fish kitchen, too, and they were in the middle of lecture. Chef Clark was very quiet, standing, holding his elbows, and shaking his head. He had put his class deep in the weeds today and now he was going to hammer them. He was shaking his head, evidently disgusted, when I entered. "Side of salmon for St. Andrew's?" I asked. He looked at me, angrily, angry at everything in his line of sight, and said, "See the fellow."

I hustled back with a side of salmon, which Chef De Santis butchered immediately, scaling the first piece and figuring exactly how many fillets he could get out of it. Dan handed me a large bag of pea pods—grill station had run out of peas; would I mind julienning these immediately?

I did so as fast as I could, and when I had several handfuls, I shoved them into a hotel pan and strode for the grill station. Paul met me half way. When he saw what I held, he closed his eyes for a quick moment, said *"Perfect,"* and dashed back to the station, juliennes in hand.

The kitchen closed daily at one. Today, John and Paul were still putting out plates of food at one-forty, both of them drenched with sweat.

"O.K., we had a pretty good Day One today," the chef said. He had called us to the front after all the stations had been broken down and cleaned, mise en place trays all back in the left-hand side of the cooler, knives cleaned and packed away, the kitchen quiet and cool. "We were a little busier than we expected to be. That's *good.* That's what we *want.* Tomorrow we do not have à la carte." The restaurant often filled with parties—I, for instance, had helped serve a group of Dutchess County legislators, the Chatham Seniors, and a large group of elderly women who called themselves "Not To Be Alone"—and the kitchen performed banquet service. "The best thing you can do right now, what I would recommend, is meet with your partner. Talk about how things went, what you can do to make things run smoother." Chef De Santis dismissed us and we headed downstairs for an hour lecture on vegetarianism.

This was the beginning of restaurant row, St. Andrew's kitchen, run by Chef Ron De Santis, former head cook for the United States Marine Corps in Okinawa and certified master chef.

Friday would be mainly calm after family meal because of two large parties that required more plating than cooking, and we were off for the weekend, returning again on Monday at six-forty-five for the final week of the block. Paul and John were typically in the kitchen early to get all their mise en place done, but today I saw only Paul. Mimi and Manning had been permanently demoted to family meal with me. As a result of their trek to New York City to see Mimi's favorite band, the Cocteau Twins, after the last day of table service, they didn't make it home till early on Day One of the kitchen and were too exhausted to get to class. The blond-haired, baby-faced Manning now questioned their judgment: "Maybe it was a bad decision," he said. Mimi said she wouldn't have missed the Cocteau Twins for anything. Mimi and Manning lived together in Rhinebeck. Manning liked kitchen work but didn't like to cook. Mimi, who had been an English major at SUNY Binghamton, where she did a televised cooking show called *Chicken Lips and Lizard Hips*, was a passionate cook and had come here in pursuit of that passion.

For better or worse, the three of us were as one on family meal, today jambalaya, with shrimp, grilled chicken legs, and andouille sausage, and corn bread by Mimi. But very little of our Friday order came in on Monday and we scrambled all morning to put the meal together. By the end of the week we would have patched together a total of 350 meals, and this turned out to be a good deal of work.

I took charge of grilling the chicken because I liked to grill, and asked Paul if we could fire old Bessie up. He said yes, after we cleaned her out. As I helped him lug last week's cinders out the back door and down a path to an underground ash can, he grumbled, "Man, the worst day he could have chosen not to be here." This would be John Marshall, his grill partner, who had yet to show.

"Do you know why he's not here?" I asked.

"Yeah, I know," Paul said bitterly. "He worked the weekend, so he's tired and sleeping in."

I had a little more sympathy at that point than Paul. Each day, John would leave the Culinary, having worked the lunch service and sat through two lectures, and drive an hour north, change clothes, and go straight to his job as chef of the Mashomack Shooting Preserve, typically cooking for about sixty people. He was a kitchen staff of one, worked brunch through dinner on weekends, and got Wednesdays off, the only moments he had with his wife. He woke a little after five Monday through Friday and typically would not finish his day till ten-thirty or eleven, to be asleep by midnight, then up again at five. This seemed to me a pretty rugged schedule and I did not begrudge him a morning in the sack. Then again, I didn't have to prep the grill station by myself.

At St. Andrew's, even family meal attempted to follow the dictates of nutritional concerns; thus I was instructed to remove all the skin of the chicken legs, then marinate them in oil, black pepper, and cayenne pepper. I'd watched the chef's demo on grilling, and Chef Pardus—oh, how long ago Skills seemed! Standard daily mise en place, béchamel, brown sauce, consommé—had once discussed the method of zones. This was crucial given the number of legs and the time they'd need to be on the grill. The top of the grill, which measured about three feet square in all, would be the hot-hot zone and would get progressively cooler the farther down on it one moved. So I would begin a row of fifteen or so legs, get them nice and seared, move them down a notch, and replace them with a fresh row to be seared.

It quickly grew tricky. The legs themselves were half mangled, some boned completely, others opened along the bone, sort of butterflied, but still connected—evidently botched pieces from meat fab. Family meal. The grill wasn't perfectly even so there were hot spots and cool spots. And by the time I had all fifty legs on, I couldn't keep track of which ones I'd shifted from a cool spot to a hot spot. I lost track, and pretty much had to stick with them the whole way through. But it must have looked good—searing at the top of the grill, cooking them through on the bottom, because the chef wandered past, saw I'd stacked about thirty in the warm zone and was searing another ten on top. Teeth gritted, lips curled into a saurian smile, nodding slowly. "Man, you are makin' my day," he said. "*That's* the way to do it. Cook 'em through there, but you gotta *ro*-tate 'em. I do not understand people who throw them on a sheet pan and finish them in the oven. Might as well *started* 'em in the oven!" And he departed.

The chef was beginning to know me just as I was beginning to know him. On Friday we were prepped beautifully, everything ticking along, plenty of time with the pork loins and their honey mustard glaze. Our sauce was left over from the roast beef—I simply added some Pommery mustard for a sort of bastard sauce Robert. Scott even had time to simmer the ribs we'd boned out—we'd been told to toss them—in water seasoned with vinegar, peppercorns, and bay leaf, and then roasted them with leftover barbecue sauce.

The problem came at nine-forty-five, a half hour before family meal was to be served. The loins were only at 120 degrees. Rare was defined as 130 to 140 degrees, so this was not good. We needed to get them up to 150 degrees before taking them out of the oven; they'd carry over to 155 degrees, the safety standard set by the Food and Drug Administration. Dan shook his head at the thermometer and cranked the oven. Fifteen minutes later we realized the convection ovens the roasts were cooking in had gone out. Dan cut the roasts in half, put them in conventional ovens at 500 degrees, and hoped they'd be done in fifteen minutes.

The chef, we all knew, got excited when family meal was late.

Manning had set the carving station and there was to be a service line plating sauce, polenta, and vegetables with the pork. "Get that fork out of here, I don't want to *see* a fork," the chef said to Manning. Manning raced the carving fork to the back of the kitchen—"Why doesn't he want a fork?" he wondered aloud. The chef himself, having been told that the roasts weren't hot enough, cut the meat. The end piece was done perfectly. Which meant the rest was too cool to serve, as the chef proved with the next few cuts.

A certain panic set in just then, sparked not by anything the chef said (which happened to be "We can't serve this") but rather by his expression. I more or less blurted out, "I'll panfry 'em!" The chef scowled at the rare pork. This was unacceptable, but it was ten-twenty—we had fifty plates to make—so there was little choice. "O.K.," he said. I ran for five large sauté pans and grabbed the nearest jug of oil, olive as it happened. I set the pans clankingly onto the pasta station's range. The chef said, "Get those burners on!" and departed.

The pans got smoking hot way too fast, the oil turned brown, and the first pieces stuck. But the chef, who had returned to carve sent me thicker cuts to fry, which, in the cooled-off pans, cooked perfectly, about twenty seconds a side; I then dumped them in a hotel pan, which went to Manning. As soon as I finished one pan, Dan was there with a huge chunk of roast. He plunked it down in the hot empty pan, and it fanned out into ten pieces, sizzling and smoking while the three other pans demanded attention. Dan said, rather more casual than I thought one had the right to be at that moment, "The ovens screwed us."

Part of being, well, not a good cook, necessarily, but a cool cook, was the ability to have five thousand pans going at once and still be able to carry on a conversation about, say, the differing properties of peanut oil and grape-seed oil with regard to heat and flavor, so I did the best I could and said, "Good thing this didn't happen during service."

Dan said, "It's happened to me. It's not fun."

And pretty much by the time that conversation ended, I had one hundred pork cutlets up to temperature. I hadn't had time to overcook them if I'd wanted. They proved to be hot and juicy. The spare ribs were superb. Three people I didn't know and who probably didn't know who'd cooked family meal, said, "Good family meal." No one could escape the wave of gratification these words sent across those preparing family meal. Mimi just had pizza, which was provided daily by the grill station, and this too was excellent.

Preparation of Monday's family meal, the jambalaya with grilled chicken, was similarly botched. We pulled the huge roasting pans filled with jam-balaya out of the oven. They weren't at a simmer, which meant that the shrimp Manning had tossed in at the last minute wouldn't be cooked through. A check of one confirmed this. We had to pick them out one by one into a pan and eventually dumped them on the nearest heat, which happened to be the grill. I borrowed Russ's tongs to scrape up the sauce-covered crustaceans and flip them. Russell Cobb, thirty-three, garde manger station, was a born and bred Long Islander who'd spent most of his adult life in the automotive busi-ness (gas station attendant, mechanic, auto parts sales) and was changing careers. He was very happy to be at the Culinary and was the perpetual embodiment of cheerful hard work; he loaned his tongs happily. Grilled shrimp are tastier than stewed shrimp, and the finished product was better than we'd planned on, but the way we got there was typical of our style.

After family meal, Manning, Mimi, and I discussed Tuesday's family meal. Chef De Santis appeared, moved rather close, and said quietly to me, "You helped those guys on grill station the other day, didn't you?"

I lifted my eyebrows.

He said, "You help out Paul today," and moved on.

The restaurant opened in five minutes. What exactly did he mean by help out? I washed my hands at the hand sink and went to see what I could do for Paul.

Paul had gotten just about everything prepped and he was reciting his mise en place as if in a trance, tapping the appropriate bain-maries and ricotta cheese containers as he named their contents: "relish, tomato coulis, poblano coulis, mushrooms, scallions . . ." The grill station's setup was

roomy and efficient. A tray to Paul's right held his mise en place. He had
four burners to himself with two holding shelves above the burners—food
stayed hot here from the rising heat of the burners. Immediately to his left
was the grill; beside the grill was a stand holding hotel pans, on ice, where
ordered meat was placed before it went on the grill. The beef pan contained
a dry rub of pepper, onion powder, garlic powder, chili powder, dry mustard, brown sugar, and salt. On the bottom shelf were grill tools, charcoal,
and a rag tightly bound and saturated with oil to mop the grill to keep it perfectly clean and slick, though sometimes if John put too much oil on the rag
and the fire was really hot, a cloud of flame worthy of the Wizard of Oz
engulfed John. Sometimes this happened in the middle of service with
steaks and salmon on parts of the grill, and John would have to wipe the
patina of carbon off the salmon.

Mise en place for the entire station ran as follows:

On tray beside stove

Tomato relish
Roasted poblano coulis
Grilled tomato coulis
Fresh peas
Sliced scallions
Vegetable stock
Olive oil
Raw whole cloves of garlic
Sesame seeds
Salt
Pepper
Chef's knife

In the lower reach-in cooler (lowboy)

Hotel pan of beef filets
Hotel pan of salmon filets
Backup tomato relish
Sliced button mushrooms
Oyster mushrooms
Backup julienned pea pods

ON STOVE

Saucepan with fond de veau and two-ounce ladle
Saucepan with boiling water and slotted spoon
Tongs

ON SHELVES ABOVE STOVE

Two sauté pans
Three sizzle platters
Half-sheet tray with rack
Hotel pan with roasted potatoes
Hotel pan with grilled bruschetta

In front of the grill station was the Y-shaped service table, which got very hot; below we stored plates and a pastry bag filled with mashed potatoes and they grew almost too hot to hold.

Every day before service Paul would recite his entire mise en place to himself, then say, "O.K., I'm good." Then as if shocked, "Oh! I need my tools. I need my knife, I need my tongs."

"Paul," I said, "the chef asked me to help you on grill."

"Great," was all he said, and not casually either, but rather emphatically. Russ said, "Hey, Mike, ya got my tongs?"

I had completely forgotten Russ's tongs, which he'd parted with so cheerfully during family meal. I said no, I had no idea where his tongs were. This annoyed Russ—he needed them for service, which was beginning *now*, and had to leave his station to look for them. I left mine, too, running off to the dishwashers to see if they were there, running back to the grill station to see if Russ had found them. "Sorry, Russ," I said. He looked like he wanted to grab me by the neck and shake me. I was about to run back to look for Manning, who did in fact have them and who eventually got them back to Russ, but I heard the chef, in that first-order Old Testament voice, say, "Ordering: two beef, one medium, one medium rare." This stunned me; I froze. Paul said, "Ordering two beef, one medium, one medium rare." Then to Martin, the departing fellow, "Do we have any more beef yet?" We had only two filets at this point. Martin nodded. Tenderloins had just come in and he was on his way to portion it.

"Ordering one beef medium well."

"Ordering one beef medium well," I said.

"Ordering, firing, and picking up one sausage ap," the chef said, reading from tickets that rolled out of a small box in front of him.

"ORDERING, FIRING, AND PICKING UP ONE SAUSAGE AP!" David Sellers shouted from the very back of the kitchen with marine volume that must have been audible in the dining room.

The chef smiled broadly to Dan, chuckled, and said, "I *luv* it."

Soon orders began to fly and pickups were called. The chef said, "Where's that bruschetta?"

I hadn't even heard it ordered. Paul, popping a sizzler with a bruschetta heaped with oyster mushrooms into the oven, said, "Coming right up, Chef."

"I need that bruschetta," the chef said, called another order, then said, "Where's that bruschetta?! I need it now!" He looked at another ticket. "Fire two beef, one medium, one medium rare."

"Firing two beef, one medium, one medium rare," I said, and popped two freshly butchered filets onto the grill.

Service had started and I had begun to cook. Almost before I knew it, I had four steaks and two salmon fillets grilling and one steak holding on the rack above the stove waiting for pickup; Paul was sautéing mushrooms, cooking peas, bringing his knife down on a large bruschetta piled two inches high with sautéed oyster mushrooms, plating the food and explaining it to me as he did when pickup was called so I could help plate. After about twenty minutes, entrées began to pour in. Paul stopped for one instant while mushrooms cooked to say, "*This* is when it's *fun*. You are *in* it."

I felt it, too. If we'd both been wearing helmets, I would have grunted and cracked heads with him. You needed that energy—it helped you focus; you forgot about the heat and were unaware of time. I would at various moments have on my grill five tenderloins, and one or two salmons, which had gone on at intervals and required different internal temperatures. I relied on touch and sight to judge doneness.

I made one mistake early. "Michael," the chef said after I'd moved the first order of salmon to the front. "Put the salmon on the grill service-side down. That way when you plate it, you don't have the fat side up." The fat had turned gray and ran in a strip across the bright orange-pink flesh. He smiled, teeth gritted, nodding.

"Ordering one pork, firing one pork," the chef called. "That's three pork all day. Firing one chicken, firing one linguine, order, fire, pick up two orzos. Michael, what's the status on that beef well?"

I spun to the grill, poked a fat fillet. My finger went deep—still very rare—and I said, "Five minutes." Where I came up with that number, I have no idea.

The chef said, "Cut it in half."

"Cut it in half," I repeated, then to Paul I said, "Cut it in half?"

Paul took the fillet off the grill and, on a sizzler, he butterflied it with his chef's knife, and slapped it back on the grill. I wasn't sure I'd want my fillet cut in half, but in a couple of minutes it was well done and, remarkably, once it was folded back together, the incision was unnoticeable. Perhaps the chef figured anyone who ordered steak well done wouldn't care or notice. When he wanted something now, he wanted it NOW! This also was a mistake on my part; I must not have put the beef on when "Fire" was called. Two mistakes. With Russ's lost tongs, three mistakes.

The chef would ask where waiters were when the food was out, sometimes nicely. Waiters streamed through on the right, picking up plates, hefting large circular trays above their shoulders, and striding out through a door on the right.

Dan would watch the chef expedite—still learning—and wipe plates as they slid up the service line.

Paul ran out of peas. "Chef," he said, "can we get some julienned pea pods?"

The chef said, "Yeah," then into the microphone, "Mimi and Manning, up front please." Mimi and Manning julienned like crazy and had two bain-maries filled in about a minute and a half.

"Teamwork," Paul said. "That's what it's all about." He was euphoric in the midst of all this heat and activity, adrenaline drumming in his head and limbs. "This is a *great* group. This is *such* a *great group*." It was like he was on truth serum.

The grill station was doing a lot of business, as usual. When there was a pause in the action, Paul said, "Leaving the station," and hustled to the drinking fountain, returned, and in a moment was back in the groove. He looked down at the instant-read thermometer in his pocket and said, "My thermometer reads a hundred twenty-four degrees." This seemed about right to me. It was hot.

"I need a large gnocchi," the chef said to the pasta station. "I also need a small gnocchi."

"Coming right up, Chef," Geoff said.

The chef checked with Dan to make sure table twenty-seven had in fact placed its order—it never occurred to me that I was standing still watching him do this—and then into the microphone, to my surprise, said, "All right. Everybody else. Break down your station."

Paul put both hands high in the air to me and said, "Yes!" I put mine up; he smacked them, delivering a good sting. Paul was having a *blast*.

After cleanup before we were dismissed, Dan the fellow called us to the front before dismissing us and asked if we wanted to hear the numbers. Numbers of each item were averaged daily by computer to give us the "mix percentage," what percent of customers ordered each item. If we were told to prep for a hundred covers, and the salmon mix percentage was 9 percent, you'd prep your station for twelve salmon, expecting to get nine orders. The method worked well, though there were occasional aberrations.

Dan read: "We projected eleven portobella, we sold six. Orzo, we projected six, sold three. Red leaf, projected eleven, sold thirteen. Bruschetta, projected six, sold six. Salmon, projected fourteen, sold thirteen. Beef, projected nine, sold eighteen." And on he went through each item.

"You don't learn to cook here," Chef De Santis said. We were sitting after service in his shared office, which was all but consumed by the two desks, two chairs, and file cabinets. "What you learn here is the mechanics."

He hadn't learned to cook here, he said, though he'd graduated in 1980, and he hadn't learned to cook in the marines before that. That's not where or how you learn "real cooking," he said.

I asked him what "real cooking" was.

"Real cooking," he said, "is all the stuff you can't explain. It's looking, it's touching, it's tasting."

De Santis said he didn't start learning to cook till he landed at the Grand Hotel Continental in Munich, Germany, shortly after graduating from the Culinary, and after that at a small restaurant in Bamberg, Germany, called Michel's Kueche Restaurant.

"The restaurant was sixty seats," he said. "The kitchen was no bigger than this room, and from Tuesday through Saturday he'd turn those tables twice." There was a single waiter. "He never walked fast," De Santis said. Apparently, Chef Michel and De Santis just cooked like mad all night and the waiter would pick up whatever happened to be ready and bring it to the person who ordered it, regardless of whether the rest of the table had their meal; it was possible that one person at the table would have already finished.

When Michelin employees came to evaluate the restaurant, Chef Michel kicked them out, according to De Santis.

"He cared about freshness," De Santis continued, "and doneness, and seasonality. He showed me local seasonality. He showed me how to work fast and hard under bad conditions. In that tiny little restaurant. Under fire."

The best chefs I met at the CIA all had at least one such chef in their career.

This work takes its toll. I would have put Chef De Santis, the soul of health and vigor, at about the age of fifty-four, but he was actually thirty-nine years old, with a wife he met in Germany and two preadolescent children. I didn't know what it was, this aged quality about chefs. Maybe it was me; as a student I unconsciously put a generation between us to make him a parent-mentor-teacher figure. But this could not be so because Chef Pardus still seemed like a graduate student to me, and he was only two years younger than De Santis. Perhaps it was all professional mien and military rigor and the fact that he'd been a teacher here for a decade.

Chef Hanyzeski, the P.M. St. Andrew's chef, talked about cooking as if it were professional football; he was striving for advanced academic degrees because few could spend their entire life cooking. "You can only take so many hits," he told his students.

But there was also something visual, something in the texture of the chefs' skin that gave them this visual appearance of age. I could think of one possible reason for this, and it was especially clear to me after my maiden voyage on grill station.

All that work over grills, fire, hot metal, boiling water, heads in the oven, day after day, year after year. *They literally cooked themselves.* They were medium well before everyone else was even *rare.* And madmen to boot, touched by the moon. Cooks worked fifty- to eighty-hour weeks moving like they were in a time-lapse film. It seemed completely possible that aging might have less to do with chronological time than with how much living and working you did in your life. Cooks got more done than most people by working faster longer. Cooks put in more hours of life in less time and therefore got older faster than most people. This solution for the question of age, combined with the physical fact that they baked their flesh daily in 120-degree heat, gradually caramelizing it, made sense to me.

Taste

The following day, our Day Five in the kitchen, Day Twelve of the block, would be our tasting day. Each station would cook and plate two of every item they were responsible for, have it on the service line by ten, not a second later, and we were to taste the entire menu. Chef De Santis mentioned it straight away, after we'd gathered in the downstairs classroom, in his morning lecture.

"A reminder once again," he said, "class tasting today. That means the food's on the plate ready to *eat* at ten o'clock, not *thinking* about getting on the plate. Then we'll take ten minutes, thereabouts, get a good taste of these things, break down, set up, get family meal rolling. Then we go eat some more." He smiled. "This is a great life!" He nodded. "Let me tell you, this is a good living.

"O.K., plan for seventy-five again," he continued. "While you're planning Thursday, Friday, you need to plan Monday. Monday I have to have everything I need for the sixty-five customers coming in. That means when you walk out of here on Friday, Monday's got to be ready to go." A new class was in first thing next week, so this preparation was essential for a restaurant whose staff changed every seven days. "They basically have to heat it, plate it, Monday. You really have to keep me prepped out on Monday. Busy, busy day for Day One.

"When you leave your station, do not leave any *notes* on your *trays*. And when you walk into Caterina"—the next restaurant of restaurant row, Caterina de Medici, Italian cuisine—"you're gonna have a lot of little *notes* all over everything. My advice: be very cautious of all the *cute* little *notes* they leave on the mise en place trays. You don't know who was writing them. Here, we don't leave little notes. When I came to St. Andrew's, we got rid of those notes *real* fast."

He stepped back to the desk, looked down at it, then looked up and stepped forward.

"I'd like to talk today about food," he said. "That's an interesting idea, isn't it? I want to begin with fond de veau lié. We finally got a finished product yesterday. This is about a three-day affair."

Once every seven days, Chef De Santis talked about St. Andrew's food and the St. Andrew's philosophy, but he would begin with what was evidently one of his favorite substances on earth: brown veal stock. I hardly need to explain, then, my affection for the man. If there were any doubts about the sort of cook he was, he put them to rest in his analysis and explanation of the recipe, on page 182 of *Techniques of Healthy Cooking*, for fond de veau lié, the ultimate brown veal stock.

The idea was simple: take really good brown veal stock, with a rich flavor, deep clear color, sturdy body, and make it better. The recipe was clear and simple, too; you could say that it was a standard recipe for brown stock, only you didn't use water, you used that really good brown veal stock instead. Chef De Santis, though, was like an Oxford don, deconstructing a classic text from the Western canon, and bringing it to life for the students with the zeal of a hard-boiled preacherman.

Step one from the recipe book: "Sauté the onions, carrots, leeks, and celery in hot oil until the onions and carrots are well browned."

Chef De Santis: "That very first step, sauté the onions in hot oil?" He paused, glanced around the room. "My suggestion to you is to do that slowly. My suggestion to *you* is to put it into a roasting pan, and put it into an oven at three-hundred-twenty-five degrees, and put in that very moist vegetable: the celery. When it starts to get *color*, add carrots, and cook them out. As the carrots start to get *color*," his voice rising to a crescendo, "add the onions! And let all that brown up nicely, and then add the tomato paste! If we take our time, we're going to get even browning." He paused, nodding, his fixed smile not a smile. Then he shouted, "What's the *purpose* of this mirepoix preparation?!"

A soft voice from the back of the room called out, "Color and flavor?"

"Color is primary," Professor De Santis said. "Flavor is secondary.

We've got a ton of veal bones going into veal *stock*. Veal bones, roasted. Do *not* make them *real brown*. Roast them till they have a great roasted aroma. If they start getting too roasted, with a natural reduction you'll have a bitterness in flavor that you certainly don't want. So," he said, raising his eyebrows, "there's a lot going on here and we didn't even get past the first step."

Fond de veau, he repeated, was a natural reduction, a contemporary sauce. "What are some other contemporary sauces?" he asked.

Slowly then gathering, we called out, "jus" and "beurre blanc" and "coulis" and "salsas" and "chutney" and "broth."

"Broths!" De Santis shouted, rising to his toes. "Beautiful, a whole *category*, considered a contemporary sauce. Vinaigrettes, that's a whole *other* category. You're seeing them on grilled items, you see those citrus vinaigrettes on grilled this and that. How about juices? Vegetable *juices*? You've got those really neat juicers, you push it in, it comes out the bottom. Instant sauce." In his evil whisper. *"Luv that."*

De Santis returned to the fond de veau and its two main stages. "The first stage would be fortification," he said, volume again rising to theatrical levels. "Strengthen, right? POWER! FORTE! STRONG!" And then he whispered, "We're gonna fortify this already good brown veal stock. We're gonna take bones and aromatics and wine and mirepoix, and BOOST that flavor, *fortify* that flavor. Now when you hear the words 'good brown veal stock,' certain things come to mind."

He paused as we called them out: color, flavor, body, aroma.

"Those are four key characteristics, that's when we say good brown veal stock, we say, yeah, those things make sense," De Santis said. "But the cook did something very fundamental to get all of those things happening. What did that cook do properly to make all of those good things happen?"

"Brown the bones right?" someone asked.

"Yes, brown the bones," Chef De Santis agreed, but this was not what he was after.

"Simmered properly for the right time?"

"Yeah, O.K.," he conceded.

"Skimming?"

"O.K., yes, slow simmer, that's very important, take all the impurities off. What else, something *extremely*, VERY valuable did that cook do?"

"Good pincage?

"Yes."

"Color?"

"Keep going."

Everyone was stumped. No one could come up with it. At last, Russ, way in the back in a tentative soft voice, said, "The correct amount of mirepoix to bones to water."

"YEAH!" the chef shouted, all but launching me from my seat. "You GOT that?! That cook *MEA-SURED! Counted.* We got a certain amount of bones here, we need a certain amount of water, *here.* And everything is *beautiful,* whether it's brown or white stock. Everything works beautifully then. You," dipping into his Jack Nicholson whisper, "have to *mea-sure.*

"So now we've got that good veal stock and we fortify it. Second stage, two things happen, one is reduction, and at the same time, clarification." He described how one pulled the pot off the center of the burner so that only half the pot bubbled. "The beauty of this is that your impurities will collect on the cooler side of the pot, and you keep skimming it off. That's how that clarification takes place. It happens naturally. So you've got these two things happening naturally to give it that very beautiful *clear* finish.

"Now, how do we know it's reduced far enough. How do we know when it's *time* to *stop?*"

Russ falls back on measure again, it had worked so well before. The chef said don't do that. Another said put some on a plate? He looked around the room. *No one knows?*

A quiet voice, I knew not whose, said, "Taste it?"

"TASTE!!!" the chef shouted, his index finger zooming into the air, veins popping in his neck, his whole frame lifting several inches into the air. "THE ONLY THING WE'RE DOING! I SAID YESTERDAY! HERE YOU ARE! ALL THAT *TIME*!" He paused. "To make it *taste* good." He held his hands out. "Taste. Taste, taste, taste, we have to constantly taste it. And when it tastes," he dropped to a whisper, "sooooo good that it HURTS! You *know* you're there. Then you know you're there.

"Now!" he continued. "It may or may *not* be the correct consistency. Most of the time it's too loose. What did you just mention, Paul, about putting it on a plate? Well that would be the perfect way to check consistency. *Not* on a ladle, because you're not gonna *serve* it on a ladle. You're gonna serve it"—whisper—"on a *plate.* Probably a warm *dinner* plate. Put a portion on a plate and move it around on the plate. If it has a nice light consistency, that is a judgment call—but if you put it on a plate and it sits there like chocolate sauce, you got a problem, you got a big problem. You need to thin it. Taste, that's the most important thing, check consistency on a warm dinner plate, then we strain it, it's ready to use. It's a finished product."

He paused, satisfied.

"Any questions? O.K., so it's a finished product. It's ready to use. We can just take it, warm it up, put it on a plate, out the door, don't have to do anything to it. So here you are." His lips curl into a sinister smile. "*Hot.* On the *line*, *million* pans, *plates* goin' out the door. You're turned around, you're plating it, you turn around, and that sauce that you're just warming up in there just to serve suddenly looks like chocolate sauce. It's too thick. What do you do? What do you add to the pan?"

"Water," said John.

"Water! Why?!"

"Because that's what cooked out of it."

"Right! Don't reach for the stock. Water's cheaper, it's always at the tap, and all you did was cook the water out. We just said it's at the flavor profile we wanted. Add water and it will be right back up to that flavor profile you started with.

"So, we really hammered that recipe around, didn't we?" he said, smiling, this time playfully. "But that's a way to *look* at something like this. I could have just taken a recipe and said, why, when, where, and how. Well, there's also a *concept* behind it. There's a lot of stuff going on in that thing. This is what cooking's *about*, right here. There's intuition and feeling and other things, gut feelings, that you're dealing with, but if you look at it in these ways and you always come back to this one right here, it's always going to work right for you. And that's the base right there, that's what you always have to work on is that base.

"This is an ideal," he concluded. "What we just went through, that is the best way to go. Not all of you will follow career paths that will allow you to do that. You will walk into places and they will have containers of base, and *that* is what *you—will—use*. Now, you can turn your nose up at it, and say this is no good. Or, you can be a chef and say, 'How can I make that stuff taste *better*?' Because you're gonna have some vegetable trimmings and meat trimmings, you'll have a variety of seasonings and herbs and stems. You can really boost the flavor of those bases and *make* them something."

He asked for questions.

Bill Scepansky said, "Do you always take it in a certain flavor direction or would you serve it just like that?"

"The beauty of it is," De Santis said, "by itself it tastes great, but it picks up flavors"—*snap!*—"just like that. So if you had some venison bones, and you roasted them off, and you put them in a pot and add some fond de veau and simmered it, no reduction, just simmered it for about fifteen minutes, turned the heat off, put a lid on, let it sit there for forty-five minutes, strained it out"—*snap!*—"tastes like venison, with all those characteristics, tastes *just* like venison. That's the beauty of that one. It's got a certain neutrality, but by itself still tastes delicious. All right, I've *killed* that one. I'm runnin' out of time. I *luv* talkin' about that. That food is good as it gets. Let's shoot over to one ninety-two."

And for the rest of class he ran through base recipes from *Techniques of Healthy Cooking*, fascinating, even ingenious recipes. This was not a health-food book, not with items like "Sausage-Stuffed French Toast with Winter Fruit Compote" and "Grilled Quail Wrapped in Prosciutto with Figs and Wild Mushrooms," but it was concerned with making good food reasonably healthful.

Page 192 described a basic creamy velouté that used evaporated skim milk for body and texture—a technique.

Twenty pages later, another technique, this one for a vinaigrette. "Now here's what we're doing in this place," De Santis said proudly. "It uses stock in place of two of the three parts oil. Still got four parts finished product, only five grams of fat, trace of cholesterol. My recommendation is to use vegetable stock. When you got that reduced chicken stock and start pouring it over your nice little greens, it tastes like cold chicken soup with lettuce. It's no good, believe me. Vegetable stock is nice; it's got a good vegetable flavor that goes nice with salad and all those things." Simply thicken hot tasty vegetable stock with a pure starch to the consistency of oil and cool it, he said, then add half as much oil. "If you stop at that point, if you combine only these two, I call it a vinaigrette base. Because all I need to do is take three parts of base, add one part of vinegar or any acid to it, I've got a vinaigrette, I can make all kinds of good stuff, just like you would take oil off the shelf. And yet it's different than what we do traditionally, but we've got a great product."

"I like it better," said Theresa, who was on garde manger with Russ.

"Yeah, I love this thing, too," De Santis said. "I think this is the way to go. It's lighter on the palate, you don't have that real oily feel to it. You have the same characteristics, because you've thickened it, and it coats the leaves real nice."

St. Andrew's ice cream was called glace, because there wasn't any cream in it. It replaced all cream and milk with ricotta cheese and yogurt, all the sugar with maple syrup. St. Andrew's used ricotta in creamy dressings, in pastry dough, in ice cream and dessert sauces—it had the binding properties of eggs and the feel and texture of fat. Simple. All you had to do was purée it to death.

"Dairy base," De Santis said. "Again, here's that ricotta cheese action going on. First step, purée the ricotta cheese. That's the important step. If you take the ricotta cheese, then you add your yogurt, maple syrup, and vanilla, you have vanilla sauce." Evil whisper: "It's ready to go. You just have to turn on a processor, blender, make it all smooth, pour it on a plate, and you can serve it as vanilla sauce! And it tastes really good all by itself, just like it is; you don't have to do anything to it! You can add some flavorings to it, maybe some instant coffee, dissolved with a tablespoon of hot water, so it's *really intense*; you'd never want to drink it; pour it in there and make a little cappuccino kind of sauce. You can do *all kinds* of craziness with it. But it's a base recipe. You can use it as your sauce. It's got a beautiful consistency for that."

Put it in your ice cream maker—*snap!*—you got glace. I had tasted this glace, as passion fruit glace, chocolate glace, and raspberry glace, and it was every bit as satisfying as ice cream. But there was a problem, De Santis said.

"It's not a stable product. What that means is if you leave it in the freezer overnight, and you come with your scoop the next day, it's gonna be like scooping this tabletop." He smacked the table with his knuckle. "That stuff is very hard because it's very low in fat." It was important to put it in the refrigerator the night before you wanted to serve it, he said.

And on he went—forcemeats (rice instead of fatback), the gumbo (a dry roux, baked flour), a soufflé that used skim milk, cornmeal, and puréed fruit—till it was time to head up to the kitchen and start prepping for the tasting and for service. We would stuff ourselves with bites of gnocchi, salmon, beef, the pork, the chicken and shrimp in saffron broth, and then we would break that down and put family meal up and eat again. And then we would cook some more for people who had come to taste the food and dig the scene.

"Now is the time to plan, now is the time to get ready for the graduation," Chef De Santis said. "The industry is a lot different now than even five years ago, and you've got some serious challenges in front of you. You need to be aware of what's expected of tomorrow's chef. Things you will need to do and to know when you get out in the field."

We sat in the quiet lecture room on our final day in St. Andrew's, and Chef De Santis launched softly at first, but with gathering volume, into the lecture he delivered every seven days. The food world was changing rapidly, he told us, and he wanted to touch on a few ideas that we might want to turn over in our minds before we graduated and moved into the field. For a man or woman trained as a cook, there were today far more dangers and opportunities than ever before.

"You need to have good technical skills," he began, "and I know that people who graduate from here are great technicians. I'd be willing to argue with *anybody* that formally trained American chefs are the *best* in the world. I say that because when I graduated, I went to Europe and worked elbow to elbow with first-, second-, and third-year apprentices, *and* chefs, and after I was there for a number of years, I trained apprentices, and I'm still convinced that formally trained American chefs are the *best* chefs in the world. And this technical ability is part of what really helps us to do that. Great technical skills, to know the where, why, and when of things—not just, 'Hey, do it because I told you to.'

"Where you'll have to continue to grow, continue to practice, like knife skills, is your conceptual skills. Those are the ones we don't work on a whole lot, so they're not real comfortable, but, like when you first picked up that knife in Skills, those of you who hadn't been cooking for years, you started to handle it, it was a little awkward maybe, maybe a little uncomfortable. And now it's second nature to have that knife at the end of your hand.

"Well, things like conceptual skills are things you can practice and build on and learn to use as well. Conceptual skills, things like *vision* and *creativity*. And vision is something that you will have to be able to explain and talk about when you go out into the field. As tomorrow's chef you'll have to have certain philosophies, certain convictions, ideals, to be able to see where the heck *you personally* are going, and where your staff and the operation and everything else is going to go also. You're going to have to have some vision in terms of what your life should be like. And along with that, you're going to have to be more creative.

"And *not* just in terms of putting food on a plate, which we're still *real* good at. But other things—how to get people in the door. You gotta be creative with that. How to keep people on the job, that's going to be a *huge challenge* for you. You do *not* want employee turnover, that's not a good way to go. You'll find it's very time-consuming, very expensive. So you need to be creative to keep them there. You can only pay people a certain amount. You'll find *that* out real fast, too. You've got a certain limit on what you can pay employees, so you'll have to have other incentives to keep people, front of the house and back of the house as well. There's a lot that has to happen under these conceptual skills. You'll have to realize there's a whole lot more to management than having people work together to get *food* out the door.

"You'll have to have financial skills," he said, writing the words on the board. "Gave you a little piece on Day Two, the gross sales analysis and how to use the mix percentage to plan, forecast—that's a piece of financial management. You'll have to be able to read, understand, analyze, and *act* upon a profit and loss statement. See, the days are gone where, 'Hey, their chef is great, the food is delicious,' and that was enough. That doesn't *fly* anymore, it just doesn't work. *You better know how to make the bottom work.* You *have* to be able to *do* that. 'Cause if you can't, see ya later, we'll find someone who can. Maybe that person's food is *just* a little bit lower quality than yours"—De Santis pinched his thumb and index finger together, squinting—"but the *bottom line* works.

"You'll have to know certain things about marketing. Start with marketing you. How to sell you. Every single individual here, you gotta sell you. Take what you've learned here, understand it, and *sell* that to people. Sell *you*. And that's just the beginning of marketing.

"We used to have pizzas mixed in with the other things. Did I tell you about that?" De Santis recounted a story about a friend of his in the industry who came to look at St. Andrew's and later talked about how to improve business at the restaurant. Once again, De Santis became the actor, playing both parts with equal vigor.

"We got together that evening and he said, 'It was really good and I know the nutritional thing, but what's something unique about St. Andrew's?' I said, we got pizzas. He said, 'You got *pizzas*?' I said, 'Yeah!' He said, '*Where are they?!*' I said, 'They're on the *menu*!' He said, '*Where ARE they?!*' I said, 'In the starter category.' And he said, 'What is the *matter* with you?! Highlight it! Put it someplace where people are gonna open it up and say, 'WHOA! They got *pizza* here!'

"So they took that, on his suggestion—menu item, placement, marketing—took it from the bottom of the starter category, lifted it out, said

St. Andrew's Cafe, lunch, *slammed* it right smack in the middle! Wood-fired pizzas, top middle—*we sell wood-fired pizzas.*

"Pizza sales are now doubled from what they were before that. Now that's a *real* simple thing about marketing, but I never knew that. We have to continuously learn those kinds of things, you've gotta keep marketing things. A real important thing that management will have to deal with.

"The *big difference* for tomorrow's chef," he continued, "is a broad-based knowledge. You'll have to know a whole lot more than just good cooking. You have to know how to research, for a variety of reasons, for a variety of things. You have to be able to write, in *clear,* complete sentences, punctuationally correct, GRAMMATICALLY CORRECT!" He paused and the walls stopped quivering from the volume. "Come on, everybody, we've got to start to write like we're a group of intelligent professionals. You'll have to know at least *one* language, *fluently, articulately, completely,* so people *know* what you're trying to say. When you know two languages, then you're really rollin'. You know three or more, you can write your own *check* in places.

"You'll have to know a whole lot more about science. You're gonna be faced with all the things that are going on out there, sustainable agriculture, selective breeding, aquaculture. You'll have to know about things like genetic engineering. Most chefs don't have a clue. Find out what it's about. Whether you think you like it or not, that's something that you—*will*—*have*—to *deal* with in your careers. You *will* be faced with the issue of genetic engineering. You need to know what it's all about.

"And then it's good to know some things about the arts. That'll round you off. That is what tomorrow's chef is going to look like. The old way of doing business is not good enough anymore. You're going out into a very different workforce—even as food preparers—than five years ago, ten years ago, and certainly when I went into the workforce.

"Our food service industry is projected to gross three hundred twelve billion dollars in 1996. Three hundred twelve *billion* dollars. Some countries don't have GNPs that big, and we're doing it selling *food.*" He dropped to a whisper. "And everybody here wants a chunk of it.

"Health care is going to be the biggest growing segment, in my opinion, in the food service industry," he concluded. "Nursing homes as well. Marriott is shutting down their least productive resorts and turning them into nursing homes. Everybody's gettin' *old!* Baby boomers are gettin' old. They're gonna need someone to take care of them and feed them.

"There's a big change in the way things are happening out there. Super-markets, that's another segment you might want to look into as more people are looking at HMRs—home meal replacement. Also education. You may consider teaching this stuff that you've learned. There's a lot out there for you. So as you continue and you start to think about your careers, get real broad in your approach to it; there's a lot of good things to do out there. The industry is big. Three hundred and twelve billion dollars does not come from restaurants. Uh-un, comes from a lot of places. Any comments, any questions? You *get* all that?

"Get yourself planned now, everyone. Take a look at the industry and see where you want to go.

"Anybody, questions? All right, now. We need to have a good prep when you walk out today. I also need demo plates from each station, wrapped with plastic, and we'll put them on a rack in the walk-in so Monday I'll have demo plates for the group that walks in. Desserts as well. Anytime you want to do it. But we got seventy-three à la carte on Monday, Day One. I need a heavy setup for the group that walks in here. Oh *YEAH*!" he said.

He leaned forward and whispered, "The weekend doesn't start till we're all cleaned up in there. Stay focused. Staaaaaay *FO-cused*."

A half hour later, the chef was in back at the pizza station, using a rosewood-handled paring knife to open quail eggs. He did this on the last day of every block. David and Craig worked with him, paddling cream cheese till it was smooth and slicing fresh dill and chives to add to the cream cheese. While everyone else prepped their stations for this day and Monday as well, pizza station worked on a breakfast pizza for President Metz. A quail egg and caviar pizza.

Because it was a graduation day, Mr. Metz entertained the graduation speaker, Dieter Hannig, of Walt Disney World, and guests, beginning with breakfast in his private dining room. Among the offerings at today's break-fast was a St. Andrew's pizza. For many months Mr. Metz had favored a smoked salmon pizza, created for him by Chef De Santis. "It was a good pizza," De Santis said. "He just got tired of it. I said, 'What would you like?' He said, 'Come up with a new one.' "

De Santis fooled around with bacon and pancetta until he realized that such pizzas were everywhere and therefore his would be undistinguished at best. He thought "breakfast" and "bacon and eggs" and this led him to consider the possibility of using quail eggs. He liked the quail egg idea and dumped the bacon. Too cute, too ordinary. He didn't remember if it was he, the fellow, or one of the students who, as they tossed ideas around, brought up caviar, but it immediately sounded good—caviar was another kind of egg, and there was now a ring to it. Quail egg and caviar pizza. Interesting. And the sevruga and miniature egg had just the right amount of showiness to it. De Santis made a trial version, and it tasted good enough to offer to Mr. Metz and his guests. (He made the old smoked salmon pizza and sent that up, too, in case the president was displeased with the new creation.) Later that morning the call came down from the president's office. The quail egg and caviar pizza was fine. It would remain the graduation-day breakfast pizza.

When Jeremiah Tower, the San Francisco–based chef who had been invited as graduation speaker, tasted it, he suggested to Mr. Metz that they serve champagne. "Caviar needs champagne," Chef De Santis said, admiring Tower's suggestion. "Coffee just doesn't cut it." With champagne, the pizza tasted so good Tower put it on his own menu back at Stars.

Students would benefit as well. Each graduation day, Chef De Santis made two extra pizzas so that every student could try it. And our group, because everyone had gotten their tasting plates on the service line by ten on the nose on Wednesday—only the second group this year to have done it, the chef said—we, too, would drink champagne.

The pizza was not flawless, however. Craig and David had, in their zeal, built the fire too hot. Way too hot.

The chef didn't notice at first, though he was right next to it, opening a couple dozen quail eggs with his paring knife, dropping each into its own ramekin. David and Craig mixed their fresh herbs into the cream cheese. De Santis rolled out a piece of dough, put a plate on top, and cut out a perfect circle. He spread the cream cheese across it, leaving a one-inch rim. He pressed a one-ounce ladle into the cheese around the edge of the pizza, to form divots that would hold the raw eggs in place. Because the eggs set so quickly, he needed to bake the crust first, and he carefully slid the pizza through the semicircular opening onto the stone. He watched it, squinting. He got to work on the second one—he always made two in case one was dropped in transport to the president's dining room.

But something wasn't right and he could sense it. He kept turning around to look at the pizza, then slid the peel in to retrieve it. The cheese had, unfortunately, browned slightly but the crust wasn't done; the chef shook his head. He checked the temperature gauge. Eight hundred ten degrees. He shook his head.

"You guys went *way* overboard with wood," he said angrily. Then he stared into the oven, its walls glowing orange, the wood cranking away. I could see the chef was *pissed*. He had to have the pizzas ready in twenty minutes. There was no fast way to lower the temperature of a stone oven. In fact, the oven was getting hotter.

It was time for me to get back to work on family meal. When the chef was pissed off, you didn't want to be standing around gawking. As I left, I heard him say to David, "Get me a roasting pan! And some long tongs!"

Between the pasta station and grill station, which are adjacent to one another, there is an opening to the back of the kitchen and the pizza station. It's a tight squeeze but there is a small rounded counter here and I chose this spot to cut some vegetables. I'd scarcely begun when I heard the chef scream, "Get outta the way!" He carried in his hands a roasting pan filled with flaming logs, and he was barreling toward me with a crazed look in his eyes. I only had time to drop my knife and dive. The chef slammed the pan on the grill station's stove, heaved the top of the grill off, and dumped the wood into the grill. This was an effective way to halt the temperature of the oven, and, being indoors, a clever place to put fifty pounds of flaming wood. Also, the chef knew he had to move that wood real fast from stone oven to under the exhaust hood of grill station or he'd set off the sprinkler system and send a shower of foam chemicals into everybody's mise en place and shut the whole kitchen down.

The president's pizza would be fine.

It only took a few days to get the hang of a station and all its mise en place, so seven days in one kitchen seemed enough. Service that last day came and went smoothly, the student cooks steady as timepieces. And when the kitchen was clean Chef De Santis called the class to the front. Many were already there, their knives packed, their hats off, hovering over an issue of *Food Arts* magazine, which had a picture of Paul in it with two other young cooks. The magazine had done a story on culinary students and externships and had quoted Paul, then an extern at the El Tovar. "Say it into the microphone," someone shouted. And Paul eagerly and willingly, with a deep and serious voice, said, "It's taking theory and putting it into practice," his voice amplified throughout the entire kitchen. Chef De Santis was watching, chuckling, and shaking his head.

When we settled down, the chef stepped up to speak.

"I'd like to thank you very, very much for making it enjoyable to come in in the morning," he said. "I really appreciated your sense of humor. I really appreciated your work. The food you did was great. I hope you'll continue building on what you've done here as you move through the other restaurants. You'll have a great time. The better time you have, the more you're going to learn. Stop by and see me every now and then. I get calls from friends in the industry. Sometimes I'll know about job opportunities out there."

And then, one by one, the students shook his hand and thanked him as they left.

O f the two enduring memories I would leave with, one had occurred that morning. The pizzas were up and cut, and the entire class got a piece and, along with that, a glass of champagne. It was like being at a cocktail party where everyone wore the same thing. Chef De Santis gave us one warning on the pizza: "Be careful. The eggs can be tricky. They tend to run down your chin if you're not careful." I *was* very careful, and the yolk ran right down the center of my chin before I knew what had happened. The champagne proved to be key to the tasting experience, as the chef had said. Paul looked at me, chewing, a fluted glass in his hand, and said, "Now *this* is what culinary school is all about." It was a happy moment indeed. Friday, the weekend near, end of a block of table service and cooking, a bright warm day, a slice of quail egg and caviar pizza in one hand, cold champagne in the other, yolk dripping down my chin.

The other memory is one that I will keep forever. It is of Chef De Santis. His index finger zooms into the air, veins pop in his neck, his feet rise an inch or so off the carpet, and from his mouth comes a single word: *"TASTE!!!"*

Part V

Bounty

Theater of Perfection

I waited nearly half a year before requesting interviews with President Metz and Senior Vice President Ryan. To know a mountain, you don't take a helicopter to the top and look down at it; you start at the bottom and climb up, which is more or less what I had done with the Culinary.

In 1982, Ferdinand Metz invited a twenty-four-year-old to be part of the team that would open the American Bounty Restaurant, the CIA restaurant devoted to America's regional cuisines. At the time, Tim Ryan, a 1977 graduate of the Culinary, was executive chef at La Normande in Pittsburgh, the city where Metz worked as senior experimental chef for Heinz. That Ryan had become a chef-instructor at the age of twenty-four was part of the pattern of his career. He seemed always to be the youngest at everything he did. He was the youngest member ever, in 1984, of a culinary olympic team. He was the youngest cook ever, at the age of twenty-six, to become a certified master chef. At the age of thirty-seven, he became the youngest president of the American Culinary Federation, a group of some twenty-five thousand industry professionals. A year later, he would become chairman of the board of that group, all the while remaining second in command at the Culinary, and, almost by-the-way, picking up his M.B.A. degree.

There's a revealing clip of Ryan cooking in the opening credits of the Culinary's PBS show *Cooking Secrets of the CIA*. He's in uniform, beside a steaming kettle, holding a green bean. "How does a *professional* chef tell if a vegetable is done?" he asks the camera, clearly about to impart secret wisdom to the masses. Ryan takes a bite of the green bean, pauses, nods, and says, "It's done." He was just goofing around, he said, and making fun of TV cooks who would suggest that there is any better way of knowing when a green vegetable is cooked, but that is his general manner. While Metz's Germanic formality was often confused with aloofness, Tim Ryan was casual, "one of the guys," according to one instructor I talked with.

I had two main questions for Ryan and met with him in his office in the oak-floored baccalaureate wing of Roth Hall. I had only seen him in a suit—his style was thoroughly corporate—but to my first question he responded as a cook: "I don't make brown sauce very much anymore." He paused. "But I prefer a brown roux."

"Why is that?" I asked.

"I like the deep brown color. Brown sauce made with pale roux looks pale to me." He also noted the appealing nutty flavor of a brown roux. I felt then a decided vindication for my Skills teacher.

Ryan evidently saw my interest in and respect for roux and noted that the year before, he had become concerned as to whether or not he should recommend modernizing the Skills curriculum, notably by not teaching the classical mother sauces at all. He surveyed about forty people in the industry whom he respected. "It really surprised me," he said. "It was unanimous. I don't recall one person who thought we should change." All thought the basics were essential. "We're not trendy here," Ryan said.

My next question concerned a particular student I knew, whom I wouldn't name, in a particular Skills class, who was due to take a practical during a winter storm. When Pardus had given me his we-git-there, we're-different speech, was he simply doing what any Skills teacher would do? Or was there, mixed in with the truth, a thread of self-aggrandizement, an attempt to inflate the importance of Skills class and therefore the whole notion of a culinary education beyond what it really was? People cut classes all the time and didn't go through what Pardus had put me through. Wasn't that whole we-git-there business a tad overdramatic?

Ryan nodded as though he'd heard this before and said, "Here's our philosophy and we publish it several times each winter. Unless the power goes out, we're gonna go on. One, over eighty percent of the students are here. Two, the culture of the school is our faculty will get here."

"Why?" I asked.

"Don't know," he said. "They'll *get* here. It's been that way historically."

"Why do you think that is?"

"I think they're just dedicated, and in our industry you show up for work. That's the way it goes, and that *is* a value we're trying to instill. So here's what we tell students. We never want to endanger anyone, but in your life you have to make your own decisions, and you have to accept responsibility for those decisions. Please, if you're going to endanger yourself or whatever, that's, you know, your decision. The school's going to continue. That's just the way that it is. Our rules will go on. It's no different from life outside. Restaurants will be open. You work in a hotel, the hotel is going to be open. And if you don't show up, will you get paid? No. That's our philosophy. It can seem harsh, but that's what life is. If you don't show up for work, even for good reason—you had a car accident, you couldn't get in, what have you—you won't get paid that day. And that's part of professionalism. And that's one of the problems the industry has, too. People changing jobs, people acting irresponsibly, people burning bridges, people not showing up for work, and we don't want that to be folks who come from the CIA. And though we would never want to put anybody in a situation that would endanger them and *trust* that they would be smart enough not to go out if it truly was dangerous, you'd be surprised what kind of response you can get from people when you don't leave them a back door. Not everybody here is young, but people are at least in some moldable shape of their life because they're going through a career transformation, or they're entering a new career. If you take away all the options to do it the easy way—well I don't really feel like it, I'd have to dig the driveway out, I'd have to salt, I'd have to get up an hour earlier, or whatever—a lot of people take the easy way out. If they don't have the option to take the easy way out, they'll be surprised what they can do."

Of course Pardus had been right, and I was grateful to him. I knew, beneath my skepticism, that what he had said was true, and not puffery. It wasn't a game here, it wasn't make-believe and it wasn't play. If it had been I wouldn't have reacted so strongly, and I certainly wouldn't have driven twenty-five miles on icy roads to make béchamel sauce. There was more to it than that.

The Culinary Institute is often criticized by its own students for being make-believe, for being not-real-life. I'm not sure why this is. Also, cooks and chefs throughout the industry who did not graduate from or work for the CIA often put the place down and deride its graduates. Detractors claim graduates of the Culinary are unqualified and demand more money than they're worth, or that the Culinary Institute of America is an ivory tower cut

off from the industry and filled with old-men chefs making creamed broccoli and cauliflower polonaise.

I hadn't come to answer either of those claims—neither of which seemed
to me to be true—but I was repeatedly struck by the forcefulness of the
detractors' emotions. They were without exception vehement. Why? If what
they believed was true, then they needn't hire CIA graduates or concern
themselves with what happened inside the school. But it obviously did
matter to them.

The reason, clearly, was because the Culinary Institute of America is
enormously influential, unquestionably the most influential culinary school
in the United States and perhaps the world, and it has a powerful voice in
the country's $313 billion food service industry. How could it be otherwise?
The Culinary Institute of America educates between eight thousand and ten
thousand industry professionals every year in its undergraduate degree
and continuing education programs. Assuming the West Coast campus,
Greystone, grows, that number will increase. Those eight thousand to ten
thousand people cannot help but disseminate what they learn at the Culinary to their staffs and coworkers, making the Culinary's impact exponen-
tial. Their myriad programs in other countries makes this dissemination
international in scope. With its vast resources—its facilities and the combined knowledge of all its chefs, along with all the knowledge that has
accrued during half a century of culinary education—the Culinary Institute
of America was poised to become the world center of food knowledge, information, and distribution. The Internet promised one day to make all of it
available to every home and business with a computer and modem.

So I can understand people's strong reactions to the Culinary. The steady
stream of CIA graduates—some good cooks, some inept, some famous, some
not, some greedy, some true, some old, and some young—was diverse; not
any single graduate was representative of the whole. On the other hand, the
information that the Culinary passed along, and the values that were inex-
tricably bound up in that information, soaked steadily into the industry.

In her book *Masters of American Cookery*, the food writer and historian
Betty Fussell argues that a food "revolution" began in the United States
in the 1940s, following the Second World War. Fussell suggests that as
legions of servicemen returned to America from abroad having by necessity
opened their palates to an unusual range of flavors from Europe to the Far

East, a curiosity and openness about food germinated. Before long, trans-
continental travel became available to the masses, further illuminating
a country devoted to canned soup and Coca-Cola. Following World
War II, Fussell writes, and on through the 1980s, four noncooks—M. F. K.
Fisher, Craig Claiborne, James Beard, and Julia Child—via writing and
television, propelled this food revolution, which was characterized by an
increase in the country's knowledge of, interest in, and proficiency with
food, including, importantly, the unusual notion that cooking was fun. This
revolution, which took hold in the 1960s, is ongoing.

Another arm of the revolution began at exactly that time, when an
attorney named Francis Roth—the first woman ever admitted to the
Connecticut Bar Association—was asked to become director of a cooking
school in Connecticut. The New Haven Restaurant Institute had been con-
ceived in 1944 by an association of restaurateurs who feared that, with the
war on, their restaurants would run out of cooks, who were then overseas
fighting. The school eventually opened two years later, in February 1946, in
a rented storefront with an enrollment of fifty men. Returning G.I.s in need
of a trade ensured the growth of the school; it moved to a new building after
a year and, by 1950, had graduated six hundred veterans and changed its
name to the Culinary Institute of America. Francis Roth proved to be a
dynamo, and for nearly twenty years she lectured before restaurant groups
and raised money for the school, determined to create and maintain not a
trade school or junior college, but rather the best cooking school in the
United States.

By the time the Culinary moved to its current digs in 1972, enrollment
had risen to thirteen hundred. Four years later the progressive learning year
was implemented. Tim Ryan, a student at the time, recalled how crazy the
standard school schedule had been for a cooking school, with the "mad
scramble" of eleven hundred students arriving in September. "On Day
One," Ryan said, "you could be in Advanced Patissserie. You could be
in the equivalent of Escoffier or American Bounty and never have had
Sanitation."

By 1980, when Metz became president—not without considerable Sturm
und Drang among the board of directors—enrollment exceeded eighteen
hundred; alumni had swelled to sixteen thousand. But the Culinary was, as
it had always been, a trade school, packed with blue-collar workers with a
high-school education, many of them coming from the ranks of the armed
services. Standards of dress and behavior were erratic. One story had Metz

presiding over his first graduation ceremony, mortified by a graduate who received her diploma wearing a cowboy hat and a chef's jacket she'd apparently been wearing since she'd returned from her externship. Furthermore, the Culinary had a new president almost every year during the mid-1970s, making growth of any kind difficult. *Restaurants & Institutions,* a trade magazine, devoted an entire issue to the Culinary Institute of America, mapping out in detail the history of the school in honor of its fiftieth anniversary. It mentions not a single word about anything that happened between 1975, when Jacob Rosenthal retired as president, and 1980, when Ferdinand Metz took over. Had Tim Ryan not graduated in 1977 (he himself has fond memories of the place then), it would seem as if those years didn't even happen.

When I asked Ryan what Metz had been responsible for, Ryan thought for a moment, then, off the top of his head, began a list of kitchens, classes, restaurants, and buildings but gave up in mid-list. "Just about everything we have," he said, finally. For his first five years Metz worked "like a one-man army," Ryan said, during which time he put in place several teams that would lead and direct the various arms of the Culinary into the next century.

Focusing first on excellence of culinary education, quality ingredients and equipment, and raising the standards of dress and behavior among students and instructors, Metz soon expanded his vision beyond the immediate future. He created numerous kitchens—such as the experimental kitchen, the fish kitchen and butchery, American Regional Cuisine, and Charcuterie. He initiated the Introduction to Gastronomy course to provide an overview of the culture into which the students were entering. He opened three new restaurants serving the public. St. Andrew's Cafe was one of the first restaurants in the country to focus on nutritional recipes and methods, and the American Bounty Restaurant was one of the first restaurants in the country to celebrate and explore American regional cuisine, years before "regional" became a restaurant buzzword.

Metz had instituted a degree in baking and pastry and had constructed a building for continuing education programs now serving thousands of industry professionals each year. The school had graduated last December the first class enrolled in the new bachelor's program accredited by the Board of Regents of the state of New York. A brand-new library and video center had recently been completed. In the same structure, a sprawling demonstration theater had been designed where chefs such as Daniel Boulud, Gray Kunz, and André Soltner lectured and cooked. Behind the demonstration kitchen was an audiovisual production center, which created the CIA's video cooking series, but also had the capacity to broadcast cooking demonstrations and lessons to companies across the country who could not afford to send their employees to Hyde Park. The previous fall, the school released four books on food and wine. The school offered thirty-week cooking programs in Mexico City; São Paulo, Brazil; and Puerto Rico; and taught continuing education in places as far away as India, Japan, Hong Kong, and Singapore.

By creating an Internet site, called Digital Chef, it was hoped that one day the school might send cooking demonstrations and food information into the computers of professional kitchens and home kitchens throughout the world. Visions of the future were tantalizing. The home cook, via the Internet, could call up any of the countless recipes in the Culinary's files. When the recipe instructed the cook to sauté a chicken breast, a click on the word sauté would bring to the screen a quick demonstration of proper sauté technique. When it said julienne the carrot on a mandoline, a click would define mandoline and even tell you where you could buy one if you wanted. The professional cook, finding an abundance of flank steak, asparagus, and shitakes in the walk-in, might call up the CIA home page and engage a program that scanned thousands of recipes listing flank steak, asparagus, and shitakes as ingredients; this chef now had dozens of ideas for specials to make use of his surplus.

The previous fall, Greystone, the West Coast campus of the Culinary Institute of America, opened its doors, an awesome state-of-the-art facility that would have its own organic gardens, grow its own merlot grapes, and feature, on the top floor, brightly lit and open, perhaps the best instruction kitchen in the world, what one newspaper called "the Taj Mahal of teaching kitchens."

Claims in publications such as *Nation's Restaurant News* that Ferdinand Metz, president of a cooking school, was a visionary in the industry did not seem unfounded.

Within the Hyde Park campus, Mr. Metz was regarded as a bottomless well of food knowledge. He had earned both his bachelor's and his

M.B.A. at the University of Pittsburgh while working in research for Heinz U.S.A. He had been a part of the culinary olympics, held every four years in Germany, for twenty years. He had led United States teams to a gold medal in the Hot Foods competition, the most difficult and prestigious part of the olympics, in 1984, then did it again in 1988. No country had ever won back-to-back golds in the Hot Foods competition. He had created a team, according to some, that all other countries looked to beat. But in a move that angered Metz, the American Culinary Federation, apparently worried that the team had become a private club of CIA chefs, replaced Metz. The United States fared considerably less well in the following two olympics without Metz's leadership, most recently taking a fifth place in the Hot Foods category, only a little better than its seventh-place finish in 1992.

Mr. Metz was a certified master chef, but he was a cook first, as Chef Smith had said. The previous fall, with the help of Tim Rodgers, he had cooked for and served the presidents of the United States and Russia when the two met at the estate of Franklin Roosevelt up the road from the Culinary.

What's more, Metz had arrived at the Culinary just as the food revolution had engaged a new gear; as Metz built up the Culinary, the country grew more sophisticated about food and more interested in chefs. No longer was the professional kitchen perceived to be a thuggish blue-collar man's world. It had become not just respectable but glamorous. Chefs, women and men alike, had become celebrities. "If cooking was to become our chief enter-tainment," Fussell explains, "our cooks would have to become stars." And Metz's school would not only share in the growing prestige of the trade, it would attempt to influence industry standards of dress, professional decorum, and values.

Metz was a stunning figure—a banquet cook with an M.B.A., an R-and-D man with a solid footing in the corporate world. He was as at ease in a boardroom as in a kitchen. He cooked dinner for his family and he cooked dinner for the presidents of the United States and Russia. To his staff, he was the embodiment of perfection. To his students he was like a Roman deity. When my friend Theresa cooked in the Escoffier kitchen, Metz appeared one day to speak with the chef. Afterward she said to me, "That's the closest I've ever been to him. I could even touch him." Her eyes were wide and serious.

I looked forward to meeting this man. I had questions of my own and they had little to do with corporate management and strategic plans and future-of-the-industry prognostications. I wanted to know what I'd come to find out: What must a cook know? What is a culinary education all about? I wanted to know what kind of roux *he* used for a brown sauce. And what had he done with that mache?

I arrived at Metz's office before the appointed hour of eight and I did not wait long before he arrived, said good morning from a distance, and unlocked the door to the far segment of his office. A few moments later he appeared at another door and welcomed me to his main office. We sat at a round table in a large room that was separated by a dark rococo high-backed wooden bench that had been a fixture at the New Haven campus. Already I sensed the difficulty of taking in the surroundings with Metz in the room. Even silent, he demanded your attention. His presence filled the room. I was vaguely aware of a small television set in the corner. From the south wall, a portrait of Ronald Reagan toasted me continuously with a glass of champagne. Near Ron was a framed copy of Metz's M.B.A. diploma. Cookbooks from the culinary olympic teams he'd managed displayed on a shelf faced me from another direction. The decor and furniture were luxurious and fine without calling attention to their own elegance. Except for a willed glimpse here and there, though, my eyes rarely left Metz.

We spoke briefly of his wife, Carol, who happened to be from Cleveland, and of my work. Dora Bottiglieri, the woman who'd refused me the mache— "Mr. Metz doesn't *mess around* with *boxes*"—wheeled a cart into the room and set a small buffet in the corner, then arrived at our round table to pour coffee into china cups on saucers set beside cloth napkins. She asked about juice, orange or watermelon? I asked for orange.

"He's traditional," Metz said to Dora.

Dora smiled at me.

We talked about his goals for the Institute in the coming years, the importance of professionalism in the industry, the new facility in St. Helena. He was so proud of the Greystone campus he left the table to dig up a photograph of the main kitchen there; we talked about the induction burners they'd installed, which only heat where the pan is. "I can put a pound of butter here," Metz said, extending two hands side by side, "and boil a pot of water here, and the butter will not melt." Impressive, I said, but did you get the heat you needed when you needed it? "It will boil this much water"—he indicated an inch with his fingers—"in about eight seconds."

He and Ryan had both cooked on them and found them superior to gas. He believed it was the future. He believed in quality. (The school had recently put a new roof on the sprawling Roth Hall; Metz opted for slate rather than a cheaper material.) And we talked about the baccalaureate program, which was the most important development at the Culinary in twenty years, he said, as it would "marry culinary education with business management."

All this was well and good, and of great importance, no doubt, but I was after something more specific and got straight to the point. Brown sauce. Roux. What kind?

"Obviously," he said, "you can't make a brown sauce with a pale roux, so the question becomes what kind of fat you use." He spoke for several minutes on the properties of various fats, confusing me utterly. I felt like I was being snowed. I knew Escoffier used clarified butter. Chef Delaplane, Corky Clark's P.M. counterpart and an admitted blond-roux guy, said in his gumbo lecture that he knew a cook in Louisiana who made roux with alligator fat. But that was as complicated as I got and Metz left me in the dust. When he had finished, I noted the reason I'd asked, and he seemed surprised to learn of the roux decree and asked me the reasons for it. I said I honestly didn't know, I had only been able to find out that it was considered incorrect, and there had been some hints that Skills students tended to make their brown roux too bitter.

"For me," Mr. Metz said, "bitterness doesn't come into play because if it's bitter, it's been cooked too far. If brown roux is bitter, I call it burnt roux."

I was satisfied. I could at last put the question of roux to rest.

The conversation meandered through his career at Heinz (as if he weren't already busy getting his undergraduate and postgraduate degrees, holding down a full-time job, and developing Weight Watchers meals there, he also taught gourmet cooking to approximately five thousand people in greater Pittsburgh, refining and quantifying his own recipes). He still cooks every day at home, he said. At home, he cooked to perfection. Perfection was his standard and where he cooked did not change that standard. "At home," he said, "dinner is when the food is done, dinner is not at seven o'clock or whenever." His wife had told me that her husband considered everything that he put in his mouth critically; he ate not a single bite without evaluating it.

I happened to know, I said, spotting an opening for an odd question, that he had taken with him to his home in Pennsylvania for the July Fourth weekend some mache. Would it be too forward of me to inquire how he used it?

He thought for a moment and said, "A lobster salad."

Lobster salad!

With avocado and artichokes, he explained; the mache gave it a nice appearance and flavor. I said, "I bet it did." Curiously, he did not seem surprised by the fact that I knew about his mache nor did he have any interest in how I found out.

In interviews and at his monthly A-Block reception, Metz used a few examples to illustrate a specific way of looking at food. The Reuben and cheese placement, for instance, was a regular one. He had a story about what makes an apple pie so good, which led to an examination of why a crust was flaky and to what degree (in essence, a good pie crust is simply a badly made puff pastry), and there was one about why we salt eggplant and salt's effects on water content and fat absorption in eggplant (salt leaches out water but also, Metz explained, prevents the absorption of fat, thus resulting in a leaner final product). Metz delivered such stories—they were very much question-answer narratives—as if he were the lead in a Platonic symposium.

While such tales illustrated the importance of knowing why food behaved this way or that, they didn't get to the heart of the matter. One could spend ten years at this school and not know all the whys. One graduated from here with a great deal of knowledge, but still that knowledge amounted, metaphorically speaking, to a shaft of light falling on the head of a boy as he peaks through a crack in the doorway into a great and awesome hallway of light. Certainly it is important to understand what makes a pie dough flaky, the purpose of cheese in a Reuben, and the physics of an emulsion, but these were examples, branches extending from the trunk of a culinary education.

"I think a culinary education has several components," Mr. Metz began, in an effort to describe for me the trunk itself. He was fantastically elegant in his movements and posture, projecting both ease and polish as he sipped his coffee or turned in his chair. His German accent was soft but distinct. "One is to thoroughly understand, and be able to thoroughly execute, those basic cooking principles, whether they be roasting or braising or frying, anything." He sighed heavily, as if in exclamation. "You could almost say that if you know that, and if you know all the related aspects to it, *that's* cooking. . . . Their mind is no longer occupied, 'Do I do the braising right, or do I have to look in the book and see?' No. It's *in* you. You know it, you've done it many times, you no longer have to look it up, you know the basic principles, you know how to perform it—*now* your mind can concentrate on 'I have fifty guests here, one hundred here.'

"And also creativity. Comprehension of those basic principles allows a person to become creative. Oftentimes, I talk to new students; they get attracted to this profession because they can be creative. But little do they know that—that part is very exciting—but that part only comes after a while, it doesn't come in the first week. Because in the first week your creativity is based oftentimes on a very shallow understanding of what it's all about. And if our students know that only certain meats should be used for braising and that the same meats could not necessarily be used for grilling and poaching, that's a tremendous advantage. If a student understands sautéing—I mean there are so many levels of sautéing. We talk about one thing in order to get the principle down, but the refinement of each of these concepts is done with experience and an open mind. And the only way you can have that open mind is to no longer worry about: do I understand the basics?

"So in sautéing you could say, my God, there are probably ten different temperature levels of sautéing. Surely, the principle is to encase the meat or fish by caramelizing the protein, keep the flavor in, but there are different levels that depend on what it is I'm doing. Some need a very harsh level; others need a very soft level that almost generates some moisture. It depends on what it is that you do. Whether it's chicken or bacon, all those things require different levels.

"On top of it, the one word, again, is passion. Seeking more knowledge each and every day, doing more things each and every day."

Ryan had also talked about passion—he'd take a student with passion over a student with experience any day.

"Can passion be taught?" I asked Metz.

"Yes," he said. "By example. Not by talking about it. By example. Absolutely. If the students are involved with a teacher who, when he or she talks about a fresh herb and what that means, and begins to become excited by this silly little fresh herb, that's passion. If they see that that person, being more mature and more experienced, still gets enjoyment by being able to focus on that, understanding and appreciating the difference that makes in his or her cooking, I think, yeah, by example it can be learned.

"And then there's another ingredient that's called balance. I see a lot of people, especially younger people, they involve themselves—they have an opportunity to open a restaurant—they involve themselves heart and soul, and that's good, but to the point where they may get burned out. My viewpoint is, there are other parts to life that are very important, and it's by maintaining that balance that I can always find this to be exciting and always get pleasure out of being involved in cooking. If this is the only thing I do and I do it eighteen hours a day, it becomes a drudgery and something I may not look forward to. A friend of mine felt that way: he hated to go back into the bakeshop, into the kitchen, and that's terrible if it comes to that, because then he doesn't do a good job. You're not happy, you're miserable, you don't look forward to it.

"So I would say those are the three components: basic understanding, passion, and balance."

Metz concerned himself about such abstract matters of education but he also kept his eye on the food here, ordering food from various kitchens, he noted, to see what the students and instructors were up to. He then said, "Potato salad is something out of my heritage, and a lot of people don't know how to do it well. I don't come down hard; I say try this way, try that way."

"You tried some recently from a kitchen?" I asked.

"Mm-hm," he said, nodding almost imperceptibly.

I knew by his expression that he had not been pleased. "How was it?" I asked.

"It wasn't too good," he said. Clearly Metz was not angry about this, but instead he conveyed genuine sadness; it had made him unhappy.

"Why wasn't it good?"

"You know," he said, "for the same reason some people think it's fashionable to undercook vegetables. I think it's the silliest thing there is. If they want to eat them raw, give 'em raw to me." He paused, mused. "Not cooked enough. Now, one could say, 'Well, so what?' Well, it has so many implications. A, it doesn't feel comfortable. B, the potatoes don't absorb the flavor. Texture and flavor, those are two important components of what food is all about. Again, it's the principle. You have to know how long to cook what item. Potatoes you don't cook medium rare, especially if you want to make a salad. Those are very simple things. But oftentimes, people get caught by 'I gotta do different, I gotta do it in a more modern way.' There's nothing wrong with doing something the old-fashioned way if it produces great results, nothing wrong with that. Why mess around with something that's perfect?"

As I listened to Mr. Metz speak I sensed—as I had sensed in every kitchen I'd attended at this school—that how one cooked potatoes was only a link away from a moral value judgment. Mr. Metz had told me one puts one's values on the plate; in fact, he suggested that this was the final and distinguishing element one brought to the basics of cookery. "The thing you add is your own sense of standards and quality," he said.

I asked him to clarify what he meant when he said one puts values on a plate.

"You know an artist is represented by his or her paintings or drawings or sculpture, the quality of it," he said. "I think we project our values by the food we have on the plate, not necessarily in the same artistic sense, but in the sense of flavors we offer. I always feel that when I put food on the plate for my family—*anybody*—I'm saying, 'I feel good about this. This is what I believe is good food. If it's not good food, I wouldn't put it there. This is what I like, this is my standard, this is what I believe is good food and I hope you enjoy it.' I think you make a value statement every time."

This, I realized after we'd said good-bye, truly was the final element of becoming a good cook. There was no secret and it didn't come from outside oneself. Your own values and your own standards—that, in the end, was all. This final element, as the Culinary tried to teach it, was a standard so near perfection that it would be almost impossible to reach for everyone who left this unusual world. And yet the good students here, the students with passion, the Adams and Ericas, they would always understand perfection, absolute and unattainable, if only to gauge how close or far away from it they'd landed. The standard was clear. Perfectly cooked. Perfectly clean. Perfect consistency. Date on a dime at the bottom of a gallon. Under Metz, the Culinary Institute of America had made itself into a theater of perfection.

The American Bounty Restaurant

The American Bounty Restaurant, my final kitchen, was the last stop for students and thus, ostensibly, the Culinary's best restaurant. When I met with Ryan and Chef Fritz Sonnenschmidt to discuss a book about how the Culinary trains cooks, we ate at American Bounty, as they and their guests often did. Among tourists, it was a popular restaurant, serving thirty-six thousand people annually.

I had worn my whites to introduce myself to Chef Dan Turgeon, a relatively young chef at thirty-three, as was my custom, forever hoping to be mistaken for a student, though I was, by introducing myself, calling attention to the fact that I was an outsider.

"Excuse me, Chef?" I said when I saw him moving past me. He stopped in mid-stride, grudgingly. Chef Turgeon had blond eyebrows and icy blue eyes. He maintained a rigid posture and had the sloping shoulders of someone who lifts weights. I said my name, hoping he'd been made aware of me. He winced and shook his head.

"Has Dr. Mayo—"

He squinted again, unpleasantly, but nodded—meaning that Fred Mayo, associate vice president of degree programs, had told him I would be hanging out in his kitchen. He said, "Do you know about—"

"Pre-Day One," I said. "Today, three-thirty."

"Right," Turgeon said, and walked away.

I remained standing in the same spot for several moments, perhaps expecting the chef to return with a package of information and a smile, but he didn't. Not a handshake, not a good-ta-meet-ya—nothing. I left to meet my St. Andrew's pals, who were finishing up seven days in the Escoffier kitchen. They waited in the hall shortly before three-thirty, a few of them mumbling about Chef Turgeon. Manning said, "The chef is supposed to be tough. I already had him in American Regional, but I heard he's gotten worse." Everyone nodded wearily.

At three-thirty, we filed into the restaurant and took seats at small tables now without tablecloths. Paul Angelis, working behind the glassed-in patisserie/rotisserie station on view for customers, saw us and came into the dining room. He was unhappy because he was no longer part of this group. A missed International Cuisine class had to be repeated in order to graduate and he had been scheduled into P.M. Bounty.

Gene, the group leader, said, "Go join your class."

"Shut up," Paul said. "You guys are my class."

He loitered some more and slunk off when Chef Turgeon appeared. Someone said, loud enough for Paul to hear, "He's not with us."

Turgeon, unsmiling, said, "Thank God." Then he opened an enormous three-ring binder on a table. He read from a class list, taking attendance and giving assignments as he went. "Russell Cobb, Mark Zanowski? Soup station. Scott Stearns, Scott McGowan? Fish station. Michael Ruhlman, John Marshall? Grill station."

Chef Turgeon continued down the ranks but I stopped hearing as the blood drained from my ears. The chef had plugged my name into the vacancy left by Paul. Unless there was some mistake, I'd made the hot line at the Culinary's best restaurant.

". . . The most important thing I can tell you is to read these handouts," the chef was saying when my hearing returned. "They're the most in-depth handouts in the school. I've told you how to tie your shoes. This is the bible. Follow the recipes. There's no room for interpretation."

Pre-Day One speech covered the basics, but you always got a good sense of the chef here. On his expectations and grading: "If you come to class every day and on time, you're in code, you set your station and cook your food and clean up, keep the kitchen clean, clean things when I ask you to— if you do *all* those things, you will get a C."

His philosophy toward teaching the class: "This is your job, and I'm the executive chef. And I want you to act that way. I'm not asking you to kiss my butt. When I was in the field, I'd often have people who wanted to work for me come in and work for a couple days, so I could see how they did. That's how I want you to treat this."

He broke student performance into three categories. Knowledge—knowing the handout with all the Bounty recipes and knowing your station. Skills—how well you cooked your food and ran your station. And professionalism. "I shouldn't even have to say this, but make sure your knives are sharp. I find a dull knife, I keep it. No foul language. We're based on a hundred percent performance. People do fail American Bounty and it's usually because they miss a day. The way I look at it is, you guys are already graduated. This is your first job. We serve about a hundred twenty people a day. My job is to get you ready for the industry."

His goals: education, hospitality, and to serve the best food in the school.

"If you make a mistake, tell me," he continued. "I'm not gonna take your head off. Just say, 'Chef, I torched this,' or 'I cooked this a little past what it should be.' But don't try to slip something by. These people are paying New York City prices. If you make a mistake, say so. The big thing is not sending it out."

"My fellow is Rose Ann Serpico," he continued. "If she asks you to do anything, assume it's coming from me, it's the same as coming from me. The kitchen opens at six-thirty. You don't have to be here till seven, but you can come as early as six-thirty. When you get in here the first thing I would get on my station is tasting spoons, a bain-marie, and salt and pepper. Get your stuff on sheet trays. If you need six pounds of cabbage, make sure it's on your tray. Supplemental is done at eight-thirty and there are a max of eight items on it. If you don't have something, you have to scrounge from other kitchens. During service, keep it as quiet as possible."

And then he moved into each station. Russ and Mark were responsible for the turkey broth (served with a turkey-and-herb dumpling and garnished with julienned carrots and scallion), corn and lobster chowder (with red pepper and chives), and an apple, carrot, and Vidalia-onion soup, as well as a goat-cheese-and-caramelized-onion tart. Veg station made corn cakes with dry Jack cheese and pan-roasted mushrooms, and roasted poblanos stuffed with goat cheese from nearby Coach Farm, black beans, and fresh corn. Sauté, the most difficult station because of the popularity of its dishes and numerous *à la minute* plating responsibilities, did a crab-cake starter, pan-roasted chicken with an old-fashioned mustard gravy, sprinkled with toasted garlic, and served with whipped potatoes, sautéed corn, peppers, and squash, and stewed kale, and spit-roasted leg of lamb with a rosemary-garlic-cabernet jus, cheddar scalloped potatoes, grilled summer squashes, and oven-dried potatoes.

Good, hearty American chuck.

Tomorrow, however, we would not do any of this. For the last two blocks, the schedule changed to allow students to graduate instead of cook; that is, for Escoffier and Bounty, the block began on graduation day. Tomorrow's graduation day was unusual in that it included a tri-annual graduation for the bachelor's program. The graduates and their families would dine in the American Bounty Restaurant. Tomorrow we would make 120 crab-cake aps (with coleslaw and a red pepper–dill sauce), 120 watercress-endive-apple-and-baby-beet salads with a walnut-raspberry vinaigrette, we would grill 120 already-marinating chicken breasts that would be served with a roasted tomato salsa and an onion pudding, and for dessert 120 black-bottomed banana cream pies with chocolate, vanilla, and bourbon sauces.

"We're gonna do a red pepper coulis with this," Chef Turgeon said, beginning the following morning's seven A.M. lecture with the crab cake. He had a strong baritone that created an almost humorous contrast to his words—coulis, capers, onion pudding. "Sweat the shallots and garlic till they're tender but don't give 'em any color. Add the peppers and sauté, really just to heat through, add the chicken stock and bring it up to a simmer and then purée it in a bar blender. I want this nappé consistency." He had a white board on an easel, and he designed the plate with colored markers.

He moved next to the salad. "You're gonna need to toast your walnuts. The last class burnt them." He paused to shake his head. "They burnt their walnuts on their last day at the Culinary Institute of America. After burning a hundred pounds of walnuts, after burning a hundred pounds of pine nuts, I want to tell you a little trick. It sounds stupid but it works. If you're toasting walnuts, put a walnut in the corner of your cutting board. It really works, I'm telling you.

"O.K.," he continued, "fish is doing the onion pudding. You're gonna do it five more times. I want it in the oven at ten-fifteen. . . . Grill, there's some sauce already made; it's complete except for the tequila. I want you to do that recipe four more times. Do not add the chipotles, got that? They don't want heat. We may even monté au beurre. The lime cream, which is in the poblano recipe, do that six times. Thin it with half-and-half." The chicken was to be seasoned with salt and ancho peppers roasted crunchy and ground to powder. "At ten-forty-five, I want you to mark 'em off," he said to me and John. "Nice crosshatch. First at seven o'clock, then at eleven. Don't turn the grill all the way up. I want the chicken cooked rare and I want the skin to render. Put 'em on half-sheet pans, size 'em so they cook evenly—a sheet pan with big ones, medium and small—and we'll finish 'em in a four-hundred-degree oven. I'll let you know when to fire those. Stagger fire 'em, maybe four sheets at a time.

"The important thing to remember," he concluded, "is you're working in a banquet kitchen today." This meant everybody should know what a small dice was so that if two different people were doing small dice, their dice would be identical. "The last plate should look like the first plate. You should all have the same sense of urgency here. At eleven o'clock, I want to be doing this." He tilted in place, twiddled his thumbs. "I want to be cleaning something, checking my mise en place. My goal and acceptance level is perfection. Anything less, you can do it somewhere else."

And into the kitchen we went. It was one thing, it occurred to me then, to be a hard-ass. It was something altogether more impressive to be a hard-ass at seven in the morning. Turgeon never faltered.

The banquet on Day One allowed me to get comfortable with our station and with the kitchen. Furthermore, Turgeon made sure the outgoing class had prepped our stations. I'd made a prep list and stood in the walk-in realizing everything had been done. All the restaurant kitchens had to operate this way given that they were restaffed every seven days and the chef had no idea what sort of crew would arrive. I looked at John, who rummaged through our mise en place, and asked, "What should we do?" He shrugged. I suggested that we go home for a little nap and come back for service. John didn't think this would be a good idea.

John had continued to cook at the shooting club six days a week, usually till eleven or twelve at night, and was up and on the road by five-thirty the next morning. The one good thing about his schedule, John told me, was that he'd gone from a forty-four waist to a thirty-eight. He said it had been a long year. Once, walking to the parking lot with him after service, thinking about how he would head straight to another kitchen, I said, "Your poor wife." With comic surprise, he said, "Am I married?!" and made a loud

Homer Simpson noise. He was older than I, experienced in the kitchen, and I was glad he would be my grill partner.

Grill station put out good simple food, shrimp and steak, but what landed me in the weeds every day was the prep. Though there were only two dishes, I could never seem to work fast enough to catch up on all the components that went into the dishes. On top of this, there was often a party that we'd have to grill and make a sauce for in addition to à la carte.

Our appetizer was grilled shrimp satay with a spicy peanut sauce, Oriental greens, cucumber, and mint salad. There were only three components, but each component comprised an array of other components. The shrimp had to be marinated in an elaborate curry marinade that included fish sauce, curry, honey, coconut milk, garlic, and various curry spices. Then there was the peanut sauce, which combined red curry paste, turmeric, peanut butter, coconut milk, chicken stock, fish sauce, and lime juice. For the salad, a mix of greens, we had to peel, seed, and slice cucumber, julienne red pepper, sauté, season, and julienne shiitakes, and, at service, chiffonade cilantro and mint. Onto this salad went a vinaigrette that included rice wine vinegar, lime juice, Dijon mustard, honey, minced scallions, ginger, garlic, soy sauce, ground coriander, and lastly some peanuts that had been toasted and chopped.

The entrée was more elaborate. A six-ounce filet mignon was first coated with dry marinade of paprika, salt, cumin, sugar, mustard, pepper, dried oregano, cayenne, garlic, and ancho chili powder. (Anchos—dried poblanos—made a tasty powder when roasted and ground, and gave an excellent flavor to salsas when rehydrated and chopped.) We had to cut hundreds of large french fries and blanch them in 275-degree oil before service. These couldn't simply be fried like normal potatoes. We had to spice them with onions that, before we cut a single potato, were peeled, chopped, sent through the small die of a Hobart grinder, squeezed of their liquid, and baked till they became dry, then ground in a spice grinder and mixed with salt and, of all things, a little Old Bay. There were huge colanders full of spinach to stem and clean, and shallots to mince for the sautéed spinach. Turgeon served succotash with the steak—onion (small dice), corn (cut from the cob, boiled, and shocked), and many pounds of fava beans (shucked, boiled, shocked, then peeled). This mixture was reheated to order in cream that we'd reduced to nappé. Rough chopped chervil would be added at the last minute. We wouldn't just serve this succotash on the plate—too easy. We'd put it on the plate in its own little cup made from a sweet onion. First we would boil the onions, shock them, peel them, cut them in half so that its top could be rested like a lid against the bowl soon to overflow with succotash. The onion, of course, had its own seasoning: two parts ancho chili powder, one part ground cumin, one part ground coriander. But the bane of my Bounty existence was the barbecue sauce on which the grilled filet was rested: minced onion, a head of minced garlic, dry mustard, ancho chili powder, cumin, coriander, cayenne, dried oregano, tomatoes roasted black, sherry vinegar, molasses, honey, bourbon, veal stock, brown sauce, and cilantro stems.

I scarcely made note, in reviewing the recipe before class, of the penultimate item. In order to make this delicious, elaborate barbecue sauce, first one had to make a brown sauce. And of the eighteen students in the kitchen, I was the one, by chance, whose duty it was to make it.

I arrived at six-thirty-three. John was already at our station, steeling his knife. By virtue of the fact that he'd set his cutting board closer to the grill than mine, he was in charge of grilling steak and shrimp; I'd cook the other items from our station. And for the first half hour I generally putzed, uncertain what to do, checking our mise en place to make sure it was good. Before I knew it the chef had arrived and called lecture, held in the refined, air-conditioned dining room. Lecture lasted just long enough for me to down a cup of coffee and shake my head clear. Then we were back in the kitchen with banquet assignments in addition to normal à la carte. Our peanut and barbecue sauces were good to go, which was fortunate, since the latter took all morning even if you knew what you were doing, and since John had to make three quarts of the banquet sauce for the forty-eight chicken breasts he would sear off on the grill immediately after family meal. During lecture he had instructed John to make the sauce: roast two pounds of chicken bones and caramelize a half pound of mirepoix; simmer it in six cups of chicken stock and six cups of veal stock; throw in some aromatics, bay leaf, a head of garlic cut in half, simmer, skim, toss in some basil stems, and strain; check for seasoning; lié at service.

"It's a busy little restaurant we have here," Chef Turgeon had said.

I supposed it was, but I didn't have time to think about it. Potatoes to cut, shallots to mince, onions to small dice as well as to chop, send through a grinder, dry, and pulverize. I took five minutes at ten-thirty to bolt a quick family meal and was back at my station not quite knowing whether I was going to be prepared when service rolled around in an hour. Others seemed nervous too. After the third loud object hit the floor, Turgeon said, "Man, you guys got the dropsies." Then Scott Stearn's mise en place tray smashed on the floor. I heard breaking porcelain—fish station kept all its fine cuts in soup cups or ramekins—and though I saw only a mound of julienned red pepper among shards of soup cup, the expression on Scott's face suggested he'd lost more than the red pepper. The chef screamed at them when they weren't ready for their Day One demo on time.

The chef walked everywhere in the kitchen at steady ramming speed, his neck seemingly preceding him everywhere. There was a built-in violence to everything he did. That day he strode down the line, stopped at our hotel pans filled with mise en place in small bain-marie inserts on ice and covered with plastic wrap, rammed his fingers through the wrap and into the fava beans, into the corn, into the onions, checking for sliminess, and moving on. He didn't simply remove the wrap; it was as if he was angry with it for being in his way.

Soon he was demoing our station. "Seasoning is the most important thing," he told us. "When you're weeded, the first thing to go is salt and pepper." And he was off through the demo. The ap call was pick-up and onto the grill went four shrimp on two parallel skewers. Ap plates were on the shelf above the line. A handful of greens went into a mixing bowl, with generous pinches of shiitake, red pepper, cucumber, and a quick chiffonade of cilantro and mint, with a small ladleful of the vinaigrette, tossed and mounded in the center of the plate. We wanted as much height as we could get. Flip the shrimp. Start the fillet. On the order call, mark the steak off on the grill; the chef wanted distinct hash marks, he said, so start the steak at seven o'clock and finish at eleven, flip it, then hold it very rare on a rack; finish it in a 450-degree oven at the fire call. When the shrimp were cooked, place the tail in the center of the greens in an even circle, all shrimp curling in the same direction. Drizzle a circle of the spicy peanut sauce—kept in a squeeze bottle—around the salad, sprinkle with toasted peanuts, and it was good to go.

Meanwhile, paint a hollowed Vidalia with some barbecue sauce and season it with the cumin-ancho mix; heat it on a sizzler in the oven. Melt some butter in two sauté pans. Sweat onions in one, shallots in the other. Sauté spinach in the shallot pan; add corn and fava to the onion, and about two ounces of cream; season, reduce cream—quickly add some chicken stock to the spinach to nudge it on its wilting way—reduce cream till thick and the ingredients are heated through; chiffonade and add the chervil before retrieving the Vidalia, now steaming hot, and begin plating, using a designated mark on the china as twelve o'clock. Season and serve the spinach at one o'clock on the plate. John would have by now put the steak in the oven to finish cooking, and I would have put eight blanched fries into the hot Fry-Max. Onion down at three o'clock, top resting against it, and spoon in succotash so that it overflowed onto the plate. A two-ounce ladle of sauce went down at six and on top of that the steak. Drain the fries, season them, and stack them in a log-cabin-style parallelogram at nine o'clock. Garnish with plushes of cilantro and you're good to go with entrée.

The chef moved on to sauté, then began banquet service as Rose Ann said into the microphone, "Pick up one soup sampler, pick up one shrimp." She paused. *"Grill?"* John called back, "Picking up one shrimp," ducked into the lowboy, and tossed a shrimp onto grill. The clock above the dishwasher pot room read ten of twelve.

Time melts when service begins. John fired the last of a dozen or so steaks at two o'clock, and I remembered little of what happened in the intervening two hours. At one point I found myself in the walk-in, the sweat on my face chilling, to grab trays of chicken for the banquet. Trying to keep up with the succotash, baked onion, and spinach, and plating it all, I watched Chef Turgeon barrel down the line. As he strode he told me to clean my station. It was a mess but I was otherwise occupied. The next time down the line, he said, "I want you to stop what you are doing and clean this station. Consolidate this stuff. Do you need this on your station? No. I want this station to be so clean you can eat off it." I cleaned my station.

I put a steak entrée up and Chef Turgeon squinted at it. He turned the plate to look at the succotash. "This looks overcooked. It looks like you broke the cream on this one."

"Would you like me to replace it?" I asked. It had broken while my back was turned, plating spinach.

He said no, then looked at a ticket and said, "Yeah, go ahead, you got a couple minutes."

Later, as he delivered one of our plates to a waiter, he said, "These fries are a little past golden brown, guys."

Beside me, sauté was buried. We shared six burners; they left me one. Salmon got hammered early and Chef Turgeon managed to dig up another side of salmon and get it delivered in time to butcher and cook. John kept track on a sheet of brown towel what had been ordered, fired, and picked up at our station. I was glad because what wherewithal I possessed was taxed.

I ran out of shallots and, somehow, Mimi appeared with a ramekin filled with minced shallots; I didn't remember asking and thought at the time she must surely be an angel. I recalled Paul's gratitude when I'd appeared with julienned pea pods.

Suddenly, John asked Rose Ann if we could break down our station and she said yes.

We'd gotten out all our food and gotten it out adequately, but for a few imperfections, and I'd held my own. I was hot and tired and there was little time or desire for high fives or self-congratulations. Too much prep for Tuesday, and everything to clean, wrap up, and put away before three.

As John and I shelved our mise en place in the walk-in, John turned to me with an enormous cabbage. He asked why we had a cabbage on our shelf. I said I didn't know. He handed it to me. Gene entered the walk-in. For no reason, I threw the cabbage like a medicine ball at Gene. Gene caught the cabbage and pretended to be outraged. "Don't you know anything about professionalism?" he demanded. "This is the CIA and we're professional here. There's no time for joking around." Then he said, "Oh, I forgot, you're a writer."

John, who was still organizing the mise en place on our shelf, trying to fit it all in, looked at Gene and said, "You wouldn't have known it today."

This halted me. I thanked John and left the walk-in.

At three o'clock, we gathered around the chef like an offense around a coach. "There are not many great Day Ones," he began. "I'd say this was between a D-plus and a C-minus. Fish station, I had to ask you to get a lot of things for demo. You really weren't prepared, and that sort of gives me a clue as to how the rest of the day will go. Grill station, you were all right, sauté all right. During service, grill, you were messy. Sauté, you were a little behind, a little sloppy. All in all there were a lot of knickknacks that need to be refined." He noted mismeasurement in recipes; the recipes, we were to follow exactly. "Generally, if I'm not talking to you, you're probably doing a good job. But if I'm talking to you, saying clean this or do this, then it's not good. It's a busy, busy week coming up. Let's be organized. Any questions? Have a nice weekend."

⊱⋰⋱⊰

The weekend snapped away and we were back at Bounty on Tuesday. After work that day, I tried to explain in an E-mail to a friend in the city why I'd been out of touch:

> It's been a personal challenge to actually work my way into a real kitchen, and be on the hot line. The chef is young, tough, militaristic. "You blanched those fries in *too* hot oil!" he said to me angrily in the middle of service, taking a cruise down the line. "I can tell by their color."
>
> "Yes, Chef, I did, I—"
>
> "I told you how I wanted them done. Do them that way. If you can't do it, I'll find someone who can."
>
> The thermometer in my partner's pocket reads 120 degrees and I've got two orders of succotash and spinach to get out because the pickup has been called, and the fellow, Rose Ann Serpico, cousin of the famous detective, is asking where the medium and the medium rare are. I try to be good, I try to be perfect at what I'm doing, and I actually try to write things down and remember what people say so I can write about it later.

This was work. I arrived at six-thirty and I cranked out mise en place and cooked at service and cleaned and was grateful to be gone at three, and not heading to another job as John and others were. Todd Sargent was late one day and, at family meal, when I asked why, he said, "I guess working, class, and being an R.A. is just a liiiiiiiittle too much." He said this with a twisted, squinty look on his face. He worked nights cooking and waiting tables at the Hyde Park Brew Pub. Dave Sellers nodded and said he was sometimes so tired he didn't even bother to turn off the alarm, just let it buzz away. Todd, as the resident advisor in his dorm, said he got complaints about ignored alarms all the time.

I was usually too tired and certainly too busy to taste the food. On Tuesday, the young, and by critics' accounts, brilliant chef of Le Bernardin, Eric Ripert, participating in the Great-Chef series, wandered through the kitchen. He talked with Chef Turgeon, and I was annoyed that it was the middle of service and I couldn't eavesdrop. Geoff Rasmussen managed to get away from veg station for an autograph. "To Geoffrey," Ripert, who appeared embarrassed to have been asked for an autograph, wrote in the notebook. "It will be our pleasure to tickle your taste buds at Le Bernardin one of these days. Good luck and bon appetite!"

This was work, just as Turgeon had told us at the outset. And contrary to continual student grousing that this wasn't a "real" restaurant situation because of the number of students, this wasn't unreal. At Monkey Bar, for instance, four people worked the line, not eight, as there were here. Three people worked the garde manger station; there was one prep cook, and four people worked the pastry station—twelve people in all, the size of a small CIA class.

On Wednesday, John didn't show up. I was worn down by this point (after only three days) and couldn't believe he wasn't there. He knew how much we had to do. Yes, I knew his schedule, but I couldn't believe, knowing all we, now I, had to do, he would willingly sleep in. You just didn't do that.

The chef had told Mimi, a tournant, to help me out, but she was swamped too and helped here and there with prep and then stayed on the line to sauté spinach and succotash while I did the rest. When John returned the next day he apologized. We had a banquet on again, as we did every day, and we were doing that chicken again. John was to mark off the chicken we'd finish in the oven for service and I had to do the barbecue sauce, which first required a brown sauce.

"You're responsible for this," I said to Chef Turgeon. "Why did you put brown sauce in this?"

"I tried just stock," he said. "But it wasn't right. It needed a flour-thickened sauce." There was a richness, a creamy luxuriousness to this sauce that resulted from the brown sauce. Reduced veal stock would not have been the same. I asked the chef what kind of roux he wanted in his brown sauce. He used a blond roux, he said, noting that skills classes tend to scorch brown roux. "Since leaving this place, I've made roux about thirty times," he told me. "That's over ten years." Then he said, "I'll see if I can get you some brown sauce."

Thank God, I thought. Service was in a few hours and the brown sauce, after the roux was cooked and the mirepoix was cut and caramelized, would take an hour to cook out. Fifteen minutes later, he hung up his phone and called out, "Michael, you're gonna have to make your own brown sauce." This gave me a very large headache. I was tired. We already had a million things to do. I tried to go through in my head how much roux I needed for a quart and a half of brown sauce. I knew we'd used eight ounces in Skills for forty ounces. I couldn't remember how much flour weighed, and I couldn't do the math in that state and didn't have time, anyway, so I filled a pan with flour till it looked right and shoved it in the oven to get it started while I cut the mirepoix.

All time was not the same in the kitchen. There was something about the forty-five minutes between arrival and lecture that was enormously important, far more important than, say, the forty-five minutes before service. If you used that first forty-five minutes to get everything you needed to your station and hammered out a couple of items—say I'd measured the flour, made the roux, cut and caramelized the mirepoix—the rest of the day, all the way through service, would be smooth, and you could give yourself a full fifteen minutes for family meal. But if you putzed for twenty minutes, didn't have your head together, only got one thing done instead of three, the rest of the day was a disaster no matter how fast you worked or how much time you saved. You would never catch up. It was like some kind of thermodynamic law.

You could actually watch mental disorganization. While the brown sauce was simmering, I'd walk to the dry-storage closet, about a fifteen-second trip from my station if no one got in the way, to grab another onion (I'd already gone there once for the mirepoix) and garlic, and I minced those. Then I'd run down the recipe and see that I needed sherry vinegar, also in dry storage, and all the way there I'd kick myself for not getting this when I got the onion and garlic, which I should have gotten before *that* when I collected the mirepoix. Was I *thinking*? After I'd measured the vinegar I realized I needed honey, *also* in dry storage, but where was the bourbon? "Chef," I said, "do we have any bourbon?"

"You're asking me *now* where's the bourbon?" he said. "You should be *straining* your sauce by now."

I wanted, of course, to respond, "I'm not straining my fucking sauce now; do we have any fucking bourbon?"—such was my self-loathing. But I said, "Yes, Chef," and eventually located the bourbon at the patisserie station without the chef's help.

At ten-thirty, John pulled out all the chicken breasts to get them marked off—nice crosshatch, render the skin—but the grill wasn't hot enough. This was one of those physical things that you might have figured out if you weren't swamped, but instead of noticing that the chicken didn't make a nice sizzle when it hit the grill or noticing that your hand didn't get as hot as it usually did when you slapped the chicken down, you thought about what you could get done while these things were searing. Because the grill wasn't hot enough, the skin wasn't rendering as quickly as it normally did, and it took longer to mark them, and he thus had to leave them on the grill longer than he wanted. He got some off and left others on the grill.

Chef Turgeon happened to walk down the line and, passing the grill, said, "You're *cooking* these, get these off the grill." Then he halted. He turned and saw the chicken John had taken off the grill and set on a sheet pan at his station. Turgeon jabbed at them with his fingers; he did this hard, punching them, and I was surprised his fingers didn't pop right through to the sheet pan. "Oh, *man,* these are cooked!" he shouted. "I said *rare!*" He punched at more. And then, in his anger, he picked one up in his two hands and ripped a hole through the center of the breast, stared at the pale pink flesh, threw it down on the sheet pan, and walked away. "Damn!" he shouted, throwing his hands up.

He returned moments later and evaluated each of the thirty John had cooked and kept about twelve. "Keep these separate. Give the rest to family meal." He went to his computer stand, sat on the stool there, and called the meat room. "I need 'em bad," he said. "Yeah, six whole chickens, I can take that." A few minutes later he said, "Grill! I need somebody to go to the meat room and pick up chickens." I felt bad for John and bolted. The meat room was on the other side of the building, down two flights of stairs. I raced back with six chickens and gave them to Manning, who would butcher them for their breasts, and got back to work. Service approached. The chef made a customary tour of the line, checking everyone's mise en place and tasting sauces.

He and John exchanged words. I don't know how it began, but I turned from my frantic, before-service cutting when I heard the chef say, "Don't get an attitude with *me,*" and he laughed *he-huh!*, his voice even deeper than usual, shaking his head

John said, "I didn't come to school to be restaurant labor."

The chef said, "Maybe because you're older, maybe because you have some business experience . . ." What amazed me here, aside from the fact that John was getting right in Chef Turgeon's face, which you didn't do to any chef at the Culinary, was that Turgeon, while he was saying all this, didn't pause once in his checking mise en place and sauces. While he and John were having this dialogue, he was poking his fingers into the shallots, leaning over pots, stirring to check consistency, adjusting flames. He said, "Maybe because you have some business experience . . ."

"Maybe I just don't learn that well from your teaching *style,*" said John.

I needed the chef to check my sauce, which I'd finally gotten blended and strained. He let some fall off a tasting spoon. "Nice consistency," he said. "Perfect consistency." He tasted it, nodded, winced. "Put about two tablespoons of molasses in it, and a little bit of salt, not much, and I think you'll be fine." And he was gone.

Service came and the banquet was served; à la carte was slow and, as always, the tension that built through the morning was released during service. By the end of the day, Chef Turgeon and John were chatting leisurely about D.C., where both had worked.

The kitchen was cleaned early that day and we gathered around the chef, who stood at the end of the service line next to the expediting microphone.

"Today," he said. "Better. It's getting better, but it's still not quite what I expect. Banquet was still not in sync. A la carte, again, details." We had a few minutes to kill and the chef, musing, said, "You know, I tell students to hurry and they say, 'I'm *going* as fast as I *can*.' Well, *no*, you're *not*. You will be amazed how fast you can do things. There is no limit to how fast you can go. You can never be good enough, you can never be fast enough. Remember that."

He asked each person, one by one, what they had learned today. Mimi learned about clabber cream, another type of soured cream. Geoff said, "When someone does something for you, double check it."

The chef smiled and said, "Ah, you realized that. Yeah, I see that all the time. Bill?"

Bill said, "I learned how to do a really good vegetable stock."

The chef said, "I think mushroom stems and sweating is the key to good veg stock." He liked to sweat the veg till they were nearly mush before adding them to the stock or water.

Another learned about wiping down sauce containers, and the chef said, "I've worked in places where that was huge, always wiping down containers so no crud builds up, always putting stuff in the smallest possible container. John, how about you?"

John was last in line. He said, "I learned not to share your feelings when you're in a bad mood."

The chef nodded, chuckled, and said, "O.K., see you tomorrow."

Conversation was limited in the kitchen for the obvious reason that we had work to do, and I asked the chef if we could sit down one day after service. I knew very little about Daniel Turgeon, other than that he was thirty-three, born in Chicago. He drove a shiny red American sports car. He was smart and articulate about food, though here he talked more about mechanics and hustle. He had cooked with Madeleine Kamman at her school in California—"Great lady, great lady," he said of the author and cook—and noted how surprised he was to find that "she had a cook's mentality." *I'm tougher than you, I'm faster than you, I'm* better *than you.* Turgeon himself *secreted* this mentality. And I knew that if you weren't prepared for him, if your mise en place wasn't ready or there was salt and scraps all over your station, he could be like bad weather coming down the line. One of his main themes, in the kitchen and in lecture, was how hard the life of a cook really was, and it was this I wanted to address first: why is he in this business if it's so hard?

He laughed an abrupt guttural he-huh!, smiled, and began talking with a lightness I had not seen in the kitchen.

"Ya know, it's funny. I remember when I started teaching Skill Development, after a couple weeks, in my head I was thinking, Day One, tell 'em, '*Why* are you doing this? What, are you crazy? Why are you getting into this *business*?!'"

Turgeon couldn't answer the question even for himself except to say that he'd always cooked. As a boy he wrecked the kitchen for a batch of botched sugar cookies, sugar all over the floor. His first job was busboy. And from that youthful vantage, the kitchen was the coolest place of all; he always wanted to get back there. And when he got back there all he wanted was "to move up the line, to be cooking on the hot line." He knew in high school he was headed next to culinary school, and when he visited the CIA, he knew this was the place to be, he said. He graduated in 1985.

Here is another facet of "a cook's mentality." After six years in the business, six-day, ninety-hour weeks, stressed, beaten down, and seriously considering getting out of the business, he was asked to become executive chef at a new hotel and restaurant on the Maryland shore, and he said sure. "It was crazy, but I enjoyed it," he said.

I turned the conversation toward cooking and learning to cook. As inevitably happened at this school when I brought this up, what we talked about was the basics.

"Rose Ann was talking about that this morning," he said. "She's consulting on a property, and a lot of stuff's out of a can and they just have no idea; she looks back at what she was taught here and said it's just so important. How to properly cook a green vegetable. That's what they hammer into you here. It's really, really important. If you look at these master chefs—we used to talk about this in lecture—all they've really done is perfected, mastered those basic cooking techniques. And you just kind of progress from there, but that's something you always lean on. And that's what you're always doing. They've mastered it, it's what they *always* do, it becomes a habit—every time they cook a green bean it's a *perfectly* cooked green bean."

"Are you a good cook?" I asked.

"Yeah. I think everybody has a little bit of a lazy nature to 'em, everybody does. And I think the most successful cooks are those who are the least lazy. It's an everyday struggle to be the best cook you can possibly be. That's my main goal. I don't care about being a great executive chef. I think it's learning how to be a good cook and then teaching people to be a good cook. It's something I'm always striving for, to be the best possible cook."

I said being a good cook was hard. He himself had hammered into us you can never be good enough, you can never be fast enough. Details fly out the window.

"It's funny, a situation happened today with the group leader," he said. "I talked about it in class. About speed and things, you can never be fast enough in the kitchen; the older you get the faster you get, the more efficient you will work. It was funny he made a comment today, he was a little bit behind, he kinda blurted out by accident, 'I'm movin' as fast as I can!' "

I laughed; we'd learned never to say this.

"I went back to his station—it's common sense—he was saucing something with a little teaspoon. I put a big spoon up and said, 'I think you can be a little bit *faster*.' He was in the weeds. He was starting to get mad at me. I was like, 'Don't get mad at *me*. You have this job to do here. Save that for later.' And later he apologized.

"Because there's a lot of pressure, I think it's a natural thing that's probably been done to me, and I kind of do it to them. At the time, I say, 'What's goin on here?!' And they're in the weeds and you can see they start to raise their temperature a little bit; but I think it's good to feel that pressure because eventually when they look back they're gonna say, 'Next time I'm just gonna keep a level head and go right through it, and then worry about it later.' "

"That's exactly what happened with John," I said.

"John too. I was thinking about John today. I'm like—" he laughed his guttural laugh—" 'Don't get an attitude with *me*.' And they always come back later, 'Hey, I was wrong, sorry.' But I know what that's like. On the line, you're on the line of battle, you're on the *front* lines there. And it can get very stressful, and when, you know, you're behind and things are starting to go wrong, you just start to get a little more irritated and it's a lot of pressure. It's like the first chef I worked for, he used to say it's a battle. You against the clock, every day. Jeff Buben. He'd say that. You can't let the clock win, you have to beat the clock every day.

"I had a student a couple blocks ago; she was a nurse in an emergency room and I always used to say this is probably very close to working in an emergency room except it's not a life-or-death situation. Everything has to be done very efficiently, very quickly; you have to get it out quickly. You have to keep your head at all times. I think that's the hardest thing. It's time, it's time, let's go, everything has to be done as quickly as possible, and quality. That's why in lecture I say try to find the best possible people you can work with, work with three, four, five of those chefs. You're gonna pick up so many good things from each one, whether it be speed or efficiency or quality or sanitation. It's just amazing what you can pick up."

The two most important chefs to Turgeon were the ones he worked for immediately after graduating. Jeffrey Buben and David Fye at the Nicholas Restaurant in the Mayflower Hotel set the course for his career.

"Day *One*, I was like, OH MY—scared to death," Turgeon said. "I was scared to *death*. I was scared to death for eight months. I really was. Buben had me in tears." Turgeon suddenly appeared weary, simply recalling all this. "He kicked—worst feeling for a cook—he booted me off the line. 'YOU'RE NOT GOOD ENOUGH!' I was slow, I was slow, I wasn't done, and I deserved it, I deserved it. I was like, 'Did he fire me, did he not?'

"The sous chef at that time was David Fye and he actually said, 'Give him one more chance.' And something clicked that day in me, and that was about eight months in. Something *did* click that day, where I came in that next day and I was *hustling*. I wanted to get to the point where he *yelled* at me a lot less. It was maybe once a week he'd say, ya know, 'Hey what's goin' on here, what *is* this?!' But he was always right; he never did it just to do it. Something wasn't right. He always had a reason. And I *needed* that. Not everybody can deal with that, but at certain points everybody needs just a little push. So I wasn't ready for that and not everybody can take that kind of atmosphere where somebody's on 'em. I certainly saw a lot of cooks come in and out the door, a hundred at least, last a day, two days. But that's where his expectations are and that's how he went about getting to that point.

"I know when I graduated from here," Turgeon continued, "I was probably like these students here. I can't remember, certainly I got B's and A's, but I don't know if I was a good cook when I graduated from here. I don't know. It took a while. It was probably three to five years before I started to say, I think I'm starting to become a good cook. Things *happen* in your head."

There it was again. I'd felt this—in a crude and introductory way—just as he'd said it, with the halting surprise of realizing, suddenly, you are a different person. "Things *happen* in your head." Structures form. Pieces of information and experience join, crystallize into a pattern and lock into place. A whole system of gears is gradually ratcheted in and, suddenly, it engages. And there it stays, in the kitchen and out, no matter where you are. The experience is difficult to describe. Turgeon said it was like a sixth sense. Something clicked and you knew everything that was happening in the kitchen. Some people called it kitchen sense. It's like something living that jumped inside you. A physical correlation might be this: you are carrying several heavy pieces of luggage through O'Hare Airport, walking as fast as you can to make a plane. You step onto an empty moving walkway— you are walking just as fast as you were, but, suddenly, space and time fly over you at double the rate and with ease.

What is it about this work, I wanted to know, what kind of person does this—or rather, for what kind of mind and body is cooking the only option?

"Some of the chefs I've worked for," Turgeon said, "have had a deep passion for what they do. Some of them are workaholics. That's all they want to do; they just want to be in the kitchen. Part of it is control, you're in control. I don't know how to explain it. You're in control. It's just a great feeling when all this stuff is going on around you and you're kinda controlling it. It's like a conductor to a symphony; when you pull it off nothing sounds better. Second, it's just liking to eat. Loving to eat, having an appreciation for food. I *love eating food* probably more than anything, and to get that sometimes you have to cook it yourself. You can't always afford to go out to eat. It's art too."

"Is it?"

"I think so. I think plating, presentation, is where the art part comes in. There's art, there's chemistry, there's science, there's a lot of little different facets of it.

"I just think, the people I've worked with, there's just a passion about food, they just *love food*. They love it. Part of it is wanting to make people happy. Certainly part for me is the physical nature. It sometimes feels like a workout and I like that. It's a sense of achievement too. There's just nothing like it when a service goes right, every plate, there's just nothing like it. It's probably like in baseball, pitching a shutout. That was it, that was the one. You're always trying to achieve that, you're always trying to get another no-hitter or another shutout. But then there are the negative things. It's really demanding, you're working all the time. You have to balance those things really well."

"So can you teach it?" I asked.

"You can, you definitely can, yes. Eventually it's like being able to pick out different complexities of wine, it's about training your palate. And they can train their palates also, and eventually taste something so many times that if somebody makes it properly, wow, I see the difference each time, and, wow, that is really right on the money. Yeah, you can definitely teach this, no question about it."

I asked him how I'd done.

"I thought you did well. I've kinda taken some of the pressure off. If you were on that station at night there would be one more item on there. Sometimes you guys had problems getting things done on time. I think you were probably a little bit nervous, first couple of days.

"I think your best experience in there was when John was absent that day. You're the man, you're in charge, now you have to do it. I saw a difference the next day in you, you were much more efficient, you knew exactly what had to be done.

"If you think what's the speed that's involved with that—you're clear-headed at all times, and you're movin' so fast. I know, put me on the line, sometimes I get in the weeds—I know I'm in the weeds when I start doing three-sixties, start going around in circles! It's just like, 'Stop, I have to stop here.' It happens to the best."

Just as knife skills and sauce work must be taught, how one behaves in the weeds is something that likewise can and should be taught. If you cook, somewhere down the road you're going to be in the weeds; if you're attempting to be a great cook, you're going to be in the weeds a lot. Here was what Turgeon did when he was in the weeds.

It was shortly before Saturday's service. Chen, on sauté, looked at me during prep and made a shaky motion with his hand.

"Nervous?" I asked. I was medium-dicing butternut squash. He nodded. "Why?" I asked.

He said, "Nervous."

"Is language hard?" I asked. "During service, people talking too fast, things getting crazy?"

"Yes, sometimes it is difficult."

Chen was behind on his prep; his mise en place was everywhere but en place and his station was a litter of kale and spinach scraps and shallot cores and burnt paper towel that he'd been using to light burners. It was easy for this to happen. When you were swamped, you could not rationalize spending time to clean up what was just going to become a mess again.

But Chef Turgeon walked by and said, not for the first time, "Chen, you gotta keep your station clean." Turgeon saw that Chen was frustrated and didn't feel that he could take the time. Turgeon, knowing Chen had no time to spare, stopped to chat.

"You know in the weeds, in the shits?" Turgeon asked Chen. Chen nodded. "When I was in the weeds, when I was *really* in the weeds, I'd stop. I'd say, 'Gimme a second.'" Turgeon had looked up at an imaginary expediter and put his hand up like a batter asking the ump for time to step out of the box. Turgeon had an actor's body language. He was on stage; his movements were big, a caricature of what they were meant to portray. "Gimme a second," he said, hand raised, head down toward his station. Then he reached below, pulled a blue Handi Wipe from the sanitation bucket, and again, slowly, exaggerating with large round shoulder motions, he wiped down Chen's station, thoroughly and methodically, till it was a clean open field of stainless steel, saying, "And I'd wipe down my station." Somehow he managed to convey service swirling around him, as he ignored it to methodically polish the stainless-steel station.

His demo over, Turgeon tossed the wipe into the bucket, stood straight, and said to Chen, "'Cause when you're in the weeds, this clutter starts to build up." He put his palms on the station and then lifted them slowly to chest level. "And if they cut you open," he said, "that's what your brain would look like."

When I heard this I laughed. It was exactly right. I thought of Chen's station, with all the scraps of food and burnt paper towel, littered with salt and pepper, spilled sauce hardened to crust—that is what your brain *does* look like when you're in the weeds. Two things are happening in your brain during service. The first is what you are imagining—how long you'll cook this piece of meat, how long you will cook this sauce down, what it will look like—how big the bubbles will be when it hits the right consistency, how low in the pan it will have reduced—when you're ready to plate it; you're thinking ahead to imagine each item that's going on every plate in its finished form. The second thing is what your eyes are actually recording, the moment and sight at hand, each passing second. Service can become so intense that what your eyes see and what you are imagining—that is, what your eyes will see in a few moments—melt together into one. And when your station is a mess, scraps everywhere, dirty tasting spoons all over the place, burnt towel, scraps sticking to your shoes, this mixes with what is about to happen and all but literally gets into the food. And the sensation of this is that the mess is coating the insides of your brain, making it hard to think. When you clean your station, you clean your brain; you can work more efficiently in your head just as you can work faster at your station when it's neat and organized, nothing in the way, nothing unnecessary in view.

So when Turgeon said, "If they cut you open, that's what your brain would look like," he'd described weeds so succinctly that it made me laugh out loud. When Turgeon heard me, he laughed at his own cleverness. Rose Ann had already appeared, saying, "Chef, Chef," with a food order in her hand. Turgeon wanted to enjoy what he'd said a little longer and continued to laugh hard. Again Rose Ann said, "Chef."

Turgeon stopped laughing on a dime, and shouted at Rose Ann, "HEY! I'M TALKING TO MY STUDENTS!" Rose Ann rolled her eyes. Turgeon paused, smiled again, then said to Rose Ann, smiling at her and at his own uncharacteristic silliness, "O.K., what?"

It was Saturday, the kitchen was rolling along smoothly now, and the chef could relax a little.

During service, Chen kept his station clean, but he was having a problem with the chicken. They were huge breasts, with the wing attached and frenched. The method was to sauté them fast and hot and finish them in the oven on the fire command. Chen looked at me when the chicken still wasn't done and said, "Honky chicken is big." The chef came to Chen's station. They both squatted at the oven, cranked to 500 degrees, and the chef poked at one, poked at another. "That one's just about there, that one's pretty good." Chen poked at each himself and nodded at the chef.

Meanwhile, I was reheating wild rice with medium-diced apples and butternut squash in reduced chicken stock. On the previous Thursday, during lecture, I had been fading in and out—stressing over the brown sauce I hadn't begun to make yet, trying to shake the morning fog out of my head. The chef was talking about the soups. "Turkey stocks are awesome," he said. "They're really flavorful. I'll never go back to making chicken consommé." And "I like that soup sampler. I tell ya, put that on the menu, you raise the average check."

Then he looked at John and me. He was either annoyed with John for missing class yesterday or thinking we had it too easy. He said, "Grill, for Saturday, why don't you give me some kind of special? Think about it. I'll call the meat room and see what kind of protein item is available." John nodded as though the chef had asked us to cut a couple more potatoes.

As service that day wound down, and John's chicken fiasco and words with the chef faded into the past, the chef approached our station and asked if we'd thought about the special at all. John, to my relief, said, "I was thinking about quail." The chef nodded. "Maybe do a grape sauce," John continued.

"I'm not big on grapes in sauces," the chef said.

"Maybe berries, dried berries?"

The chef said, "Let me think about it."

While we prepped for Friday, the chef floated a sheet of yellow legal paper on the service shelf above our station.

> Saturday, 12 orders
> Grilled quail stuffed with hickory-smoked chix sausage
> Wild Rice
> Apple
> Butternut squash
>
> Wild Mushrooms
>
> Other Veg

The evolution of a special was fascinating to me in its apparent whimsy. What began Thursday as wondering what kind of protein item was available in the meat room would become, by Saturday, the most interesting entrée on Saturday's menu. It was simply a response to a common question—what should we fix for dinner tonight?—taken to an artful, and marketable, level.

Chef Turgeon grew bored once he'd brought the class to autopilot proficiency; to amuse himself he made an exquisite forcemeat. First he threw some hickory chips in a small roasting pan, put it over a burner, then smoked boned chicken leg on a rack over the chips covered by another pan. The smoked meat was then ground with about 20 percent pork fat and mixed with shallots, reduced apple cider, salt and pepper, thyme, rosemary, and Pommery mustard. With a piping bag, David, a tournant, would stuff about an ounce of the forcemeat into the boned quail, then secure its legs through slits in the skin, and rub them with oil. John would mark these off on the grill at service and finish them in the oven.

John created a sauce of half veal/half chicken stock, fortified with more roasted chicken bones. He added some sage and apple cider that he'd reduced by three-quarters. The chef tasted it, then added *verjus*, rosemary, and thyme. John then strained and reduced it, and we'd monté au beurre at service.

Meanwhile I would sauté a dice of butternut squash and Granny Smith apples in butter, then add some wild rice and walnuts, a couple of ounces of chicken broth, and season the mix with salt, pepper, and fresh thyme. In another pan, I would heat butter and some bacon fat, sauté haricots verts, fava beans, spears of cooked bacon.

The plate was gorgeous. It began with a large spoonful of wild rice with bright yellow-orange squash and white apple in the center of the plate. On this bed, two stuffed quail were rested facing five and seven o'clock. Fava and haricots were sprinkled around the perimeter along with whole shitakes that had been seared and reheated in a little chicken broth. The plate was sauced, and we sprinkled tiny bright green leaves of thyme over the quail.

Not that we needed more to do, but somehow, by that time, we'd grown competent enough at our stations that the extra cutting and cooking seemed more a pleasant diversion than an unnecessary chore.

At the end of the day, as we huddled, Turgeon said, "I'm going to let you guys slide out of here. It was the best day so far; I saw very few mistakes. Have a good weekend. I'll see you Tuesday."

Tuesday was my last day working in kitchens at the Culinary. For my fellow students, it was their last day in the kitchen before graduation, the culmination of two years' work. When I asked how it felt, I was greeted with the obvious. Mimi said, "I woke up this morning and I thought this is the last time I'm gonna have to wear this uniform." When I asked John if he was glad to be leaving the kitchen, he remained completely silent with a hard smile, his mind apparently flooded by possible sarcastic remarks. Eventually, he only chuckled and said, "Yeah, I'll be glad to get out of here."

"How you guys doin' today?" the chef said, arriving in the dining room with his three-ring binder. The graduating group had had a pig roast over the weekend to celebrate their final block and graduation and that was the first thing on Turgeon's mind. "How was the pig roast?" he said. "How did the pig turn out? Good. All right. Busy day today. A la carte, we have seventy reservations. Make sure you get totally set up for that, plus business tomorrow, about fifty à la carte, plus a little party, but it's all à la carte. For the banquet, it's twenty-eight people. We're getting twenty-eight orders of crab cake; tournants are going to clean it. We have to set up twenty-eight orders plus a dozen other orders for tomorrow, plus the endive, plus the coleslaw. The entrée," he said, looking at John and me, "we're basically going to be doing your steak dish. We're doing it with a pork tenderloin. Tournants, I ordered twelve pork tenderloins that we need to trim up. We're gonna leave them whole, and marinate those like we did the tenderloin. O.K.? Sauce, we need about two quarts of sauce. Tournants, you're gonna have to help out with this, also veg station. I'll have veg station do the french fries; you need about thirty-five potatoes cut up for it. Make sure you've got the onion spice mixture for it. Veg station, I also need you to clean five bags of spinach and if you guys can set up the onions for it, I ordered extra, thirty onions, and succotash for thirty. So, grill, you guys are going to do the onions, the sauce, and the succotash."

"Did you order fava beans?" John asked.

"Yeah, I ordered four pounds." He continued through the rest of the banquet meal and then told us we needed complete mise en place for the incoming group's Day One. "As soon as you're done and have everything wrapped up," Turgeon said, "call me over so I can go through your station with you. Make sure you leave a prioritized prep list for the next class. Make sure you leave a station diagram, and kinda take your time, make sure it looks neat, how to set the station up, by the time you leave.

"Also, we were not here for two days; make sure you double-check everything, pull it out, taste it, make sure it's good to go. That's not something I want to catch at eleven-thirty, I'm going through tasting stuff and oop, this is no good, it's slimy.

"Next thing I want to do is go through your game plan today for à la carte, starting with soup station."

Soup station, then fish station went through their game plans and Turgeon said, "O.K., grill?"

John said, "We gotta do about fifty onions, succotash for thirty. We have a lot of barbecue sauce, but not enough for two quarts, so we've got to do about two quarts of barbecue sauce. Probably have to dehydrate some onions for the onion rub for tomorrow. We need to get a little more mise en place for the special today, and cut potatoes for our station."

"I'll have veg station cut potatoes for you."

And on Turgeon moved through every station, followed by a critique of Saturday, small quibbles, mainly at sauté station, but concluded by saying, "So it was by far the best day. Today, I expect it to be twice as good as that. O.K.? This should be your best cooking day here at the school. All right? That's what it's all about.

"Usually on Day Eight—I was standing in your shoes at one time, too, getting ready to graduate, I didn't have a job when I left here and for me, by far my first job was probably the most important position I ever took. I didn't know what the hell I wanted to do." Turgeon had worked at a large hotel chain and while that environment taught useful skills, such as how to have strict controls on recipes, it was not where he would grow. A friend told him about the job at the Mayflower Hotel. "I just happened to walk across the street, walked in, guy talked to me, Jeff Buben, said, 'Yeah, I need somebody, you can start in a couple days.' I ended up taking that job and that's the one where I told you, second day on the job, the chef told me he was going to fire me. But it just set me up for the rest of my career. I ended up working for him for two and a half years. It was exactly what I needed. I needed that discipline. I just remember how he worked; whenever he wasn't doing anything he was polishing stainless steel. He was wiping things down, *all* the time, all the time. He'd be sitting there talking to you, wiping down the table. He was a *fanatic*. But there are important lessons I saw in that. And in how he worked, too. Make sure your station was wiped down. Totally organized at *all* times of the *day*. When I came in there, I was late every day, getting my stuff done, and he was all over me. So it's really important. I had somebody in my face saying, 'Let's go, let's clean this up.' A lot of you may not work for somebody like that. You're gonna have to take it upon yourself to push yourself every day.

"Two pieces of information that I could give you, lessons I've learned.

When you go and work, some of you have jobs, some of you may not, some of you have talked to me. Know what you do? Find the top ten, top twenty places in that city, wherever you're gonna go, and go work there. Money really shouldn't be a big issue. Some of you it has to be, you may be older, you may have a family, you may have a wife, may have kids, or you have to worry a little more about money. But for a lot of you guys, money shouldn't be a major consideration for at least three to five years. I mean that. You make the right decisions, you work for the right people, you keep on working for places of that quality, later down the road, you're gonna be making more money than somebody who came right out and took a sous chef position at thirty-two at an average hotel; you're gonna end up passing them by a long way. Your education should be your major consideration at the beginning. Secondly, when you leave that place, this is something I've done, never take a step back in quality. Again, money can sometimes be a driving force. When you leave a job, keep going to a place that is better, and better, and better. The money comes later and the money'll be *good*, if you make the right decisions. That's real important.

"What else? I just think you have to be a hustler in this business. It's really physical, and you have to be really, really fast. A lot of people when they work, they work kind of lethargic; that's not what this business is about. It's very, very physical and it's very demanding. I look at it as kind of a war or a game, every day, me against the clock, and I don't want the clock to win. So I always—I'm in the kitchen? Get my stuff done as quickly as possible, work efficiently, work cleanly. That's probably a couple of the most important things."

Finally, he asked everyone what they had planned after graduation. Theresa was headed back to Seattle to the restaurant where she'd externed. Mark also would head to Seattle. Chen hoped to bring Escoffier's principles, and much of the food done in the Escoffier Room, to his father's hotel in Taiwan. Manning and Mimi were headed to San Francisco. John planned to go to *Food Arts* magazine and then to Germany. Russ answered, "I'm going to go to the Grand Hyatt in New York City. And hopefully in about two years I'm gonna open something of my own."

"Good," Turgeon said. "Bill?"

"I'm gonna go work for Boston Harbor Hotel."

"Good. Who's the executive chef there?"

"Daniel Bruce."

"Yeah, I heard a him, good. Gene?"

"I'm gonna relocate to Florida."

"Don't know what the hell you're gonna do, go fishing or something? Todd?"

"I'm not quite sure where I'm looking. Boston or Chicago area. I'm gonna try to use my connections from my extern."

"Where'd you extern?"

"Rattlesnake Club in Detroit."

"How often did you see Jimmy Schmidt there?"

"There was a major turnover when I got there, they just got three new chefs and were understaffed, so he was popping his head in there quite a bit."

"All right guys, that's about it; let's have a good day, seventy reservations."

And we were back in the kitchen.

"I think he does this on purpose," I said to John as we walked to our stations. "That barbecue sauce takes all day. We've got about ninety million onions to do."

"Succotash for thirty," John said.

"We'll do what we can."

"That's all we can do."

I would be making brown sauce, again, on my last day working in the kitchens in the Culinary Institute of America. I remembered the virulent roux debate of the previous winter, and I had thought at the time, "What an unusual place this is, what strange people who get passionate over brown sauce and what color you cooked your roux to." And then it occurred to me that *I'd* become one of them.

But not today. Three cups of brown sauce was the last thing I had time for, what with all the fava beans to shuck, cook, and peel, mise en place for the quail special to finish, onions to boil and shock and peel and hollow, and more onions to peel, chop, grind, dehydrate, and pulverize. What color roux did I make? Blond. Blond and that was all right, for I had learned by then that there were many things to consider when making a brown sauce.

We managed, just, to get everything done. Service was fast and smooth and over almost before it began.

"We looked pretty good," Turgeon said, before dismissing us. "Quick service. Basically worked out well. What I really try to do here, in seven days, is to give you a little sense of reality, a little bit just how things should be done, how fast you need to move. Sometimes I snap at you a bit, but my main goal is really to get you guys prepared to go out and work. I wish you all luck. Have a good one." A smattering of applause followed and Turgeon said, "Remember, tomorrow, when you're front of the house, I'm not your friend."

It was done. John would dress the next day in black pants, white shirt, bow tie, and apron to serve the food he'd been cooking for the past week. The next time he wore a chef's jacket would be for graduation, six school days away. The graduating class would be seated on stage, and one by one they would traverse the stage of Alumni Hall and bow their head to President Metz as he draped the graduation cordon over their neck—a brief moment of fanfare—and that was the end of a Culinary education. My class would disperse, some to Europe, Chen to Taiwan, some to New York City, others to the West Coast. No time to think. It was a vagabond life, this life of a cook. Just keep moving, moving perfectly.

Afterword: Benediction

The first Saturday cooking at Bounty, the day I'd begun cooking for real and my partner John had told Gene he'd never have known I was a writer, I drove out to Chef Pardus's house. In one respect, it was sort of a pilgrimage. He was the reason I was able to hold my own in Bounty, the reason I passed the practical exam, the reason I could move through any kitchen now with confidence. He had been a good teacher. I once asked Chef Turgeon who his Skills teacher had been. He named her and said, "You go through a lot of classes here, but you never forget your Skills teacher." This was true. Also, I missed Chef Pardus, missed hearing him talk about food, missed arguing about whether the hollandaise had too much acid or not enough salt.

When I called for directions—my pretext for meeting him, though I hardly needed one, was to find out how his three weeks in Brazil had gone—he said, "I live in the wilderness." He said his nearest neighbors were the kinds of folks who put broken washing machines on their front lawn. Behind his rented ranch-style house, cornfields extended for miles, it seemed, and beyond them were the Catskill Mountains, a hazy blue when I arrived on that warm bright summer afternoon. His dogs Pumpkin and Early yapped and danced as Pardus welcomed me and led me to his kitchen. He was dressed in jean shorts, newly cut off and without fray. He had been crushing ice.

"I was just about to make myself a mint julep," he said. "Care to join me?" I said I would very much care to. "I've got mint growing in the backyard," he said, noting that juleps were the very best possible use of mint he knew of. I was inclined to agree, especially on such a fine warm late afternoon as this.

We sat on a small patio in his backyard and chatted, drinking from our enormous glasses perfect examples of the mint julep, and the sun hovered over the Catskills. He told me about Brazil and how the wheat there was different, and therefore sauce making was different because the roux was different. He went through the logic, returning me instantly to Skills class. "Where is our wheat grown?" he asked me. "What are the characteristics of that wheat?" The harsher the climate, I'd learned from Chef Coppedge, the stronger the wheat; the thing that made wheat strong was protein. Wheat grown in the harsh weather of the Great Plains was very high in protein. "Where is theirs grown?" Pardus continued in his manic way. "So that means what? Theirs is going to be *low* in protein, *low* in gluten, and high *starch*. So to make a roux you need more of everything and you can cook sauces forever without getting the starchy taste and feel out." Because of their geography, his students in Brazil used pure starch, such as arrowroot, to thicken sauces. "Arrowroot *grows* down there," Pardus told me. "You can buy it fresh in the market."

He showed me pictures of the friends he'd made, pictures of the kitchen and his students.

Then we sat back and relaxed. What a fine evening to be drinking a gigantic mint julep, I thought, after a long day cooking, and now surrounded by a sea of corn, hazy and almost glowing, backlit by the sun descending over the mountains, the dogs dashing in and out between the stalks and romping throughout the herb garden. A small fig tree, a gift from Chef Griffiths, grew in a pot beside the garden. We were shaded by a young beechnut tree. It was a perfect summer evening, and, recalling the blizzards of winter, it was an apt time to say what I had wanted to for some time.

"Chef, I want to thank you," I said. "I know I'm a writer and not a cook"—I was always careful to make this distinction, especially around Pardus—"but I wouldn't be able to do what I'm doing had I not started in your Skills class."

"Hey, Michael," he said. "You're a cook. If you're working the grill station in American Bounty on a Saturday afternoon, you're a cook."

I felt a powerful surge of emotion. My God, I was a cook. This had been something that I'd wanted to achieve, to *be*, since that winter storm. John had given me a great compliment that afternoon, but now the name had been bestowed on me by the only person who could rightfully do it, my Skills teacher. I was enormously, irrationally proud. Proud to be a cook.

Appendix
The CIA Curriculum:
Associate Degree

CURRICULUM: ASSOCIATE DEGREE

CULINARY ARTS FIRST SEMESTER—15 WEEKS				
BLOCK A Introduction to Gastronomy Culinary Math	**BLOCK B** Nutrition / Sanitation / Meat Identification	**BLOCK C** Meat Fabrication / Product Identification & Food Purchasing / Culinary French	**BLOCK D** Culinary Skill Development 1	**BLOCK E** Culinary Skill Development 2
	OR	**OR**		
	Product Identification & Food Purchasing / Culinary French / Nutrition / Sanitation	Meat Identification / Meat Fabrication		

CULINARY ARTS SECOND SEMESTER—15 WEEKS				
BLOCK F Introduction to Hot Foods Supervisory Development	**BLOCK G** Seafood Cookery American Regional Cuisine	**BLOCK H** Asian Cuisine Charcuterie	**BLOCK I** Breakfast Cookery Lunch Cookery (Costing Examination)	**BLOCK J** Garde Manger (Culinary Practical Examination)

CULINARY ARTS THIRD SEMESTER—21 WEEKS
BLOCK K Externship (18 weeks required)

CULINARY ARTS FOURTH SEMESTER—15 WEEKS			
BLOCK L Bread Baking Pastry Skills Development	**BLOCK M** Pâtisserie	**BLOCK N & O** Menus and Facilities Planning Management of Wines and Spirits Restaurant Law	**BLOCK P** International Cookery Advanced Culinary Principles
	Cost Control		

CULINARY ARTS FIFTH SEMESTER—15 WEEKS				
BLOCK Q Classical Banquet Cuisine Introduction to Table Service and Catering	**BLOCK R** À la Carte Service St. Andrew's Cafe Kitchen	**BLOCK S** Table d'Hôte Service Caterina de Medici Kitchen (Culinary Practical Examination) (Costing Examination)	**BLOCK T** Formal Service Escoffier Kitchen	**BLOCK U** American Service and Dining Room Management American Bounty Kitchen